MW01055710

Second to None

Second to None
The History of the NASCAR Busch Series

BY RICK HOUSTON

DESIGN BY TOM MORGAN

 **DAVID BULL** PUBLISHING

Copyright © 2001 by Rick Houston and David Bull Publishing. All rights reserved. No part of this book may be used or reproduced in any manner whatsoever without written permission from the Publisher except in the case of brief quotations embodied in critical articles and reviews.

We recognize that some words, model names, and designations mentioned in this book are the property of the trademark holder. We use them only for identification purposes.

Library of Congress Cataloging-in-Publication Data is Available
ISBN 1-893618-11-0

David Bull Publishing, logo, and colophon are trademarks of David Bull Publishing, Inc.

Book and cover design: Tom Morgan, Blue Design, Portland, Maine

Printed in Korea

10 9 8 7 6 5 4 3 2 1

David Bull Publishing
4250 East Camelback Road
Suite K150
Phoenix, AZ 85018

602-852-9500
602-852-9503 (fax)

www.bullpublishing.com

PREVIOUS PAGE: Tommy Houston's last Busch Grand National win was bittersweet. Houston made it through two spins and a record 26 cautions to capture the victory at Hickory April 18. His father, Oren, had died two days earlier. (Tommy Houston collection)
RIGHT: Joe Bessey (97), Jimmy Spencer (10), Roy Payne (27), Butch Miller (75), and Hermie Sadler (front end visible at right), crash in turn three at Bristol April 3, 1993. Michael Waltrip won the event and promptly proposed to his girlfriend, Buffy Franks, in victory lane. Two days before the race, reigning Winston Cup champion Alan Kulwicki had been killed in an airplane crash. After his win, Waltrip became the first of many drivers to honor Kulwicki with a "Polish Victory Lap" around the track in the opposite direction, just as Kulwicki had celebrated his wins. (Bryan Hallman)
FOLLOWING PAGE: Sam Ard helps push his car down pit road before a Budweiser Late Model Sportsman event at Hickory on October 17, 1982. Ard collected a paltry $730 for his 18th-place finish in the event. (David Allio)
PAGES 8-9: The field readies for the Tri-City Pontiac 200 on a gorgeous August night in 1987 at Bristol. Larry Pearson beat Jimmy Hensley for the win by two car lengths. It was Pearson's fifth victory of the season. (Dick Conway)

Contents

To Betty Jane Houston: Momma, I hope this book makes you proud; and to Gary Neice, Clifford Allison, and Adam Petty. Your contributions to the Busch Series will never be forgotten.

LEFT: Mark Martin ended his Busch Series career after the 2000 season with more wins than any other driver in the division's 19-year history. He posted 45 victories, with 1987 his only full-time season on the tour. (Phil Cavali) RIGHT: Although Jack Ingram had not won in two years, he still had the look of a fiery competitor in 1989. Ingram led the standings as late as August, but he faded to fifth by the end of the season. (Dick Conway)

Prologue
What the Busch Series Is All About

In the NASCAR hierarchy, the Busch Series has always been in the shadow of the Winston Cup circuit. Considered something of a Triple A minor league to its Winston Cup counterpart, the Busch Series is much more of a close-knit community with a completely different atmosphere. The biggest reason is that there's more at stake financially in Winston Cup racing.

The Busch Series' point fund paid Jeff Green $735,487 for winning the 2000 championship, while Bobby Labonte earned $3,386,640 for capturing the Winston Cup title that same year. Green's take wasn't meager by any means, especially given the fact Anheuser-Busch's first title sponsorship in 1982 was worth $50,000. Still, Green's total winnings of $1,929,937—the most money ever won by a Busch Series driver in a single season—was far short of Labonte's take.

Competitive Winston Cup team sponsorships begin at about $10 million per year, compared to about $2.5 million to $3 million for the Busch Series. But the cost of sponsoring a Busch Series operation has skyrocketed in recent years. Current budgets are now about 60 times the amount Tommy Ellis had to work with when he won the Late Model Sportsman championship in 1981, the final year before it was transformed into the Busch Series. Busch Series sponsors are marketing their investments as never before, placing images of their cars and drivers on all sorts of different products and in a multitude of promotions. But the Busch Series hasn't become a dog-and-pony show. Not yet.

There are some other telling differences. Interviews with Winston Cup Director Gary Nelson generally need to be scheduled in advance through at least one public relations representative. Often out of necessity, Nelson does his talking at massive press conferences. Busch Series Director John Darby, with very few exceptions, has an open-door policy, and he even returns phone calls. He's a big fish in a much smaller pond.

A Winston Cup transporter can be like a fortress, with a charged atmosphere that suggests the backstage of a high-profile rock concert. By comparison, a Busch Series transporter feels almost like a visiting a family member's house. Most crew members, drivers, and team owners are quick to welcome visitors and offer food and drinks.

When someone in the Busch Series community unexpectedly misses a race, competitors will often call their home or shop to see that everything's OK.

The Busch Series is also something of a feeder circuit because many young drivers use it as a way to get noticed for a highly coveted Winston Cup ride. Many of Winston Cup racing's most successful drivers came up through the Busch Series ranks, including Bobby Labonte, Dale Jarrett, and Jeff Gordon. But many other very successful competitors, such as Jack Ingram, Tommy Houston, Randy LaJoie, Mike McLaughlin, and Elton Sawyer, have chosen to make a career out of the Busch Series. So the division is more than just a stepping stone to bigger things.

There's virtually no difference in the appearance of Winston Cup and Busch Series cars and certainly none in cost. Because of new rules for the 2001 season, Busch Series engines have the same 12-to-1 compression ratio as those of Winston Cup cars. Speeds are still generally slower in the Busch Series because of carburetor restrictions that were mandated to help keep costs down. Teams usually are allowed to change only three sets of tires under caution per race in another effort to control expenses.

Winston Cup cars weigh 3,400 pounds without their drivers, just 100 pounds more than those in the Busch Series. The 105-inch wheelbase found in the Busch Series is five inches shorter than that of a Winston Cup car. Why the difference? Bigger cars, with wheelbases of up to 112 inches, were eligible for competition in the early years of the Busch Series. Older models were still in service in the mid-1980s. It wasn't uncommon to see cars that were seven and eight years old in competition.

In an attempt to encourage Detroit manufacturers' involvement, NASCAR allowed shorter, current-year models in 1986 and mandated the 105-inch wheelbase, as well as the smaller V-6 engines that were then popular. Although V-8 engines returned in

1995, the 105-inch wheelbase remains unchanged.

During the 2000 season, approximately 35 full-time Busch Series teams ran the division's 32 races, 21 of which were held in conjunction with the Winston Cup tour. Typically, on a shared weekend, the Busch Series race is run on Saturday as a prelude to the Winston Cup show on Sunday. The overlapping events allow many Winston Cup stars to compete regularly in the Busch Series, which is an issue that has been hotly debated since the beginning of the division.

Mark Martin ran only one full-time Busch Series season, in 1987, but has the most wins in the circuit's history—45—of which all but three were

earned while he was a full-time Winston Cup driver. The presence of Winston Cup drivers is good for promoters who contend they need big names to draw fans for their supporting races, but it's bad for young competitors who fail to qualify for races because those stars claim some of the 43 starting spots.

When events overlap, Winston Cup drivers get practice time in both cars, which many in both the Busch and the Winston Cup garages feel is an unfair advantage. Almost every weekend, crossover competitors will make changes to their Busch Series car just before a race, based on the conditions they've discovered during the Winston Cup practice session that morning.

Nevertheless, the competitive character of the Busch Series regulars has meant that Winston Cup racers have never been guaranteed easy victories. Sam Ard whipped a host of Winston Cup regulars at Charlotte in 1983, and 17 years later, series champion Jeff Green did the same to Jeff Burton in a one-lap shoot-out to the checkered flag at Rockingham, N.C. In between, there

were plenty of times when Winston Cup drivers blinked first in a duel with their Busch Series counterparts.

The Busch Series has always been about racing hard and having fun doing it. What follows are stories of fierce competition and strong camaraderie in the quest for the championship between Sam Ard and Jack Ingram in the series' infancy, on through other famous rivals, such as Tommy Houston and Tommy Ellis, Dale Jarrett and Jimmy Spencer, Mike Alexander and Larry Pearson, and Randy LaJoie and Buckshot Jones. There's a rich tradition about the Busch Series, one that's all its own.

ABOVE: Dale Shaw (left) confronts Mark Martin (far right) and his crew chief, after the IRP event in 1988. Shaw spun on the frontstretch after they collided on lap 173 while battling for third. Martin maintained control and finished seventh, while Shaw dropped to 25th. (Dick Conway) **OPPOSITE:** Although Tommy Ellis protested the scoring of the race, Mike Alexander was allowed to keep his win at Hickory February 28, 1988. Ellis was credited with a fourth-place finish, nine seconds behind Alexander. (Dick Conway)

Late Model Sportsman
In the Beginning

When the Sportsman Series was formed in 1950, races were run with cars that had been driven to the track. Drivers drove for the thrill and little else. Open-wheeled Modifieds and full-bodied Sportsman cars ran in the same events, and there weren't a lot of rules about what could go under the hood.

The Late Model Sportsman and Modified divisions split into separate entities in 1968.

LEFT: Sam Ard and Richie Evans receive their trophies for winning the Late Model Sportsman and Modified portions of the 1980 Cardinal 500 Classic at Martinsville. Evans was a Modified legend, winning nine championships. He would be killed at Martinsville five years later. From left to right in the photo are Ard's car owner, Howard Thomas; Jo Ard, Sam's wife; Ard; Ard's crew chief, Jesse Coke; Billy Nacewicz, Evans' crew chief; and Evans. (Jesse Coke Collection) RIGHT: Bob Pressley was one of the Late Model Sportsman division's toughest competitors, and stories of his run-ins with Jack Ingram is the stuff legends are made of. Pressley's sons are involved in racing today: Charley is a veteran mechanic and crew chief, while Robert drives for Jasper Motorsports in Winston Cup competition. (David Allio)

Hundreds of local race tracks featured Late Model Sportsman cars from Canada, Vermont and Maine, Virginia and the Carolinas, down to Georgia and Florida.

Drivers could race exclusively in weekly events at local tracks, each of which paid points toward a track championship. The next step was to go after a state title by collecting points at several tracks in the area. Finally, a third tier offered a national championship to drivers who raced anywhere from 60 to 90 times a year all over the country.

There was no set schedule for drivers trying to win the national title. Two drivers competing for the same championship could have done so at different tracks hundreds of miles apart on the same night.

Most Late Model Sportsman events paid the minimum of 50 points to win, but NASCAR often doled out more based on a track's purse. Bigger purses meant more points. The lure of big money and additional points was hard to resist, and the so-called national championship events amounted to all-star races. Still, to win the championship, it was just as important to run three or four weekly races worth the minimum points as it was to enter events with big points payouts.

"In order to win a national title, we had to run the weekly events also because they paid a small amount of points," said Jack Ingram, who won three straight Late Model Sportsman championships from 1972-74. "A championship race paid 175 points or so, and a weekly race paid 50 points toward the track title, state title, and the national title. Those same 50 points counted in three places."

Ingram was often a "hired gun," brought in by track promoters to take on local hotshoes who'd been winning

a little too often. He stopped Darrell Waltrip at Nashville a few times in the early 1970s and often went at it with hometown heroes in Virginia. Ingram wasn't out to win friends. He was just out to win.

"I've got a headline from a paper in Richmond that says, 'Ingram Bang Proves Fatal To Richmond Gang,'" Ingram said with a satisfied smile. "I got into a bangin' contest with a couple of them, and I came out on top. That's the way they liked to race, so I just obliged them."

Ingram won the division's ultimate prize three years running, but Virginian Bill Dennis went to victory lane in the biggest race in each of those seasons. One Daytona win is a career highlight for most drivers, but to do it three years in a row is nothing short of astounding, particularly given the competition from Winston Cup stars entered in the races.

The 1973 event featured one of Daytona's wildest finishes among Dennis, Ingram, Red Farmer, and Dennis Gireaux. Ingram finally scored the first of his two Daytona Late Model Sportsman wins in 1975.

"All day, you could put a blanket over us," said Dennis, who ran only a handful of Late Model Sportsman races in each of those seasons. "I took the white flag leading, and then on the backstretch, I was running fourth. When I got to turn three, I came back around them.

"In the other races I won, there was [Darrell] Waltrip, [Neil] Bonnett, Bobby and Donnie Allison—a lot of the big boys. You were running against some of the best Winston Cup drivers, and it wasn't no easy pickings. I'm like your typical race car driver. You go to win."

Trickery among drivers vying for the championship wasn't uncommon.

"Drivers would lie to each other about who was going where," recalled Lance Childress, NASCAR's field director for the division. "There was a big race in Oxford, Maine. At that time, we had Jack Ingram, Butch Lindley, Bosco Lowe, and Harry Gant running for points. They all got together on Saturday night and agreed not to go to Oxford on Sunday night.

ABOVE: Although L.D. Ottinger (seated, with glasses) and Tiny Lund (dark T-shirt) were friends, Ottinger once tried to sneak away to a race in Asheville, N.C. to gain points on Lund in their battle for the 1975 Late Model Sportsman championship. Also shown in this drivers' meeting photo from that year are Morgan Shepherd (to the left of Ottinger) and Dick Brooks (to the left of Lund). Tragically, just a few weeks after this snapshot was taken, Lund was killed in a Winston Cup event at Talladega. (L.D. Ottinger Collection) **RIGHT:** A completely exhausted Harry Gant spun three times at Bristol in May 1977. His final crash was on the next-to-last lap, and he limped around the track on flat tires to barely hold off Tommy Houston for the win. Houston protested the scoring of the race, and then Darrell Waltrip filed a grievance over Gant's engine. Both protests were denied. (David Allio) **OPPOSITE:** Before they were split into separate divisions in 1967, open-wheel Modifieds and Sportsman cars raced in the same events as part of NASCAR's Sportsman Series. They also wrecked together as shown by this mid-1960s photo from Martinsville. The post-1967 Late Model Sportsman division would become what is now the Busch Series. (Martinsville Speedway Archives)

We all ended up on the same airplane leaving out of Boston on the way to Oxford."

Although L. D. Ottinger and Tiny Lund got to be "the best of friends" as they battled each other for the 1975 Late Model Sportsman championship, Ottinger once tried his best to get one over on Lund.

Both were in Hampton, Va., for a race that was rained out on a Saturday and rescheduled for the next day. It was raining then, too, with another event slated for Sunday night in Asheville, N.C. Ken "Bear" Hunley, Ottinger's crew chief, made a deal with Lund that neither would try to make the Asheville event.

Hunley must've had his fingers crossed. Ottinger needed the points to pad his lead in the standings over Lund.

"I didn't really want to do it, but Bear wanted me to slip off, go on to Asheville, and pull a fast one on Tiny," Ottinger said. "Tiny got to missing me. Well, he knew a lot of people, and he fooled around there and got a flight.

"He had to fly somewhere—maybe up to Cleveland—and then made it into Asheville. Meanwhile, we ran wide open in the pickup truck. It's a wonder we didn't get killed. We got there, and the cars were lined up. We went up to get tickets, and I'll be damned, here came Tiny in a highway patrol car mad enough to kill me.

"I said, 'Now, Tiny, it wasn't my doings. That there crazy Bear made me do this.'"

A few weeks later, Lund was killed in the early laps of a Winston Cup race at Talladega. Ottinger went on to win the 1975 and '76 Late Model Sportsman championships.

Gant's week-long stretch in May 1977 was typical of the grueling pace many competitors maintained. Gant practiced and qualified at Charlotte on May 24 and 25 for one of the first Winston Cup races of his career. He then raced and won a Late Model Sportsman event on May 26 in Columbia, S.C.

On May 27, it was back to Charlotte, where he damaged an engine practicing for a Modified race that was to be held the following day at the track. Gant then hustled up the interstate to Kingsport, Tenn., for another Late Model Sportsman race that night, which he won.

Afterward, he drove to Asheville to pick up the repaired Modified engine, arriving at about 3:30 a.m. on May 28. About 2 1/2 hours later, Gant got back to his rag-tag team's motel in Charlotte. Sleep eluded him,

so he headed for the track and that afternoon's Modified race. Again, he won. And, again, he was off to another Late Model Sportsman race the same day, this time at Hickory, N.C. Gant scored a third-place finish.

Driving a car owned by Joe Frasson, "Handsome Harry" finished 30th in the May 29 Winston Cup race at Charlotte. Still, the weekend wasn't finished. There was a big 300-lap Late Model Sportsman race on May 30 at Bristol, Tenn. Gant had to be there in body, if not in spirit.

After working on their car until about 2 a.m., Gant and his few crew members headed to Bristol, getting there about five hours later. The race wasn't until that night, and by that time, Gant was barely conscious. He hadn't slept much, if at all, in five days.

"Finally, it was race time," Gant said. "I'm leading the race, and I get me a lap lead. But I'm just so dazed. I'm just running against the wall all the way around. I didn't even look at it. I was just sort of floppin' around in the car."

Midway through the race, Gant smacked the wall on the backstretch. He spun, blew a tire, and smashed into a guardrail. After pitting for fresh tires, Gant

OPPOSITE: Tracks often had to come up with promotional gimmicks to draw a crowd. Here, L.D. Ottinger packs at least eight children into his car for a ride around Lonesome Pine Speedway in Coeburn, Va. (L.D. Ottinger Collection) ABOVE: Racing was always in Dale Earnhardt's blood, but the dirt-poor driver had to race for several years in Late Model Sportsman competition before landing his first full-time Winston Cup ride. The No. 8 is a family tradition. His father, Ralph, used it, and now so does his son, Dale Jr., in the Winston Cup ranks. (David Allio)

came back out in about fifth place. He lapped the field again, but hit the wall a second time.

Gant was exhausted, and on the next-to-last lap, he smacked the wall a third time. The race to the checkered flag was on.

"I'm going down the backstretch trying to steer that thing with the tires blown out, and Tommy [Houston]—zoom!—he went by me like a rocket," Gant said. "I come off of [turn] four, and the white flag's waving. I look over and Tommy's going down the backstretch. I tried to give it gas, but it's turned sideways with the flat tire.

"I come down the backstretch. I look over, and I didn't see him. I look up, and here he's coming. I'm only doing 60 miles an hour. He's flat out. Just as I got it pointed for the flagstand, he's there. I just nailed it to the floor. The rim was on the ground, showering sparks out."

Gant won. Houston protested the scoring of the race, which was resolved in Gant's favor well after midnight. Then, when he got back to the infield, Waltrip had filed a protest over Gant's engine. It was one heck of a way to win a race. And for all Gant's troubles, the 1977 Late Model Sportsman championship went to Butch Lindley.

Tommy Ellis won the final Late Model Sportsman championship in 1981 with a $20,000 sponsorship deal from Industrial Boiler, plus a tire deal from Goodyear and an engine deal with a company in Richmond.

Limited financial backing meant no paid crew members. "You might not have the same guys one week as you did the other," Ellis said. "I had two or three guys that were there every week, but then again, you'd have two or three that couldn't get off from work. There were a few teams that had full-time help, but I'd say 98 percent of them were all volunteer crews."

The trials of being on the road forged a bond between competitors. Hundreds of stories deserve to be told, like this one from Tommy Houston of a long-ago race at Orange County Speedway in Rougemont, N.C.

"Ray Hendrick blows up in front of us," Houston said. "He knocks the fence down, went through it. I hit that oil, and I'm flipping through there and catch on fire. I tore my car all to pieces. Jerry Shepherd winds up out in the pond upside down.

"Bobby Allison goes on and wins the race. Clayton Mitchell (who owned Hendrick's car), brought out a jar of moonshine, and he was chewin' tobacco, spittin' and a-goin' on. He told Bobby Allison, 'You might've won the race, but you didn't outrun nobody. All the good stuff's laying outside the track.'"

Adding insult to injury, Houston's deal money from the track promoter for showing up at the event was 90 $1 bills.

Gere Kennon, a veteran mechanic and current Busch Series crew chief, offered a story that clearly illustrates not only the hardcore racing style of the young up-and-coming Dale Earnhardt, but also the Wild West gunslinger atmosphere of the Late Model Sportsman Series itself.

"Earnhardt came to Caraway [Speedway in Asheboro, N.C.] and was leading the race with about three laps to go. Sam Ard had come in and put tires on and was going to pass Earnhardt going down the backstretch for the checkered flag. Earnhardt ran Sam into the infield, and they both wrecked.

"After it was over," Kennon continued, "everybody was all up in each other's face. It wasn't a fight, just kind of an argument. Sam went up to Earnhardt and asked, 'Why did you wreck me? Why did you wreck me?' Earnhardt looked right at him and said, 'If I couldn't win, you weren't going to win.' Earnhardt turned around and walked off."

As Late Model Sportsman cars—and stars—became more expensive in the late 1970s and early '80s, tracks turned to Late Model Stock machines for their weekly main events. These cars were much closer to an actual passenger car, and their lower operating costs were

ABOVE: Gene Glover says that Late Model Sportsman racing "was just a way of life. That's what we enjoyed doing. We had a lot of fun back then. There wasn't as much pressure, sponsor-wise back then as there is now." Here, Glover is shown at his home track in Kingsport, Tenn. (David Allio) RIGHT: Sonny Hutchens (foreground) and Ray Hendrick (on the outside) sandwich an unidentified competitor in the middle during the Late Model Sportsman portion of Martinsville's annual Dogwood 500 Classic on March 16, 1980. Seconds later, they crashed. Tommy Ellis won the event. (David Allio) OPPOSITE: Tommy Houston receives his trophy for winning at Hickory in 1979. Houston says that it took running in several events to average $2,800 a week in winnings. In front of Houston are two of his three sons, Andy (on left) and Marty. (Bob Dudley)

"The salvation for the tracks were the Late Model Stock cars. Go back to a cheaper car, and get it to be more of a localized division. But what do you do with the Jack Ingrams and all these guys that had normally run all over the country?"

As Ellis was in the midst of putting together his championship season in 1981, rumors cropped up that NASCAR would soon do away with the division and form a bona fide touring series in its place.

Something had to be done, Childress told a gathering of track promoters in November or December of that year. If not, he said, the facilities were going to be left with nothing to run in their feature events. Beginning at Daytona in February 1982, NASCAR officials had decided that the Late Model Sportsman Series would be a touring division, with a set schedule.

"There were no other choices," Childress said. "We told the promoters, 'If we don't do this, it's going to go away. All these guys with race cars, they're gonna put them out behind the barn.' The handwriting was on the wall. The weekly race tracks were not going to run Late Model Sportsman cars much longer, and they didn't."

Reaction to the new series was less than enthusiastic.

"There were a lot of people that didn't think it would work," Childress concluded. "I worked out a schedule, but we didn't stick with it because of the fact that so many tracks really surprised me when they said they didn't want [a date].

"Some of the promoters didn't like it. They didn't like us telling them what they had to pay, telling them when they could run, how many races they could run and who they could get there."

Still, Childress and NASCAR forged ahead with plans for the series. What is now the Busch Series was about to be born.

much more attractive to local weekly racers on limited budgets. The Late Model Stock cars were much cheaper to run than their Sportsman counterparts, mostly because of reduced engine costs. Cylinder heads were strictly stock and cost about $400 per set, as opposed to $4,000 to $6,000 for the highly refined Late Model Sportsman heads. Various other parts, such as the carburetor, brakes, and tires, were also simpler and less expensive. Jack Ingram estimated that when tracks went to Late Model Stock machines, car costs were cut by more than half.

Old Dominion Speedway in Manassas, Va., was the first to make the switch to Late Model Stocks in 1979, and car counts at other facilities dwindled to the point that only a handful of tracks planned to hold Late Model Sportsman events in 1982.

"Tracks were trying to compete with each other for the stars," Childress said. "It got to be a bidding war. It got to be where the tracks were putting themselves out of business.

ABOVE: Jack Ingram leads Morgan Shepherd at Martinsville in 1980. Ingram won three consecutive Late Model Sportsman championships in the 1970s, but says that winning two of the division's races at Daytona made him "a big-name race car driver." (Bob Dudley) OPPOSITE: Dale Jarrett (on the inside) does battle with his older brother, Glenn, during a 1980 event at Hickory. Their father, two-time Grand National (now Winston Cup) champion, Ned Jarrett, had been the track's promoter, but chose to pursue a broadcasting career. Glenn would follow in his father's broadcasting footsteps, while "D. J." continued to drive. (Bob Dudley)

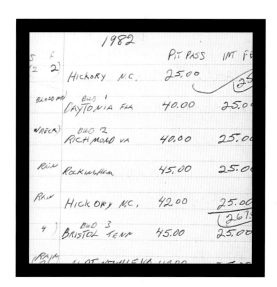

1982
The Start of
Something Great

There weren't a lot of obvious changes for the Late Model Sportsman division when the 1982 season began in Daytona.

Drivers were using cars they'd raced the year before. Points from a few races on the tour still counted toward track championships at the local level. Even its name was the same, because Anheuser-Busch's famed Budweiser brand did not become the division's title sponsor until later in the year.

FT: Sam Ard straps into his car at ckory prior to the next-to-last race the 1982 season. Note how clean d sparse Ard kept the cockpit of his chine. He finished 18th in the race n by Jack Ingram. (David Allio) HT: This is a detail of Jack Ingram's gerbook, which he used to keep ck of entry fees and pit-pass costs larger view appears on page 28.)

The overall records of Late Model Sportsman drivers through 1981 no longer count toward career totals, although champions of the division are still listed in the Busch Series record book. Gone forever, it seems, are the estimated 275 races Ingram won. The same goes for the achievements of Tommy Ellis, Morgan Shepherd, L. D. Ottinger, and all the rest who made the transition. All might as well have been fresh-faced rookies.

Andy Hall, who joined NASCAR in October 1982 as a public relations assistant for the division, insists that the sanctioning body's reasoning for wiping the slate clean was sound. Because drivers ran such varied schedules at tracks where record keeping was inadequate at best, accurate tallies were impossible.

"The main reason [the results were dropped] is there was no way to go back and keep records of all that stuff," he said. "There was no disrespect intended. It was just that you had to start somewhere."

Other differences were in place. A standardized purse required most tracks to pay in the range from $2,000 to win to $500 to finish 10th and $200 to start, according to Childress. And, to entice the stars of the Late Model Sportsman wars to keep showing up, a Winner's Circle program was established.

Tracks that hosted weekly NASCAR races paid $500 to each of the drivers on the plan, and those that didn't shelled out $750 per competitor. Superspeedways such as Daytona and Charlotte put up $1,000 per driver. Four drivers were initially on the Winner's Circle plan—Ingram, Ellis, Sam Ard, and Geoffrey Bodine, who'd been a Late Model Sportsman track champion at South Boston the previous year.

There was some stonewalling at first, because the star drivers were hesitant to commit to a series that some thought might not last. A few, like former Late Model Sportsman champion Butch Lindley, turned down NASCAR's offer to join the Winner's Circle program.

"We offered it to them in order of the way they finished in the previous year's championship," Childress said. "We offered it to them, but they didn't all jump right on board. In fact, Jack Ingram made the statement, 'I get more deal money than this to go to some of the races.' But he didn't get that much to go to all the races."

A firm final schedule for the new series didn't exist when Dale Earnhardt held off Jody Ridley in the closing laps of the first race at Daytona on February 13. Third went to Ard. From the time he'd first laid a tire on Daytona's racing surface in the early '70s, Ard said he "fell in love with the speedways."

"The speedways are so much easier to drive," Ard admitted. "You've got to hustle a car on the short track. On a speedway, you don't have to do that. You've just got to have good equipment. You've got to know where to make moves and how to make them."

The next two races filled open spots on the Winner's Circle program. Houston won a crash-filled thriller February 20 at Richmond, and Phil Parsons beat David Pearson March 13 at Bristol. The following month, Bodine vacated his Winner's Circle slot. Two weeks after he gained notice in the Winston Cup garage with a Budweiser Late Model Sportsman win April 3 at Darlington, Bodine accepted a ride with team owner Cliff Stewart. That made him the first driver from the newly formed division to use it as a stepping stone to the Winston Cup circuit. Many more would follow in the years to come.

Meanwhile, it didn't take long for Ard and Ingram to distance themselves from the rest of the pack and begin staging a two-man show for the championship.

Ard had won his first race of the season at Martinsville on March 28, while Ingram was third. Ingram scored his first official Budweiser Late Model Sportsman victory April 10 at Hickory. Ard was second. On April 18 at South Boston, Va., the order was reversed—Ard won and Ingram claimed the runner-up spot.

ABOVE: Driver David Rogers waits as a crew member removes a shredded tire during a pit stop at Daytona. Rogers finished 14th, five laps down to Earnhardt, and collected $2,120 in winnings. (Graham Niven) **OPPOSITE:** Dale Earnhardt (15) leads Jody Ridley (98) around Tommy Ellis's lapped car in the first race of what is now the Busch Series on February 13, 1982. Ridley's attempts to pass were repeatedly foiled by slower cars allowing Earnhardt to capture the victory. (Graham Niven)

1982

S F		PIT PASS	INT FEE	
MAY 2 (2-4)	BUD 9 RICHMOND VA	36.00	25.00	JULY 9 (
MAY 8 (4-1)	BUD 10 HAMPTON VA.	48.00	20.00	JULY 10 (
MAY 15 (3-2)	BUD 11 DOVER DEL	40.00	25.00	JULY 16
MAY 23 (5-3)	BUD 12 HICKORY N.C.	48.00	20.00	JULY 17
MAY 29 (2-17)	BUD 13 CHARLOTTE N.C.	40.00	25.00 / 327.00	JULY 23
JUNE 4 (1-1)	HICKORY N.C.	36.00		JULY 24
JUNE 11 (2 1)	BUD 14 ASHEVILLE N.C.	40.00	20.00	JULY 25 (
JUNE 12 (RAIN)	HICKORY N.C.	30.00		AUG 1 (4
JUNE 18 (2 1)	ASHEVILLE N.C.	30.00		AUG 7 (2
JUNE 19 (8 4)	BUD 15 HICKORY N.C.	36.00	20.00	AUG 14 (6
JUNE 28 (2 4)	BUD 16 SOUTH BOSTON VA.	48.00	20.00	AUG 21 (3
	BUD 17 ...INGHAM N.C.	40.00	25.00 / 345.00	AUG 28 (3
	...ORY N.C.	36.00	15.00	SEPT 4 (5
	BUD 18 ...WAY	48.00	20.00	SEPT 11 (

MARTINSVILLE SPEEDWAY
MARTINSVILLE VIRGINIA

That event at South Boston also saw an impromptu driver change just before the green flag fell. Dale Jarrett didn't have a car prepared and was on the verge of missing out on those all-important points toward the championship.

"Gary Neice got out of his car on the starting line," recalled Jarrett, who went on to finish 10th. "I don't know if he saw something in my eyes or whatever it was, but he literally unbuckled, took his helmet off, got out, and let me get in the car."

Three more times during the summer, Ard and Ingram finished 1-2. Although Ard led in the standings, it wasn't by much.

"Jack was one of the toughest competitors I had," Ard said. "He was like a shadow. Every time you looked around, there he was."

After the May 2 race in Richmond, Va., Ard had a 100-point advantage on Ingram. Ard then trailed Ingram to the checkered flag May 8 at Langley Speedway in Hampton, Va. Only 17 cars started the event, the smallest car count in the history of the division.

With such small fields, officials had to overlook minor technical infractions to get drivers for certain events.

"NASCAR was very lenient, and they had to be, with the local competitors," Ingram said. "The things that really counted—the weight of the cars, the size of the motor, the size of the carburetor, the kind of tires you used—had to pretty much come in line, which wasn't hard to do.

"But their bodies might not have been fixed exactly like the specs. That really wasn't a factor as far as them having a good finish. NASCAR would work with the guys that came in from a weekly race track. If they started following the circuit, they would make them get more in line if they had something wrong with the body."

As a result of the rather loose inspection procedures, it wasn't uncommon to bend the rules a little—or a lot.

"We did all we could get by with," Ellis said. "We learned from the school of hard knocks. I worked hard at it, believe me. I stayed up at night, awake, thinking about ways to get by with stuff."

What's the best trick he ever devised? Ellis won't say.

"I'm gonna let that dog lie," he said with a laugh. "We never did get caught at it."

Ard's lead stabilized at between 30 and 50 points

for most of the summer, but he stumbled badly August 13 at Indianapolis Raceway Park. He completed only 12 laps because of engine failure and was credited with a 28th-place finish. Ingram finished fifth behind Shepherd, the winner, and a wild scramble for second place among Ellis, Houston, and Jimmy Hensley. Ingram took the lead in the standings and kept it the rest of the season.

"I almost knew for sure that the only person who could possibly beat me for the championship was Sam Ard," Ingram said. "If he had a little worse luck than I had, I would beat him. He and I were basically winning all the races."

The IRP race was important for more than just its significance in the championship battle. It was the first

ABOVE: Sam Ard (right) poses with his crew before the Kroger NASCAR 200 at Indianapolis Raceway Park, August 13, the division's first race outside the stock-car friendly confines of the Southeast. Engine failure after only 12 laps dropped Ard to 28th in the finishing order. Jack Ingram finished fifth, taking the lead in the Budweiser Late Model Sportsman standings from Ard. Jesse Coke, Ard's crew chief, is third from the left. (Jesse Coke Collection) OPPOSITE TOP: Jack Ingram kept track of his 1982 entry fees and pit-pass costs in this ledgerbook. He notes races on the Budweiser Late Model Sportsman tour with "Bud 1", "Bud 2" and so on. Notice the number of races he ran in addition to his BLMS schedule. Ingram won $122,100 as the circuit's inaugural champion, including a $31,069.60 share of the point fund from Anheuser-Busch. (Jack Ingram Collection) OPPOSITE BOTTOM: Phil Parsons has the advantage over Butch Lindley under caution at Martinsville March 28. Lindley led the event twice for 17 laps, while Parsons was out front once for eight laps. Lindley finished second behind Sam Ard. Engine failure dropped Parsons to 36th in the final rundown after he completed 35 laps. (Jerry Haislip)

event for the division outside the stock-car friendly confines of the South, and quite a few people were pessimistic about its chances for success.

"They went out there, and it was a packed house," Hall said. "It ended with Morgan Shepherd winning. Jimmy Hensley, Tommy Ellis, and Tommy Houston all spun and wrecked across the finish line going for second on the last lap. The crowd just went nuts.

"1982 was the year that Gordon Johncock and Rick Mears had one of the closest finishes in Indianapolis 500 history. Then, in August, these NASCAR boys come into town, and look what they do on the last lap. The town got really fired up, and the event was a total success the first year."

Free tires from Goodyear helped ease some of the financial sting for teams that made the trip to IRP that first year. Most competitors were a long way from home, and the help was greatly appreciated.

"Basically, all our regulars that went out there got at least a set of tires," Childress said. "Some of them got more than one set, and it wasn't the Jack Ingrams that got more than one set. The guys that couldn't really afford to go, they got more help than the guys that had the money to go.

"Until now, nobody really knew that [we gave more tires to smaller teams] other than myself, Goodyear, and probably Bill Gazaway [NASCAR's head of competition at the time]. It wasn't a thing that we promised anybody anything. We waited until we got there and saw who we had, and then we helped them out."

Although that event was a success, the series was struggling. This was a time when top teams were willing to accept $1,000 per race in sponsorship and crowds were small. In a 1990 Associated Press story, Houston said, "I remember the first year. It looked like it would be hard to start a fight up there in the stands because there were so few people."

Ingram won October 17 at Hickory, N.C., while Ard was 18th. That made Ingram's cushion more comfortable, but in the final race of the year, on October 31 at Martinsville, Ingram and Ellis crashed on the 122nd lap. Still, Ingram's 26th-place finish was enough to give him the championship over Ard, who was a lap behind race winner Lindley in sixth.

Ingram collected a $31,069.60 share of the point fund for winning the inaugural Budweiser Late Model Sportsman championship. His total earnings were $122,100 for the year. Lindley, on the other hand, competed in only 14 of the 29 races that year and nevertheless finished 10th in the standings. His share of the points fund came to the grand total of $3,910.44.

Although Ard lost the Budweiser Late Model Sportsman crown, he won the Winston Racing Series Mid-Atlantic regional championship by continuing to compete at the local level. He was just getting warmed up.

OPPOSITE: NASCAR's Andy Hall presents Sam Ard with a trophy for his runner-up finish in the Budweiser Late Model Sportsman standings. Ard won $122,099 in 1982, $1 less than the champion, Ingram. Looking on is a bearded Dale Jarrett, who was sixth in points that season. (Andy Hall Collection)
BELOW: Because full-time help was scarce, competitors often "borrowed" help from Winston Cup crews at combination events. Here, members of Harry Gant's Winston Cup team service Jack Ingram at Charlotte on October 9. Ingram finished fifth behind winner Darrell Waltrip. (Lowe's Motor Speedway Archives)

LEFT: Sam Ard ducks under Dale Earnhardt during the Miller Time 300 at Charlotte on October 8, 1983. Ard led the final 22 laps, to beat Earnhardt to the finish line by seven and one-half seconds. It was the last of Ard's four consecutive victories that fall. (Graham Niven) RIGHT: When a young Davey Allison struggled during preparations for Charlotte's Miller Time 300, his father, the legendary Bobby Allison, stepped in to help. The advice must have worked, because Davey finished seventh in the event. (Dick Conway)

1983
One Legend
Challenges Another

Ard didn't take losing the inaugural Budweiser Late Model Sportsman championship lightly. He came out swinging in 1983, sitting on the pole and finishing sixth in the February 19 season opener at Daytona and then winning a week later, on February 26 at Richmond.

Ard would win 10 races on the way to winning the championship that season, including four in a row late in the year. Both feats are still records.

Reflecting on that magical year, Ard said with a smile, "I must've been doing something right. I don't know what. It means a lot to know that I've still got something out there for them to shoot at."

Another mark established by Ard in 1983, his 10 poles, would stand for nine years.

Despite changing crew chiefs midway through the season, the team was in good shape to overcome Ingram. Ard credits Ken Bingham's 311-cubic-inch engines for much of his success. Nine of his 10 wins

were on short tracks, where he was powered by engines built by Bingham. A weight rule—cars had to weigh nine pounds for each cubic inch in the engine—added to the advantage.

"Ken just didn't quit," Ard said. "He just kept on until he was better than the rest of them. It was just like me driving the car. I worked on my car all the time. I slept with them things. I dreamed about them, what I could do to make it better. Ken was the same way about the engine. We made a real good combination."

Ingram knew what he was up against. Ard's team, which was owned by Howard Thomas, was a formidable foe.

ABOVE: Sam Ard heads into turn one during the Mello Yello 300 at Charlotte, May 28. Although he would complete only 76 laps and finish 32nd, Ard would have much better luck at the track in the fall. It would be a history-making year for him. (Graham Niven) OPPOSITE: Diane Teel watches as her car is pushed through inspection at Martinsville, March 20. She would finish 10th. A year before, also at Martinsville, Teel had become the first female to compete in a Budweiser Late Model Sportsman event. With 10 career starts, Teel registered two top 10s and collected $5,065 in winnings. (Jerry Haislip)

"They were spending more money than anyone at any race," Ingram said. "Sam was running the whole team, building his own cars. That's what I admired about him. He wound up with these extremely powerful motors.

"Howard hired people to work on that car. They had multiple cars and a couple of tow trucks. They didn't have no better organization than I had, but they had a better one than most everyone at the race track. Sam was able to capitalize on it."

Was he ever.

After winning at Richmond, Ard next won at Martinsville on March 20, starting from the pole and leading 212 of 250 laps. He followed that up with another win April 3 at North Wilkesboro, N.C., by a lap over runner-up Houston. Only 10 cars were still running at the end of the race, a mark that's also still on the books.

Ard had taken the lead in North Wilkesboro from Lindley on the 34th circuit and led the rest of the 200-lap event. While other drivers were continually falling out because of mechanical problems and wrecks, Ard couldn't afford to rest easy.

"Any time you were racing with Butch Lindley and Jack Ingram, you didn't hold back," Ard said. "I had a good engine, and I had made some changes in the car just for that one particular race. I hit it right on the head. It would go whenever I wanted, where I wanted it to go."

Ard, however, wouldn't win again for nearly four months. Disaster struck at the very next race. Ard completed just eight laps before crashing on April 16 at South Boston. The car, the team's primary machine, sustained serious chassis damage in the accident. Although crew chief Jesse Coke said he tried to convince Ard there was a problem, the damage wasn't discovered until after Coke left the team in late June.

"The crash at South Boston bent the car up, the front snout, the tail clip, and everything," Coke recalled. "We straightened the tail clip and put a new front snout on it, but there were some brackets bent underneath the tail end of it that we didn't find at the time. The rear end just wasn't in the location it was supposed to be."

The performance lull cost Ard ground in the championship chase, and on June 25 at South Boston, he fell out early and finished 15th. Ingram's second-place finish gave him a 35-point cushion in the standings, the

ABOVE: Tommy Ellis pushes Sam Ard through the turns at South Boston. Ellis, a native of Virginia, swept both of South Boston's races that June. (Dick Conway) LEFT: Jack Ingram (11), and Tommy Ellis, fight it out for the Coca-Cola 200 at South Boston July 23. Ellis won the race, and three others during that year at the tiny 0.357-mile bullring. Ingram had to settle for second. (Dick Conway) OPPOSITE: Darrell Waltrip finished second at IRP after Tommy Houston shoved Tommy Ellis out of the way on the last lap to take the win. Pepsi sponsored Waltrip's Junior Johnson-owned Winston Cup entry, and he brought the backing along with him when he drove this Pontiac owned by Jack Ingram. Waltrip's star presence helped fill the grandstand. (Dick Conway)

beginning of a lead he would keep the rest of the summer and into the fall.

Coke, who split time between the race shop and a fleet of trucks that serviced Thomas's country ham business, left the team about that time and was replaced by Gere Kennon, who eventually discovered the bent rear end on the primary car. After it was repaired, the team's results improved dramatically.

Kennon's first race with Ard was at Caraway Speedway in Asheboro, N.C., on July 6, and it was an eventful debut.

"We qualified on the pole and led about the whole thing," Kennon said. "With about 15 [laps] to go, Butch [Lindley] ran him down, spun him out, and won the race. They had played golf that morning, and then he spun us out in the race.

"Sam didn't wreck. He just spun around. He was sitting down there in turn four, and he come on the radio said, 'I ain't never playing golf with him again.' It was hilarious."

Ard finally won again July 30 at Hickory, leading all 200 laps. Ingram responded with a victory August 6 at Langley, Va. Ard finished seventh, dropping him 90 points behind Ingram.

The next race, on August 13 at IRP, featured a stirring confrontation between Houston and Ellis. Racing for the lead on the last lap, Houston tapped Ellis into a spin coming off the second corner. Houston won, with Ellis recovering to finish fifth.

That was little consolation to Ellis, whose response to the incident has grown to epic proportions. Although stories abound, all that's for certain is that Ellis used a baseball bat to knock the gauges off air bottles in Houston's pit area.

"He wrecked me on the last lap," Ellis said. "I've heard stories that I knocked his toolbox over, set fire to his pits, threatened to beat his crew up. None of that was true. I went over to the damn victory lane and told him what a no-good son-of-a-bitch he was."

The memory of the rough-and-tumble good ol' days brings Houston to fits of laughter. He might've been mad then, but time—and winning the race—have tempered his outlook.

"After the race was over, Tommy was sitting in the back of the NASCAR truck," Houston said, laughing harder as the story progresses. "I walked up to him and said, 'Tommy, why in the world do you want to tear up my pit equipment like that?' He said, 'You're just a blankety-blank, blank, blank. You're just lucky I didn't tear up your head.' I couldn't help but laugh at him."

Houston learned before he left the track that a fine would be forthcoming. Ironically, he'd already arranged to fly from Indianapolis back home to Hickory with NASCAR officials. It could have been an awkward flight, but Houston shrugged off the penalty.

"Tommy had already been told he was going to be fined $2,000," Hall said. "He kind of leaned back in his seat and said, 'Well, I might as well enjoy this ride, because I'm paying for it.' There was talk of a one-race suspension. Tommy Ellis actually came to Tommy Houston's defense and said, 'No, don't suspend him. He's racing for a living just like I am.'"

Ard had avoided the Houston-Ellis fracas to finish third, but Ingram was 20th in the final rundown. Ingram's lead in the standings was chopped to 28 points, and from there, Ard was on the charge.

Ard won at Bristol on August 26 and finished second to Neil Bonnett at Darlington on September 4, despite miserable weather that nearly forced him out of his car.

"It was blistering hot, and the caution came out with about 15 laps to go," Kennon said. "He'd been complaining all day about his heel burning, and he said, 'If I come down pit road, I'm getting out of this hot son-of-a-bitch.' So he didn't pit. Bonnett pitted, put four tires on, and he beat us.

"Sam came screeching up to the gas pumps after the race and jumped out. There was some guy standing there

with a cooler. He knocked the cooler out of the guy's hand, opened the lid, and just stuck his foot in the guy's cooler. He was just standing there, going, 'Ooooo . . .'"

Ard again avoided disaster on September 11 at North Wilkesboro. He and Parsons spun shortly after a late restart and collected Ingram in the process. All three would come back to finish in the top 10—Ard fifth, Ingram sixth, and Parsons seventh. The Ard Express was still on track.

A win at South Boston on September 17 narrowed Ard's deficit to just 19 points. He regained the lead in the standings with another win September 24 at Martinsville, while Ingram was fifth. Then on October 1 at Orange County, Ard was in victory lane once more. A fourth consecutive win came October 8 at Charlotte, an event that was usually a sure win for the visiting Winston Cup drivers.

Ard beat Earnhardt to the checkered flag by some 7 1/2 seconds.

"A lot of that Cup crowd came back and raced with us," Ard said. "They had better stuff, but I tried to make my stuff as good as what they had. The only other thing was that they had more experience, so I had to get as good as they were. When I beat them, I had beat the best."

Ingram finally broke the streak by outlasting Ard October 16 at Hickory. Ard took the loss in stride.

"Jack come along, and I couldn't hold him off," Ard said. "Jack was tough. He run me hard to start with, but I didn't hit the setup quite right. I wasn't really disappointed. When you got beat by Jack Ingram, you got beat by one of the best."

It was at Hickory where Ingram hooked up with the sponsor that would be with him until his retirement in 1991. U.S. Tobacco and its Skoal brand were already involved in Winston Cup competition with Gant, who helped set up the meeting with Ingram.

Skoal, which also had backed Phil Parsons in 1982 and '83, was the first national corporate sponsor in the division. Most drivers at that time considered themselves fortunate to get a few bucks from local businesses. Other sponsors were simply companies associated with the driver or car owner. Owner Howard Thomas, for instance, advertised his Thomas Brothers Country Ham products on the cars he fielded for Ard.

Although Skoal was bringing corporate credibility to the sport, it wasn't a huge financial deal for Ingram, who accepted $50,000 for the entire upcoming season. The figure is paltry by today's standards, but Ingram wasn't complaining.

"I was obviously not gonna be able to maintain that kind of performance because of my age," said Ingram, who was in his mid-40s at the time. "They didn't take advantage of me. I agreed to everything. I appreciated what they did. They came along and offered me a corporate sponsor, and there weren't many of those around."

With one race to go, Ard led Ingram by 72 points. The title was up for grabs October 30 at Martinsville, but Ard was too strong for Ingram to overcome. Ard led three times for 211 of the race's 250 laps to capture his fifth win in the last six races of 1983 and clinch the championship by 87 points over Ingram.

An astounding season—the last with Budweiser as the tour's title sponsor—was over.

"I never took any time to know how many records I had set or anything like that, because all I did was race," Ard said. "When I went there to race, I went there to win. I didn't go there for second or third or nothing like that. Whenever I do something, I try to do my best at it."

ABOVE: Tommy Houston races Joe Thurman (04) for position at Martinsville September 24. In 1967, Thurman had won the final Sportsman championship. The next year, the Late Model Sportsman and Modified divisions were split. (Graham Niven)
OPPOSITE: Sam Ard and Phil Parsons spin in turn one at North Wilkesboro, September 11, seconds after a late restart. Jack Ingram was also involved in the incident. Ard salvaged a fifth-place finish in the event, moving him closer to Ingram in the battle for the championship. (Wilkes Journal-Patriot Archives)

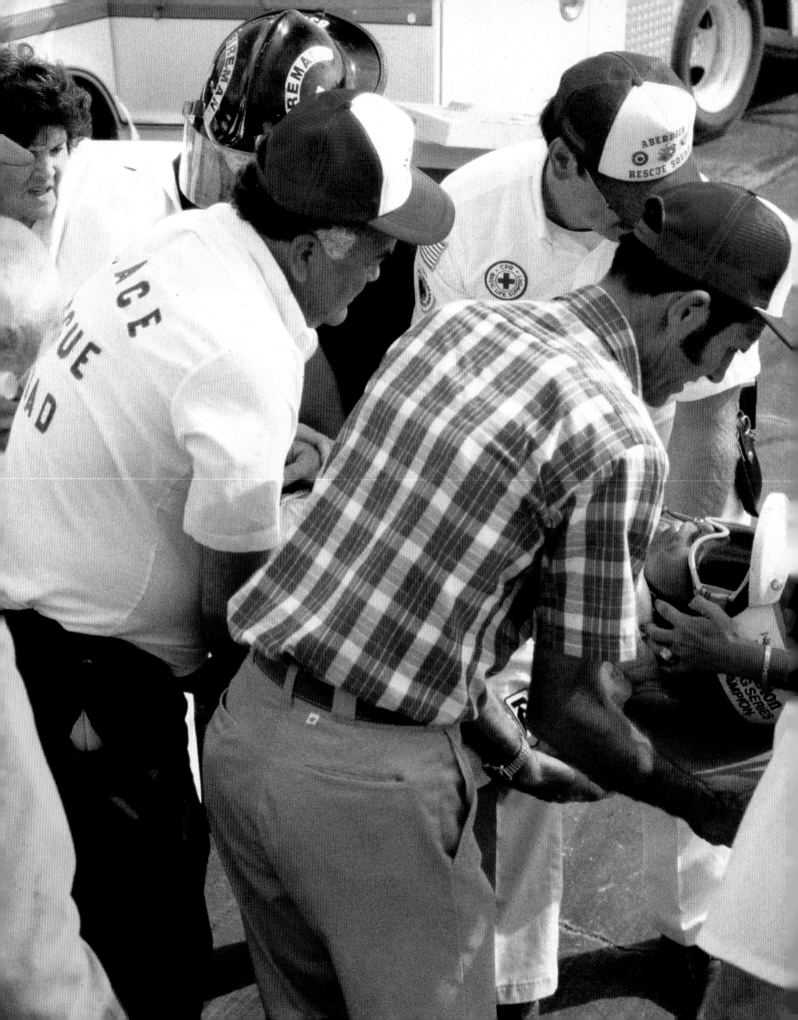

LEFT: An unconscious Sam Ard is taken out of his car by a bevy of safety workers after his career-ending crash the October 20, 1984 event at Rockingham. Steve Hmiel, then a Petty Enterprises crew member, was one of the first to the car, and said Ard had already started to turn blue. (Sam Ard collection) RIGHT: Sam Ard opens up a small lead over pole-sitter Tommy Ellis at Martinsville March 25. Although Ard didn't win this race — he finished ninth, two laps down — it would be a very good year for him. And a very bad one. (Dick Conway)

1984
A Life Changes in an Instant

As good as 1983 had been for Sam Ard, 1984 was even better. And it was also worse, much, much worse.

He began the Busch Late Model Sportsman season disappointed with a fourth-place finish at Daytona in February, but finished it clinging to life after an October accident at Rockingham, N.C., that ended his driving career. Ard would go from being virtually unbeatable to wondering if he'd ever walk again, much less race.

Few other drivers in history have been as dominant as Ard was in 1984. In 28 starts that year, he posted 24 top-five finishes and 26 top 10s. Entering the next-to-last race on the schedule, Ard led Ingram by an amazing 583 points, having long since clinched the championship.

Ard was giving his rivals fits. What made his team so good in general and during 1984 in particular?

ABOVE: Ron Bouchard closes on Sam Ard in the final laps of the Budweiser 200 at Dover May 19, but comes up a foot short at the checkered flag. It was Ard's fifth win of the season, and his third in a row. (David Chobat)

Tommy Houston suggests one reason was that Bingham and partner Ronnie Reavis made liberal interpretations of the rulebook when putting together Ard's engines.

"They had the intakes raised up with spacers," Houston said. "When NASCAR would say that you couldn't run aluminum spacers, they'd come back the next week and have an inch-and-a-half gasket. They stayed on top of the ball game."

There's a twinkle in Kennon's eye as he refutes Houston's claim. By almost all accounts, Houston himself wasn't exactly a saint when it came to tinkering with the innards of his race car.

"We had the manifold spaced up, but the rulebook didn't say you couldn't do that," Kennon began. "People could complain about B&R motors all they want. Dale Jarrett had them. He couldn't beat us. Geoff Bodine had them. He didn't beat us all the time. We beat him.

"I know for a fact Tommy did some serious stuff. I've heard from more than one person he'd run cheater carburetors. He was bad about soaking his tires. Howard Thomas would've had a fit over getting caught cheating. There were times the car might've been a little bit low, but nothing motorwise."

Ard finished fourth at Daytona despite stiff competition from several Winston Cup stars. He battled Bobby Allison, Ron Bouchard, Neil Bonnett, and Geoffrey Bodine throughout the race and wound up leading eight times for 52 laps. He was out front with just four laps to go.

"I had them beat bad," Ard recalled.

Backing off would have been a good strategy had his fuel filter not been clogged. Others closed in on Ard, and his engine shut down in the middle of a torrid battle for the lead with Darrell Waltrip.

"When my car shut off, I had pulled back up alongside Darrell and almost in front of him," Ard said. "It was starved for fuel. When we got in the corner, the car caught back up, sort of. I went through the corner pretty good. When we started down the front straightaway, it shut off again."

A Busch Series regular would not win the season opener until 1995, when Chad Little turned the trick.

After Daytona, Ard won at Richmond and Rockingham, giving him a lead of 117 points in just three races. Ingram answered Ard's early season wins by notching firsts in four of the next five races and had closed to within 57 points following a victory April 28 at Nashville. But then Ard went on a tear of his own and posted three more wins in a row—at Langley, Milwaukee, and Dover, Del.

Conserving his equipment almost cost Ard the win May 19 at Dover, when Ron Bouchard crept up from behind during the closing stages and mounted a charge to the outside coming off turn four on the final circuit.

"I backed off too much, and I didn't realize he could close the gap that quick," Ard said. "He did. He came on strong. I did almost give it away. I picked it back up,

ABOVE: Busch Late Model Sportsman Director Robert Black conducts the drivers' meeting prior to the Roses Stores 300 at South Boston June 23. Among the competitors pictured are Ed Berrier (sitting left, leaning on one arm); Joe Thurman (sitting left, dark cap); Geoffrey Bodine (sitting to right of Thurman); Sam Ard (sitting, Goody's logo on back of uniform); Jack Ingram (standing, Skoal uniform); Dickie Boswell (standing in front of Ingram); Bosco Lowe (to Ingram's left); Tommy Ellis (sitting, to Lowe's left); Glenn Jarrett (leaning against left side of truck); Dale Jarrett (sitting on truck bumper); Eddie Falk (red uniform, blue stripe, sitting on truck bumper); Jeff Hensley (standing, red uniform); Tommy Houston (sitting on truck bumper, partially obscured by Hensley); and Rick Mast (leaning against right side of truck). Tim Hudson (seated in front of Black) is currently NASCAR's chief scorer. Charles Hudson (seated to left of his father) is currently one of Jeff Gordon's public relations representatives. (Dick Conway) RIGHT: Tommy Ellis gets serviced on a nearly-empty pit road at Orange County July 7. Ellis finished 12th, 30 laps down, because of a flat tire. Drivers had few crew members in those days, so the closest thing to a team uniform in this photo are the L.D. Ottinger T-shirts in the stall to the left of Ellis's. Also note that Ellis's gasman isn't wearing a fireproof uniform. (Dick Conway)

ABOVE: Jack Ingram waits for the start of the Goody's 200 at Hickory July 28, a race he went on to win. It was his seventh victory of the season, tying him with Sam Ard for most wins at that point in the schedule. (Dick Conway) OPPOSITE: Dale Jarrett's Pontiac shows more than a few battle scars prior to the Coca-Cola 300 at North Wilkesboro September 16. His car may not have looked pretty, but Jarrett finished eighth, two laps down. Sam Ard captured the last win of his career in the event. (Dick Conway)

but he had such a running start on me, he almost got me anyway."

Ard's margin of victory is listed as one foot.

Ard was sixth May 26 at Charlotte, behind a heated battle for the win among Bobby Allison, Darrell Waltrip, and Lake Speed. Allison and Waltrip banged doors coming off the fourth turn, and the leader of the "Alabama Gang" nipped his longtime nemesis by a yard or so. Speed was right behind, looking for either to bobble.

Allison would win the next day's World 600 Winston Cup race, making him the first driver to sweep both events in a combination weekend since the formation of the Busch Late Model Sportsman division as a touring series two years earlier.

Ingram was an early casualty at Charlotte, completing only 52 of the race's 200 laps because of transmission failure. That put Ard's cushion in the standings at 212 points. With 17 races to go in 1984, the battle for the championship was all but over.

Ingram didn't have a horrible season in 1984; he eventually won eight races. Yet Ard was always right on Ingram's heels, preventing him from gaining any substantial ground.

Ingram, the driver called "Iron Man" long before Terry Labonte, won June 16 at Orange County. Ard, however, was third. Ingram won another race at the 0.375-mile bullring on July 7, but again Ard was just two spots behind at the finish. Ingram took the checkered flag in the next race, on July 28 at Hickory, but Ard was again third. A fourth win by Ingram, this time on August 11 at Langley, broke the string. This time, Ard was second.

Ingram won that event in a car borrowed from longtime friend and fellow driver, Ronnie Silver. Silver, in turn, took over newcomer Elton Sawyer's Pontiac and drove it to a fifth-place finish. Today, such swapping would be unthinkable.

"In the last practice session, we had an engine problem," Ingram said. "We didn't have time to change it, so I time-trialed Ronnie's car. Ronnie started his racing career helping me, and his daddy painted my first race car."

Ingram had to have been one of the sport's most frustrated winners. Ard, never stumbling, kept posting one top-10 finish after another. But Ard wasn't biding his time simply to tally points toward the title.

Witness the September 1 race at Darlington, S.C., where he was back at it with Bouchard. Officially, there were 13 lead changes. Unofficially, there were probably 25 or more. In the end, fading brakes spoiled Ard's shot at capturing his eighth win of the year.

"When I'd pump the brakes up, it'd slow the car down," Ard said. "I'd go in the corner, and the car would skate up the track. When it did, Ron got by me. Coming off [turn] two and down the back straightaway, I passed him back. We went in the next corner, and the car shot up the track real high because I was in there too hard.

"He cut down and got under me coming off the corner. I came all the way off the track, down into the sand. The car started getting a little squirrelly getting under him. I eased back up on the track. I was right on his back bumper when we crossed the finish line."

Ard finished out of the top 10 in only one of his 27 starts before heading to Rockingham in October. He finished 11th September 8 at Richmond—two laps down—after getting spun by a lapped car. As disappointments go, it was a minor one. Ingram came home 27th, the victim of early engine failure.

"It didn't upset me too much, because I was so far out in front of them," Ard said. "They just about couldn't catch me anyhow. What upset me was a lapped car took me out. They got the move-over flag, and then he just didn't heed it enough. He went in the corner too hard and took me out. That made me ill."

Ard captured his final win on September 16 at North Wilkesboro. He led the first circuit, regained the advantage from Houston on the fourth lap, and was never headed during the rest of the 150-lap event.

Ard experienced little trouble in 1984 until the 15th lap of the October 20 Komfort Koach 200 at Rockingham. Having qualified second, Ard was racing pole-sitter

Geoffrey Bodine for the lead as they charged into the third turn, Bob Shreeves's car apparently had broken a water hose, and dropped fluid on the track. Ard hit the standing water as he entered turn three and crashed hard into the wall. His accident also collected Bobby Allison, L. D. Ottinger, Ed Berrier, and Shepherd.

Kennon can still remember the temperature of that October day, the sickening feeling of seeing Ard's battered car, and the sense of loss he felt as Ard was taken, unconscious, to Moore County Hospital in nearby Pinehurst, N.C.

"After he hit the wall, he came down and stopped on the inside of the track. The car was sitting down there running wide open," Kennon said. "Steve Hmiel and Dale Inman, they climbed over the fence and shut the motor off. Steve said he was blue then.

"He was all wound up under the dash. After that, we just loaded the car up and went to Pinehurst to the hospital. It was killing me. It was like losing my dad."

Ingram also knew his longtime adversary was seriously injured as he passed the accident site.

"When Sam wrecked, he'd always get out to direct people and help them load it up, but his head was hanging over," Ingram said. "I had just an eerie feeling. I just hoped Sam was all right. I didn't want to win a championship, races, or anything in the future without Sam Ard, but that's the way it wound up being."

Two hours after he was extracted from the wreckage of his car, Ard was still drifting in and out of consciousness. Listed in critical condition in the facility's intensive care unit, he was suffering from severe swelling of the brain, a half-dollar sized blood clot in his brain, and a dislocated right shoulder. Three days later, medication had greatly reduced the size of the blood clot, and by the next day, he'd regained consciousness.

He still had a long way to go in his recovery, however.

"When I got out of the hospital, I couldn't do nothing," Ard said. "I couldn't walk. I couldn't talk. As a matter of fact, [a doctor] suggested that my wife put me in a nursing home. He said I would probably never be able to do anything for myself again. But she wouldn't do it. She carried me home."

Behind his home near Asheboro, N.C., there was a big pile of sawdust. And it was on that spot, which provided padding when he fell, that Sam Ard took his first tentative steps.

"I had a walker, and I finally got so I could use that," Ard said. "I took it, and I'd walk down through the woods until I could get to the sawdust pile. That is where I learned to walk again. If I fell down, it didn't hurt."

Ard recovered enough to enjoy his championship banquet in Charlotte in January 1985. Later that year, he raced a couple of Late Model Stock races at Caraway, winning both over current Winston Cup regular Mike Skinner. He just didn't have the same abilities, and he knew it.

"I drove that car, and I won it just on instincts, because really, I couldn't see from one end of the track to the other," Ard admitted. "I knew the track real good. I guess that helped me through it."

When Ard's doctor learned that his patient had been racing, he delivered an ultimatum.

"I told him what I had done, and man, he hit the ceiling," Ard said. "He said, 'Man, you've gotta be crazy. Don't you know you ain't put together like you used to be? If you take another lick, you ain't gonna survive. You can't do that no more.' So I took him at his word, and I never drove again."

LEFT: Sam Ard pits for tires at Charlotte October 6. Although he didn't repeat his win of the previous year, Ard finished third behind winner Darrell Waltrip and runner-up Phil Parsons. Ard led Jack Ingram by an incredible 598 points after the race. (Lowe's Motor Speedway Archives) ABOVE: A fabulous career ended with this wreck at Rockingham October 20. After hitting water on the track left by another competitor, Sam Ard slammed into the third-turn wall. Also involved in the crash was Bobby Allison (22), but Jack Ingram (11) was able to weave his way through the melee unscathed. (Sam Ard Collection) OPPOSITE: Although Sam Ard was able to attend the banquet in honor of his 1984 Busch Late Model Sportsman championship, he had a long way to go in his recovery. Here, Ard is shown with car owner Howard Thomas (center), crew chief Gere Kennon, and a few of their trophies. (Gere Kennon Collection)

LEFT. With one race remaining, Jimmy Hensley's fifth-place finish at Rockingham October 19, 1985 moved him to within 39 points of Jack Ingram for the championship. Hensley finished third, and Ingram fifth, October 27 at the season finale at Martinsville, but the points gain for Hensley wasn't enough. (Jerry Haislip) RIGHT. Jack Ingram headed into the season without his longtime rival, Sam Ard, who was still recovering from the injuries he received the year before. Ingram faced stiff competition for the championship from Jimmy Hensley, who'd taken over Ard's car. (Dick Conway)

1985
Another Title
for the Iron Man

Jimmy Hensley replaced one legend in 1985 and came close to beating another for the championship.

Car owner Howard Thomas picked Hensley to fill the void created by Sam Ard's career-ending injuries. The Virginia native would win three races and finish just 29 points behind Jack Ingram in the title chase. It was almost as if Thomas's white-and-red, No. 00 Oldsmobile were meant to do battle with Ingram, no matter who was behind the wheel.

Taking over for Ard wasn't easy, but Hensley was determined to do well in his first real shot in the Busch Series. Previously, he'd driven a car owned by his uncle, Hubert.

"Sam was a big part of the mechanical end of [Thomas's team]," Hensley said. "He built the cars. He understood them. He was a good mechanic as well as being a driver. Without him, some of the magic was gone, yet we still had an opportunity to win.

"I had never really raced for the championship. I'd never had the big money deals. We might've run all but two or three races a year, but that was enough to knock you out of the points. [The ride with Thomas] was an opportunity where I thought I had good chance at the championship."

Ard or no Ard, Ingram was supremely confident as the season began. Only nine of the season's 27 races were held on tracks of more than a mile in length, which Ingram felt gave him a distinct advantage. Experience pays on short tracks, and Ingram certainly had it.

"No one could compete with me as a driver. I was so good on the race tracks that we were going to," Ingram said. "When I went to South Boston, Orange County, Hickory, or wherever, it was a 'gimme' almost, because Sam wasn't around. Other guys probably hadn't raced there very much in their careers, or maybe never.

"I'd been very successful on all those tracks before the series ever started. It was just fortunate for me that we had two, three, or four races a year on those

race tracks. I was able to capitalize on it."

Ingram wasn't unbeatable on short tracks, however. After wins by Geoffrey Bodine and Dale Earnhardt in the season's first two races, Hensley captured his first career victory March 10 at Hickory by going head to head with the master. The win moved Hensley atop the point standings, with Ingram fourth.

"I had never run well at Hickory, but that day, I remember passing Jack Ingram on the outside," Hensley said. "He and two or three other guys had dominated races there, and I just drove away from him."

Ingram remembers well an incident with Bodine March 30 at Bristol that left him 17th in the race and fifth in the standings.

"I was quicker than he was," Ingram said. "I couldn't get under him, so I decided I'd pass him on the outside. For about three trips around that race track, he wouldn't give me enough room. The next time, I caught him in the right rear with my left front. He went into the wall, and I spun down the frontstretch."

Unfortunately for Ingram, the damage was about to get worse.

"I couldn't get the car in reverse. It wouldn't start," he said. "My pit crew pushed me off, and I went across the access road between [turns] one and two trying to get back out on the speedway.

"Robert Ingram Jr. [no relation] decided that he would make a late entrance to backstretch pits, and we hit. I was sitting dead still. He didn't see me. It didn't work for either one of us."

The next week, Hensley started from the pole and led the first 61 laps April 6 at Martinsville but finished 20th and fell to second in the standings.

"Jack and I got together, and I wrecked," said Hensley, the memory still fresh in his mind. "I had pitted, and I was trying to take third place away from him. Somehow or another, we got together on the straightaway coming off turn four. That probably cost me the championship, because I was gonna win that race."

Gere Kennon, still on board as the crew chief for Thomas's team, said that afternoon was the only time he'd ever seen Hensley angry. The drivers discussed the incident after the race, which Brett Bodine won and Ingram finished sixth.

"It was typical, 'You came down on me,' and 'No, you came up on me,'" Hensley said. "We raced the rest

ABOVE: Bosco Lowe's Oldsmobile burst into flames when it was struck by Robert Ingram Jr. at Charlotte May 25. Although Lowe escaped unharmed, his car was a total loss. (Graham Niven) RIGHT: There wasn't much left in the cockpit of Lowe's machine. Note the melted windshield. (Dick Conway) OPPOSITE: A bout with high blood pressure forced Jack Ingram to turn his car over to Harry Gant (right) early in the Dixie Cup 200 at Darlington April 13. Gant took the lead with three laps to go, and won. (Dick Conway)

of the year and really didn't have any other problems."

Still, Hensley considers that race as the year's turning point.

"You can look back and find 29 points anywhere," Hensley said. "I'm looking at a race that I dominated and didn't win. Instead of winning, I wound up 20th. That's a lot of points. That's the reason I keep going back to that race. There was nobody even close to me that day, and as far as I'm concerned, I got taken out."

Secretly, in the midst of this war, Ingram had developed health problems and called on Harry Gant for relief April 13 at Darlington. Ingram completed the first 31 laps, but turned his Oldsmobile over to Gant following a rain delay.

"I didn't want to tell the public at the time, or even want my sponsor to know it, but I had wound up with extremely high blood pressure," Ingram said. "A week or two before at Bristol, when I got in that deal with Bodine, I didn't feel good. I felt like I was gonna pass out.

"Of course, I went to my physician. I asked about

racing, and he said, 'If you get hot and excited, you could black out.' My doctor advised me not to race at Darlington. I wasn't evasive with anybody. I just said that I was having stomach cramps."

Gant passed Brad Teague for the lead three laps from the end of the race. The tag-team win moved Ingram to third in the standings, 23 points behind Houston and just two behind Hensley.

"Harry was probably the best driver 1 ever saw at Darlington," Ingram said. "I was running about the same speed as Earnhardt, [Darrell] Waltrip, and all those guys. Harry got in the car, and he turned the time up about three-tenths of a second over what they were doing and did it the rest of the day."

"That ol' car just flew," Gant added in his typically understated manner.

Hensley won again April 20 at South Boston, with Ingram in second. Ingram, however, took the lead in the standings for the first time in 1985 with a third-place showing May 4 at Langley Speedway. Hensley finished ninth, which dropped him to third in the title chase behind Ingram and runner-up Houston.

The dust settled during the next several races, with Ingram up front and Hensley and Houston swapping second. Then the championship battle heated up again in mid-August.

Ingram blew an engine August 10 at Hickory and finished 23rd in the 25-car field. Hensley took a four-point lead in the standings with his fifth-place effort. Ingram came back with a win August 18 at Milwaukee, retaking the points lead from Hensley, who finished third.

Ingram lost yet another engine August 31 at Darlington, resulting in a 31st-place finish. Hensley finished fourth to post a 71-point lead in the standings. Two weeks later, Ingram scored the first win for a six-cylinder engine in the division at North Wilkesboro.

The more fuel efficient six-cylinder powerplants were being phased into passenger car production by Detroit, and in a race car, they had a much different tone than the throaty roar of a V-8 engine. The age of cars sounding like bumble bees had arrived.

"Basically, the motor companies wanted that situation [for race engines to mirror street engines]. They supplied almost everybody in the field with some parts or a whole motor," Ingram said. "In my case, I think I wound up with about three or four motors."

The win left Ingram 38 points behind Hensley. A second consecutive victory September 28 at Orange County, combined with Hensley's 12th-place finish, set Ingram atop the standings with four races remaining in the season. For the October 27 finale at Martinsville, Ingram opted to run an eight-cylinder engine.

"I had run awful good with the six-cylinder engines, but at Martinsville, I went back to the V-8," Ingram said. "That year, you could use either kind. I felt the V-8 would possibly be more dependable in a long race like that. I was so concerned with what Jimmy might be able to do at the last race."

The strategy worked. Although Hensley finished third, Ingram came home fifth to clinch the championship. The joy of the occasion was tempered by the death of Modified star Richie Evans in a practice accident earlier that weekend at Martinsville.

"A good, longtime friend of mine died here this week, and all he did makes my five championships seem pretty insignificant," Ingram said at the time. "Richie won [the Modified title] nine times, and I've got a long way to go to catch him."

The 1985 dogfight had ended, and Ingram was looking forward to more success in 1986. Yet what happened the following year would be one of the most crushing and embarrassing disappointments of his racing career.

OPPOSITE: As safety workers tend to an accident on the frontstretch at Bristol August 23, Tommy Houston limps onto pit road with his blown powerplant. Houston led the standings briefly earlier in the season, but a variety of problems moved him to fourth in points by the end of the year. (Dick Conway)
BELOW LEFT: Sam Ard made it back to the track in 1985 as the crew chief for driver Charlie Luck. Ard stayed with Luck's team for a couple of years, then formed his own operation. (Dick Conway)
BELOW RIGHT: Tommy Houston stays in front of a battle for position between Jimmy Hensley and Ed Berrier (53) at Bristol. Hensley finished 10th, Houston 18th, and Berrier 21st. Like Houston, Berrier was a victim of engine failure. (Dick Conway)

FT: Dale Earnhardt pits during the
oody's 300 at Daytona February
5, 1986. Earnhardt beat fellow
Vinston Cup regular Geoffrey Bodine
the finish line by a car length to
ollect his second victory in the tour's
nnual season opener. (Dick Conway)
IGHT: Brett Bodine, Orvil Reedy (08),
nd Daryl Lacks (black car), get
gether at Richmond September 6.
arry Pearson (21) was able to
eave his way through the mishap,
his way to a fourth-place finish.
ick Conway)

1986
New Name,
Strange Season

The division changed its name to the Busch
Grand National Series in 1986, and shorter
cars with wheelbases of 105 inches made
their first appearances on the tour.

For the first time, NASCAR allowed current-
year cars—hence, the smaller wheelbase—with
the hope of drawing manufacturer interest to the
series. It was a big change for the division, and
a bizarre turn of events late in the year gave the
tour a new champion to go along with its new
name and new cars.

Ingram had a healthy lead in the standings over Larry Pearson and Brett Bodine in mid-September, then was suspended for two races after an altercation with another driver in a Late Model Stock race in Asheville, N.C.

Next, a race scheduled for October 11 at Hickory was canceled, which took away a chance for Bodine to close the points gap on Pearson for the Busch Grand National crown. This was indeed one of the strangest years in the division's history.

Would Pearson and Bodine have been able to battle for the championship had Ingram not missed those two races? That's a good question.

"It would've been close," Pearson said. "I think we could've gained ground on him, but I really don't know if we could've caught him."

The first seven months of the season were typical Jack Ingram. He held on for a sixth-place finish February 15 at Daytona and virtually owned the short tracks. He trailed winner Ronnie Silver to the finish line March 9 at Hickory to capture the top spot in the standings. Ingram won in April, May, June, and July at South Boston and on July 26 at Hickory.

After that Hickory win, his last of the season, Ingram led Pearson by 343 points and Bodine by 432.

Although his cushion shrunk considerably during the next six races, "It was all over with for the championship," Ingram said matter of factly.

Bodine, however, wasn't so sure.

"I think we could've caught Jack," Bodine said. "His experience was keeping Jack competitive, but we were starting to out-race him. I think Larry's team and our team raised the bar, and Jack couldn't keep up."

Bodine finished third September 13 at Dover, with Pearson fifth and Ingram 15th. At that point, Ingram led Brett Bodine by 246 points and Larry Pearson by 265 with six races left on the schedule. Ingram returned overnight to Asheville, arriving at about 7 a.m. the next day. Shortly thereafter, he headed to New Asheville Speedway for that afternoon's 200-lap main event, a race that had absolutely nothing to do with the Busch Grand National Series.

Although Ingram planned to run the race just for fun and an extra paycheck, it would be far from a joyride.

The race began as hundreds of others had for Ingram—with him leading and trading a little paint. On lap 172, he and local competitor Ronnie Pressley touched as they headed into turn three. Both spun, and Ingram was collected by Larry Ogle.

As Pressley turned his car around on the backstretch, Ingram backed his in reverse to about the start-finish line. As Pressley came off the fourth turn, Ingram's car lurched forward and hit Pressley's head-on at the entrance to pit road.

"My car wouldn't respond to the steering," Ingram said. "I tried to head it up pit road. I dropped the clutch to spin it around, but it wouldn't. It went straight. About that time, Ronnie came around the edge of the inside wall.

"If you looked real close, you might've seen the roof of the car. But I didn't see him. When I tried to spin around and head up pit road, I hit him coming into the pits."

Pressley was distracted by Ogle and never saw the impact coming.

"Larry was coming down the race track carrying something like he was gonna throw it through my windshield," said Pressley, whose cousin, Robert, won the race. "That got my attention. And then as I turned back to cut into the pit road, the last thing I remember was hearing an engine wide open and a black hood. It caught me off guard. I wasn't prepared for a lick."

Safety crews cut Pressley from the wreckage, and he was taken to Memorial Mission Hospital in Asheville with strained chest muscles, a slight concussion, and an injured left wrist.

ABOVE: Always a hands-on driver and owner, Jack Ingram works on his car prior to the April 12 event at Darlington. He qualified 13th and finished eighth. Ingram had already been at the top of the newly renamed Busch Grand National standings for more than a month. (Dick Conway) RIGHT: Tim Richmond pulls onto pit road after trouncing the field at Charlotte May 24. His was the only car on the lead lap. Brett Bodine finished second, a total of 37 seconds behind Richmond. (Jerry Haislip) OPPOSITE: Ronnie Silver gives Brett Bodine a tap during the Busch 200 at South Boston April 19. Silver finished third, the last car on the lead lap. Bodine, who'd taken over Jimmy Hensley's ride from the year before, finished eighth. (Dick Conway)

ABOVE: The most controversial incident of Jack Ingram's career, had nothing to do with the Busch Grand National circuit. After Ingram (11) and Ronnie Pressley (white car) collided during a Late Model Stock race in Asheville, N.C. September 14, they hit again at the pit road entrance. NASCAR ruled Ingram rammed Pressley intentionally, and as a consequence Ingram missed two Busch events, which cost him the 1986 championship. (Barb Saunders) RIGHT: Brett Bodine's Oldsmobile shows the effects of a vicious hit in the passenger's side door at IRP June 21. Bodine was credited with a 26th-place finish which dropped him from second to fourth in the standings. (Dick Conway) OPPOSITE: After a four-car tangle at Richmond, September 6, Brett Bodine was nearly 300 points behind Jack Ingram in the chase for the championship. Larry Pearson was just nine points behind Bodine in third place. The battle was going to be for the standings' runner-up spot ... or so they thought. (Dick Conway)

Chaos ensued.

"I had my truck there, and I was taking my driver's suit off when some police officers arrived and told me that I'd have to leave the speedway," Ingram said. "I said, 'I can't leave the speedway until I get my equipment.' They said, 'No, you're leaving now.'

"The police officers, who were moonlighting for the speedway, proceeded to beat me up, broke some ribs, drug me all over that speedway handcuffed. They lifted me plumb up off the ground with my hands behind me. It still makes me hurt."

Ed Cox, a competition administrator for NASCAR, happened to be at the race. He saw what he felt was intentional contact at pit road between Ingram and Pressley, and worse, he saw what was happening with the off-duty police officers. The situation was tense, explosive.

"The crowd was very, very vocal. They were booing," Cox recalled. "They put handcuffs on Ingram and started to bring him across the track. I was standing in front of the VIP tower with Banjo Matthews, and I told Banjo, 'We can't have this.' If they'd brought him out into where the fans were, there was going to be a mob, an ugly scene."

Ingram was released, and he left the facility. He'd had many a scrap with other drivers, but none had the dire consequences of this one. Notice of his indefinite suspension and a $5,000 fine arrived a couple of days after the incident. Ingram filed an appeal, but couldn't get an immediate hearing.

"A federal judge gave my lawyer the green light to get a restraining order against NASCAR to let me start racing or give me a hearing," Ingram said. "I refused to let him do it. U.S. Tobacco [the parent company of his primary sponsor, Skoal] and Chevrolet were sponsoring me.

"They were both afraid they'd get caught up in some kind of a bad situation. I told them that I'd get rid of that deal the best way I could without stirring up a big stink."

Pearson remembers hearing about Ingram's melee on the news the night it happened. He didn't celebrate.

"Actually, I felt sorry for him and wondered what the hell he was doing there," Pearson said. "Asheville, back then, was known for roughness. Jack was running Busch, and I guess all the guys up there were gunning for him."

Pearson finished second September 21 at Martinsville, Bodine fourth and Harry Gant, Ingram's substitute, was eighth. Pearson took the lead in the standings with a win September 28 at Orange County, while Bodine moved to second. Phil Parsons filled in for Ingram at Orange County, but came home 16th due to an accident. Ingram returned to competition October 4 at Charlotte and finished 15th, but Pearson finished third and Bodine seventh.

After the Charlotte race, Pearson led Bodine by 25 points and Ingram by 132 with just three races left. Ingram's shot at the championship was all but over.

"I was so hurt inside by something I had believed in for so long, and still do," Ingram said. "But in my opinion, I had been dealt an unfair blow. It totally consumed me. I almost never could perform to the level I had on the race track."

The next race on the schedule was a 200-lap event October 11 at Hickory. Bodine captured the pole during time trials October 10. Then Patty Moise crashed during a practice session, damaging a light pole. One veteran Busch Series official claims that the track's promoter, desperate for the race to be canceled, was later caught trying to saw the pole so there wouldn't be enough light to run the next night's race. Today most claim that the race wasn't run because the stands were nearly empty and that the promoter couldn't—or wouldn't—pay the purse, which had been a little more than $35,000 for another Busch Grand National event just a few weeks earlier.

Stranger still, although the promoter claimed it wasn't possible to run the Busch Grand National Series event because of light rain that greeted crews the day of the race, a preliminary Late Model Stock race went off as planned. According to Benny Yount, whose local car dealership was to have sponsored the Busch Grand National race and who shortly thereafter took control of the facility, a car owned by the promoter won the Late Model Stock event.

"I was upset because it took away an opportunity for us to close the gap at a track where we knew how good we were," Bodine said. "We knew we were going to be the team to beat there. I'm not saying that we would've won, but we would've started on the pole in a 200-lap race where you didn't change tires. We had a pretty good shot."

Although he and Pearson were close friends, the memory still angers Bodine.

"I think the people that were in charge of the Busch division at that time didn't really want me to be the champion," he said. "They didn't want me to win that championship, and they didn't want Howard Thomas's team to win the championship again.

"It would've been good for the sport for Larry Pearson to win that championship. Larry Pearson's was a name that was well recognized. Brett Bodine's name was not well recognized."

Pearson finished fourth to Bodine's fifth October 18 at Rockingham and then clinched the championship with a second-place showing behind Bodine November 2 at Martinsville. Bodine trailed Pearson by 20 points at the end of the year, and Ingram was 250 points down in third.

"I didn't rub it in Brett's face or anything," Pearson said. "He was a good guy to race with, a clean driver. He congratulated me and, of course, I would've done the same for him."

Pearson's father and car owner, the legendary David Pearson, had won three Winston Cup titles. Finally, both names were on racing's honor roll.

"It meant a lot to me because Daddy had won his Winston Cup championships," Pearson said. "I'd wanted to win one or two, just to say I'd won something also."

OPPOSITE: The cars of Larry Pearson and Brett Bodine go through the inspection line in October. After Jack Ingram was suspended the title came down to a fight between these two friends. (Dick Conway) BELOW LEFT: Jack Ingram and Joe Thurman hustle their cars through the twisting turns of Road Atlanta July 6. Darrell Waltrip won the event, the division's first on a road course. Ingram and Thurman finished 19th and 28th, respectively. (Dick Conway) BELOW RIGHT: Geoffrey Bodine, Dale Earnhardt, Brett Bodine, and Larry Pearson chat before the All Pro Auto Parts 300 at Charlotte October 4. Pearson finished third to Bodine's seventh, giving Pearson a 25-point lead over Bodine in the standings. (Lowe's Motor Speedway Archives)

FT: **The Busch Grand National** arage at Oxford Plains Speedway Maine wasn't very elaborate, as ustrated by this photo taken prior the division's July 12, 1987 event t the one-third mile bullring. Since is time, garages on the circuit have nproved greatly. (Dick Conway)

GHT: On July 5 at Georgia ternational Speedway, Mike lexander was flagged the winner the finish line, but officials found arry Pearson had been scored as sing two laps during a mid-race pit op when he'd actually only lost ne. Here Pearson emphatically akes that point to NASCAR official ister Auton. (Dick Conway)

1987
Who Needs
Good-Luck Charms?

Larry Pearson might have been the defending champion when he rolled into Daytona for the 1987 Busch Grand National opener, but he was far from worried about grabbing a second crown.

Pearson was having the time of his life. Racing was too much fun and life far too short to get bogged down worrying about how to stay on top.

63

"I'd already won my championship," Pearson said. "I wanted to win another one, yeah, but there was never any pressure because I drove for my family.

"I knew going to every track, short tracks especially, that we had a chance to win the race. I never, ever felt pressure, even from Daddy. When I'd screw up, he'd tell me about it. But we never harped on anything."

So all Pearson did in 1987 was lead the division in wins, top fives, top 10s, laps led, total money won and, most important, points toward the title. Nobody, though, could have convinced Pearson he'd be so successful after his third-place finish February 14 at Daytona.

The ultra-superstitious Pearson considered it a bad omen to finish well in the season opener and a good sign to fare poorly. After all, he'd been credited with a 41st-place showing the year before at Daytona. But it wasn't just that track that brought out the voodoo in Pearson.

"You name it, I believe in it," Pearson said of his superstitions, unashamed. "Green. 13. Black cats. Ladders. Always put my left shoe on first, left glove on first, left sock. Wore certain underwear. Every race I won, I marked them with a magic marker. I marked my blue jeans, marked my shirts."

His competitors knew about Pearson's hang-up and took advantage of it every chance they got.

"He had this Chattanooga Chew hat," Brett Bodine

ABOVE: Tommy Houston (6) captured the pole at Daytona in February 1987 with a lap of 194.389 mph. It's still the fastest qualifying lap for the division. Houston had an oil cooler go bad early in the race and finished 36th. (Dick Conway)

said with a wicked grin. "After one race, I got his hat and he was in a tither about it, upset—not mad upset, but nervous upset because one of his lucky items had been taken. I gave it back to him the following week, and it was like giving back his first born."

Early in the season, Pearson faced chasing Jack Ingram for the title. Ingram captured his 31st and final Busch Grand National victory March 15 at Hickory, to lead the standings by seven points over runner-up Bodine and by 15 over third-place Pearson.

Still, Ingram's debacle at Asheville the year before was weighing heavily on his mind. A civil lawsuit had been filed by Ronnie Pressley against Ingram in late 1986, and it took nearly a year for the case to be settled out of court. Although he led the standings for the next three-and-a-half months, and at times by more than 100 points, all was not well.

"You can't be consumed by something like that and perform like you should, because it takes so much of your concentration," Ingram said. "I had to run the race team and drive the car. It was mighty tough to do all those things, alone.

"I got consumed with something I felt shouldn't have happened. If I'd been guilty of what they said I'd done, most people get a $200 fine. It still eats at me."

More controversy erupted in the May 23 Winn-Dixie 300 at Charlotte when Geoffrey Bodine made contact with the rear of Dale Earnhardt's Chevrolet on lap 186. Both drivers spun, while Pearson and Darrell Waltrip had to loop their cars as well to avoid the mishap. The incident took place just six days after Earnhardt had punted Bill Elliott into a spin that collected Bodine during Charlotte's The Winston all-star event. Following that incident, Elliott rammed Earnhardt's car on the cool-down lap, and Bodine hit Earnhardt on pit road.

Despite the incident, Waltrip finished second, Pearson third, Earnhardt fifth, and Bodine 13th.

On May 26, NASCAR announced that Bodine had been fined $15,000 and placed on probation until December 31 for wrecking Earnhardt in the Busch Grand National race. An immediate appeal was filed by Bodine's car owner, Rick Hendrick.

"Some people think I hit Earnhardt intentionally, and I've turned out to be a hero with them," Bodine said. "But the truth is, I didn't. If we don't win the appeal, we're going to follow up legally. We're not going to stand for it."

Geoffrey Bodine (15) hit Dale Earnhardt during the Winn-Dixie 300 at Charlotte May 23. The accident also involved Darrell Waltrip (17) and Larry Pearson (21). Bodine was fined $15,000 and placed on probation, but both penalties were lifted following a June 1 hearing. (Lowe's Motor Speedway Archives)

LEFT: Safety workers clean up after Rusty Wallace struck a water-barrel safety barrier during Charlotte's spring Busch Grand National event. The impact sent water spraying 50 feet into the air. Wallace completed 84 laps, and finished 33rd. (Lowe's Motor Speedway Archives) ABOVE: As Tommy Ellis climbs out of his machine in the background, Brett Bodine walks away from his battered car at Dover May 30. Ellis and Bodine were racing for second place on lap 144 when the collision took place. Ellis took a 22nd-place finish, and Bodine was listed 23rd. (Dick Conway) OPPOSITE: As Mike Alexander celebrates at Georgia International Speedway in Jefferson, Ga. July 5, Larry Pearson's crew begins its protest in the background. Once he was awarded the win, Pearson went from a tie for first in the standings with Jack Ingram, to leading by 71 points. (Dick Conway)

Three members of the National Stock Car Racing Commission—Jack Arute Sr., Barbara Cromarty, and Richard Gore—heard Bodine's appeal June 1 in Newark, N.J. The panel determined that while Bodine had exercised poor judgment, there was no evidence that the accident had been the result of rough driving on Bodine's part. Both the fine and probation were dropped.

Mark Martin captured his first career Busch Grand National victory May 30 at Dover just two months after Ingram won his last. Although 1987 was Martin's only full-time Busch Grand National campaign, he would break Ingram's record for most wins in the division's history 10 years later. It was also the first-ever victory for a Ford in Busch Grand National competition.

"This win is a big break for us," Martin said at the time. "Right now, we have no major sponsor, and maybe this will open some doors for us in the Winston Cup garage, too."

The door did open for Martin. Team owner Jack Roush snapped him up, and the two are still together on the Winston Cup circuit. The race was also important for Pearson, who finished second behind Martin. Ingram was 17th in the final rundown, allowing Pearson to chop 55 points off his deficit in the standings.

Pearson beat Elton Sawyer to the checkered flag by a half-car length June 6 at Indianapolis Raceway Park, moving him even closer to Ingram.

"A few laps before [the end of the race], Elton had got into the back of me going into turn one and got me sideways," Pearson said. "He'd passed me, and that ticked me off. I probably drove the fastest laps of the race trying to catch back up to him.

"Going into turn three on the last lap, I took the low line, and I trapped him behind Bosco Lowe. I got underneath Elton, and he couldn't move down to go around him. I guess I got overexcited. I just spun the tires off turn four, and he came back to make it close."

Martin won again June 27 at Orange County, while Pearson finished fourth to Ingram's 13th. That left Pearson and Ingram tied for the lead in the championship with 1,650 points each. The race wouldn't be knotted for long.

Mike Alexander was flagged the winner July 5 at Jefferson, Ga., but the victory was awarded to Pearson after a two-hour recheck of the scorecards. Officials discovered Pearson had wrongly been scored as losing two laps during a mid-race pit stop, when he'd actually lost only one. Pearson made up the lap and was credited with a 13-second win over Alexander.

Forget the fact that Pearson and Alexander were good friends off the race track. This wasn't personal. The victory, combined with Ingram's 18th-place finish, gave Pearson a 71-point lead in the standings.

"Mike took my trophy, and he wouldn't give it back," Pearson said. "They just screwed up the scoring that night."

Not so fast, said Alexander.

"I remind him about that race every time I see him," Alexander said with a laugh. "I could've caught him if they'd lined us up correctly. Instead of being able to race him for the win, I ended up getting sucker punched. I never had a chance."

Slowly, Pearson began building on his advantage in the standings over runner-up Ingram and Brett Bodine, who took third from Martin with a fourth-place effort July 18 at South Boston. Third wasn't bad, considering the scheduling nightmare Bodine faced while running the Winston Cup and Busch Grand National circuits full time.

Bodine qualified Hoss Ellington's Chevrolet fifth at Michigan on August 14 and then hustled to the Detroit airport for a flight to Charlotte. He attended his sister-in-law's wedding that night, then afterward, it was back to the airport for a flight to Chicago. He rented a car and drove back to the race track, arriving at 7 a.m. on August 15 for practice.

As soon as the morning session was completed, Bodine once again headed to the Detroit airport. After landing at the Raleigh-Durham airport, he hustled to Orange County for that night's Busch Grand National race. He qualified second and was leading when he and Alexander made contact on the sixth lap.

"Mike Alexander tried to pass me on the inside. He just clipped me and spun me," Bodine said. "Tommy Houston came along and T-boned me in the passenger's side. If he'd hit me in the driver's side, it would've killed me. It just destroyed my race car, and I know I had cracked ribs."

Dale Jarrett was also running both events, and they were able to fly back to Michigan on NASCAR's plane. Arriving about 1 a.m. and still hurting from the Orange County mishap, Bodine figured it'd be safe for him and Jarrett to sleep in a bit the morning of the Winston Cup race.

"We got up too late and underestimated the traffic," Bodine said. "We had to go down the side of the road. People were cutting us off, running us off in the ditch, giving us the finger. We weren't going to make the start of the race, much less the drivers' meeting."

"Finally, I got to a stoplight, and a patrolman stopped me," Jarrett added. "Of course, he didn't know who Brett Bodine and Dale Jarrett were and didn't care at that time. We finally showed him our NASCAR licenses, and he got us through there."

Pearson finished fourth October 24 at Rockingham to clinch his second consecutive championship.

"Nowadays, the Busch Series is tough. Don't get me wrong," Pearson said. "It's very tough to even make a race. Back then, it wasn't as hard, necessarily, to make the races because there wasn't as many cars, but, dadgum, it was hard to win."

Second place in the standings was still up for grabs. Jimmy Hensley—driving a car owned by Sam Ard—won the November 1 season finale at Martinsville to move from fourth to second in the standings. Bodine maintained third, while Ingram's 20th-place finish dropped him from second to fourth in the title chase.

Jimmy Hensley's win in the event came in a backup car, because he'd crashed the team's only other machine during practice. That, combined with the emotion surrounding the injury that ended Ard's driving career, made the win all the more special.

"He'd almost lost his life," Hensley said of Ard. "Even before he started talking about starting up a team, we'd go visit and try to give him a little encouragement. It was great to stand with him in victory lane."

A veteran would run away with the 1988 Busch Grand National championship, but it wouldn't be Pearson.

BELOW: Mark Martin leads Rusty Wallace (90) and Ken Bouchard at Dover May 30. Martin beat Larry Pearson to the finish line by five seconds. It was Martin's first win on the circuit, and there would be many, many more. (Dick Conway)

LEFT: Rob Moroso chats with Larry Pearson late in the 1988 season. While Moroso had another eventful season of Busch Grand National competition ahead of him in 1989, Pearson planned to test the Winston Cup waters. One of his biggest regrets was leaving his friends behind. (Jerry Haislip) RIGHT: Tommy Ellis had several options for the 1988 season, but chose to drive for J&J Racing. The decision paid off when Ellis won the championship with a budget of $300,000 from team owner John Jackson. (Dick Conway)

1988
The Old School Meets Generation Next

After a few years of trying to make a go of the Winston Cup circuit, Tommy Ellis came back to the Busch Grand National Series in 1988 expecting nothing less than the championship. All he had to do was land with the right team.

Sponsorship for a car owned by Rick Hendrick and prepared by famed mechanic Robert Gee had fallen through, and he'd also talked with Howard Thomas about replacing

Brett Bodine. But when Thomas wavered in whether to run a full schedule, that all but sealed a deal with J&J Racing owners John Jackson and Bill Papke.

"I told John Jackson the only way I would do it was to have the team where I could work on it and oversee it," said Ellis, who had the team moved close to his home in Richmond. "He gave me a budget of $300,000, which was not much money, but it was enough.

"I told him then, 'I can win the championship. I'm as sure of it as I'm living.' He really didn't think we could."

The investment paid off handsomely, but not immediately. Bobby Allison won February 13 at Daytona, a day before his legendary victory over son Davey in the Winston Cup opener.

Mike Alexander won the next race on February 28 at Hickory, but Ellis protested the event's scoring. Officials finally determined Ellis illegally gained 11 seconds on the track when his scorer missed a lap prior to a pit stop. When his time was adjusted, Ellis was listed as finishing fourth, nine seconds behind Alexander.

"Tommy was a thorn in our side," Alexander said. "He worked the officials more than he did on his car. Larry Pearson thought it was funny. I didn't think it was funny worth a damn."

The win gave Alexander, whose shop was located in Franklin, Tenn., a lead in the Busch Grand National standings he would not lose for the next four-and-a-half months. His Hickory scrap with Ellis notwithstanding, Alexander was on top of the world with buddies Larry Pearson, Larry Pollard, and others.

"If they have more fun now than we did then, God bless them," Alexander said with a smile. "We had a big time. We raced hard, but we loved each other at the same time. Sometimes, we didn't come home. We'd use Sam Ard's or Hubert Hensley's shops while we were on the road and lean on them for pieces and parts."

Dale Jarrett missed the April 30 race at Langley because of a Winston Cup event in Talladega, Ala., making Tommy Houston the only driver to have competed in each of

the tour's 185 races to that point. Meanwhile, Ellis led more than half the race until a flat right front tire forced him to pit and lose a lap.

Ellis regained the lost lap and passed Ingram—who went the entire race on one set of tires—14 laps from the end to collect his first victory of the season. It moved him from fifth to second in the standings, 61 points behind Alexander.

A rocker arm broke in the engine of Jarrett's Oldsmobile after 80 laps May 28 at Charlotte, and he ran on five cylinders until a halfway break. His crew fixed the problem as cars reformed on the track after the break, and Jarrett went on to post his first superspeedway victory.

The race was also the first on a superspeedway in which every car used a V-6 engine. Nineteen-year-old Rob Moroso was the highest-finishing Busch Grand National regular in fourth, despite having spun on the frontstretch under a caution just before the halfway break.

"I had just put on new tires, and I was trying to warm them up," Moroso said. "I'm gaining experience. That was an experience, and I'll never do it again."

Tommy Houston won the June 11 event at Orange County to become the 13th winner in the season's first 13 races, but his victory the following week at Lanier in Braselton, Ga., broke the streak. That same day, June 19, Bobby Allison was critically injured in the Winston Cup race at Pocono.

"I called home, and Liz, my wife, said Davey had called," Alexander said. "I knew Bobby had crashed

ABOVE: Sam Ard (center) talks with his team's driver, Jimmy Hensley, and Elton Sawyer prior to the April 30 event at Langley. Sawyer finished sixth, but problems sent Hensley all the way to 22nd in the 23-car field. (Dick Conway) OPPOSITE: Tommy Ellis (99), Larry Pearson (21), and Joe Thurman (24) go three wide at Bristol April 9. Jack Ingram, who went on to finish third, runs just behind the heated battle. Although Ellis was still fifth in the standings after the race, he said his second-place finish put him in contention to win the championship. (Dick Conway)

pretty bad, so I figured it was just a call to let us know how things were. I got home, and they called back. We met with the Stavolas [Allison's car owners], and I was asked to fill in for Bobby until he got better."

Alexander finished fourth behind race-winner Ellis June 25 at Louisville, Ky., and then drove Allison's Buick to a 10th-place finish in Michigan's Winston Cup event the following afternoon. Louisville officials had to water down the track when soaring temperatures began turning the racing surface into mush. The start of the race was also delayed to offer relief from the heat.

"Man, it was hot as hell," Ellis recalled. "I think it's the hottest place I'd ever been in my life that day.

How did Ellis cope with the horrible conditions? He just toughed it out.

"I kind of come from the old school, when racing was really racing," Ellis continued. "You raced your ass off. When you got out of that car, you knew you'd been in a race." After his win, Ellis trailed Alexander by 99 points.

Moroso became the series' youngest winner to that point by passing Larry Pearson on a lap-168 restart July 2 at Myrtle Beach. At the ripe old age of 19 years, 9 months, Moroso beat Pearson to the checkered flag by 3.1 seconds.

"I couldn't believe it on that restart," Moroso said. "Pearson was driving slow, and he gave me room on the inside. I guess it was meant to be. I was ready to go, and the opening was there. I was cookin'. I was psyched. I can't believe it. Once I got that lead, I was trying to be smooth, but I wanted to pull away."

Steve Bird, Moroso's crew chief, coached his young driver from pit road.

"We were a little faster [than Pearson]," Bird said. "I said, 'Robbie, cool it. Stay behind him until he makes a mistake. Ain't no sense in pressuring him and getting in an accident.' He listened. He listened all the time."

Alexander finished 20th at Myrtle Beach and on July 10 in a 47-car field at Oxford, Me, he was 43rd as a result of engine trouble. The problems signaled the beginning of the end for Alexander's title hopes.

"We had an oil line that was collapsing and drying the motor out, so we burned up two or three motors at Oxford," Alexander said. "The frustrating part was not knowing what was causing it until we got home. We didn't detect what was wrong until Dennis Fischer got the motors back."

Again, problems bit Alexander July 16 at South Boston, where he finished 20th. Ellis took the lead in the standings with a runner-up effort behind Pearson. On July 23 at Hickory, a faulty rear end dropped Alexander to 18th in the final rundown.

Alexander went from a 99-point cushion to trailing Ellis by 63 points in just four races. Splitting his time between the Winston Cup and Busch Grand National circuits had taken its toll.

"All the guys I had with me were kind of new to the racing business," Alexander said. "I think if the main guy is not there to oversee things, the guy with the most experience, problems aren't going to be detected as quick. I'm not laying blame. We were just a bunch of kids."

OPPOSITE: At the age of 19 years, 9 months, Rob Moroso became the division's youngest winner at Myrtle Beach July 2. Moroso captured the win by passing Larry Pearson on a lap-168 restart. Here, he gets the traditional dousing in victory lane. (Ray Shough) BELOW LEFT: Gary Neice (01) and Ronnie Silver race each other at Hickory July 16 in cars fielded by Howard Thomas. Winding his career down as a car owner, Thomas ran his last race later in the year at Charlotte with Joe Millikan behind the wheel. (Dick Conway) BELOW RIGHT: Two of the sport's hardest chargers slug it out early in the Kroger NASCAR 200 at IRP August 6. Tommy Ellis led 84 laps, but finished third. Earnhardt completed only 95 laps due to engine failure. The Winston Cup star was relegated to a 29th-place finish. (Dick Conway)

Second-place finishes on August 13 at Orange County and August 26 at Bristol helped Alexander rally. After a seventh-place run September 3 at Darlington, Alexander was only eight points behind Ellis. But another mechanical failure September 10 at Richmond dashed Alexander's title hopes for good.

"A vent on top of the oil tank had kind of dry-rotted, and oil would get up there and get on the exhaust," Alexander said. "We were leading the damn race, and I smelled it. That was part of the visual

inspections that needed to happen at the shop. We came from midway in the field, took the lead, and started smoking."

Ellis slowly began pulling away in the points chase despite being black-flagged for rough driving after an incident with Moroso September 24 at Martinsville. Ellis was held in the pits for three laps and finished 15th. Moroso salvaged a 10th-place showing.

"I had Robbie sit there for 80 laps riding behind Tommy," Bird said. "Finally, Tommy made a little mistake, and Robbie got by him. In a lap or two, we would've left him. But Tommy just drove it into turn one, and he knew he wanted to put Robbie out, and that he did.

"When he came down pit road to go in the penalty box, I had a tire in my hand, and he knew I was kind of mad. I was ready to throw it at him. I was that pissed, because I really wanted to win at Martinsville."

Moroso came back to win October 8 at Charlotte after crashing hard during practice the day before. Moroso was only the second series regular to win at Charlotte,

and his $54,650 winner's purse was the division's largest at the time. The youngster was becoming a star.

Bird had led the crew's repairs to Moroso's machine until 9 p.m. the night before the race and then got back to work at 6 a.m.

"We put a hood, two fenders, and a nose on it," Bird said. "The right side chassis rail was bent in two inches. We just strung it the best we could. That was probably one of the best races I ever won."

Ellis finished sixth at Charlotte and then clinched the championship with a ninth-place showing October 22 at Rockingham. Moroso trailed winner Harry Gant to the finish line in the October 30 finale at Martinsville, which moved him past Alexander into second in the standings.

Eighteen different drivers won in 1988, more than in any other season in the division's history. It's somehow fitting that one of its fiercest drivers would come out on top of the Busch Grand National Series' most competitive season.

Alexander and Pearson (who was Winston Cup bound in 1989) had a running gag in which they'd put bananas in the other's car to draw the bad-luck "monkeys." Pearson pulled the trick on Alexander at Martinsville, and a couple of weeks later, Alexander was involved in an accident that eventually led to his retirement from Winston Cup racing in the early 1990s.

Alexander sustained a broken collarbone, several fractures and, worst of all, a closed head injury during the December 4 Snowball Derby Late Model Stock race in Pensacola, Fla. Today, Alexander still has a certain amount of memory loss. Ever the superstitious sort, it's almost as if Pearson actually blames himself for Alexander's accident.

"I wouldn't do worth a damn when he put the bananas in my car, so I started doing it to him, and he wouldn't do worth a damn," Pearson said. "I done it at Martinsville, and then he got hurt down there. That made me feel real bad. We quit the banana stuff."

Said Alexander: "I think that's just the sincerity he had for people. Larry loves me. I know he does. He would do nothing to harm me or anybody else. That wasn't Larry's fault."

With Alexander hurt and Pearson in Winston Cup, the next season would feature young buck Moroso against two more grizzled veterans—Houston and Ellis—for the division's bragging rights.

LEFT: Rob Moroso leaps into the arms of his father, Dick, after winning the All Pro Auto Parts 300 at Charlotte October 8. It was the first win for a Busch Grand National regular at the facility since Sam Ard turned the trick in October 1983. (Jerry Haislip) BELOW: Tommy Ellis holds off Harry Gant in the season finale at Martinsville October 30. Gant won the Winston Classic and Ellis finished third to put the finishing touches on his championship. (Dick Conway) OPPOSITE: The late-season woes of Mike Alexander (84) continued at Charlotte, where he finished 26th. Splitting his time between the Busch Grand National and Winston Cup circuits had taken its toll. (Dick Conway)

LEFT: A livid Jimmy Spencer is restrained by NASCAR official Buster Auton after being parked for rough driving during the Granger Select 200 at Louisville (Ky.) Motor Speedway June 24, 1989. Spencer was black-flagged after rubbing the side of Robert Pressley's car while passing for position. Spencer completed 136 laps, and was credited with a 17th-place finish. (Ray Shough) RIGHT: Rob Moroso was well on his way to becoming a superstar in 1989 as NASCAR's original "Wonder Boy." He waged a fierce war with veteran Tommy Houston for the championship, and came out on top. (Dick Conway)

1989
A Bright
and Shining Star

Rob Moroso was racing's original "Wonder Boy."

When Moroso wrestled the 1989 Busch Grand National championship from veterans Tommy Houston and Tommy Ellis, the sport had a new superstar. Moroso was the complete package; he was young, popular, good-looking, and as talented as they came when he strapped himself into a race car.

The season got off to a superb start for Moroso February 18 at Daytona. He finished third behind winner Darrell Waltrip and Rusty Wallace after dodging a last-lap tangle among Wallace, Dale Jarrett, and Geoffrey Bodine.

"There was nothing Robbie could do," said crew chief Steve Bird. "They were side by side, and he hollered on the radio, 'Who do you want to win?' I said, 'Waltrip!' He went behind Waltrip and pushed him across the line. If there'd been another lap, we should've won that race."

Houston finished sixth and had his eye on the championship that had eluded him for so long.

"When you go to Daytona, you've gotta think points," Houston said. "When you leave there and go to the next race, you've gotta think points. You take the best finish you can. You keep that thing running. You keep the wheels on it."

After regaining a lap March 4 at Rockingham, Moroso was second behind Harry Gant when the Winston Cup regular's car began smoking. Gant ignored a black flag that first waved four laps from the end and, as a result, his car was not scored for the final two circuits. That handed Moroso his first win of the year.

"For the last 20 laps or so, Harry was losing oil," Moroso said. "I really didn't think he'd last as long as he did. It was definitely oil smoke, not tires. I hope I never have to lose a race the way Harry did, but that's just the way NASCAR called it."

Gant and Dale Earnhardt got together earlier in the race, and Gant claims that's what caused the smoke.

"The starter had the checkered flag, and he waited until I went under the flagstand," Gant said. "I looked in the mirror, and I saw him wave it at Moroso. I went down to the winner's circle, too. They said it was leaking oil.

"There wasn't no oil, just a fender rubbing in the turns. They made the call too quick and wouldn't retract it. I thought they'd reverse it until about Tuesday of the next week. That's the reason I wasn't so mad."

Moroso's win gave him an edge on the rest of the pack for the championship, but the advantage was short-lived. Ellis won the next race March 12 at Martinsville despite being black-flagged earlier in the race for separate rough-driving incidents that also involved Gant and L. D. Ottinger. Moroso started from the pole, but finished 23rd after crashing with then-leader Rick Wilson on lap 162. Houston took the lead in the standings, while Moroso fell to second.

"When I hit Rick, I had no brakes," Moroso said. "I just went in the corner, and the brakes went to the floor. Then, all of a sudden, the rear brakes locked up. The car jumped and twisted the driveshaft and rear end."

Moroso climbed back atop the heap with a third-place finish March 25 at Hickory. Jack Ingram led the event with four laps to go, but slowed with a mechanical problem. Jimmy Spencer then nudged hometown favorite Dale Jarrett out of the lead and into a spin on the next-to-last circuit to take the win.

A riot nearly followed.

After the race, Jarrett bumped Spencer from behind on the frontstretch. Fans pelted the makeshift victory lane with all sorts of debris, and some tried to climb over the fence to join the fray. Jarrett jumped out of his car and made it to the window of Spencer's car before being restrained. Ed Spencer, Jimmy's father, then slugged Anheuser-Busch representative Dennis Punch as he tried to keep the younger Spencer from getting at Jarrett.

Punch said the assault was stopped when Jimmy yelled to his father, "It's OK, Dad. He's on our side." The incident led to a $2,150 fine for Spencer and a $1,000 penalty against Jarrett. Both were placed on probation for the next six races.

Other drivers spent the next three months trying to gain ground on Moroso, but Ellis thought he was handcuffed by NASCAR penalties as he chased the young upstart. Ellis was black-flagged at Darlington April 1 for jumping a restart. The combination of that black flag, the problem at Martinsville earlier in the year, and a couple of other penalties made Ellis think someone was out to get him.

Said Ellis: "I remember going to [race director] David Hoots and telling him after Darlington, 'Go look at the replay, and let me know if you made a good call.' He came back to me at Bristol and said, 'I've got to apologize to you. That was a bad call.' I said, 'That was just one of four.' "

Moroso went a lap down May 27 at Charlotte when he had to pit and have a cut right rear tire replaced on the fifth lap. He got back on the lead lap and then steadily moved through the field to take the lead from Rusty Wallace on lap 195.

It was Moroso's second win in a row at Charlotte.

"There's a great deal of satisfaction in beating the Winston Cup regulars because you know they are going to run up front," Moroso said. "If I can finish in front of them, that just puts a bigger buffer between me and the next Busch guy."

Jack Ingram took the points lead when he finished third July 22 at Hickory, while Moroso was 28th in the

LEFT: Tommy Ellis may be laughing here, but he thought that several calls by NASCAR officials cost him the 1989 championship. Ellis even claims that certain people at the sanctioning body didn't want him to capture the title. (Dick Conway)

BELOW: Chuck Bown's Pontiac lays down some tire smoke in this mishap with Martin Truex at Martinsville March 12. Despite the spin, Bown was able to come back and finish eighth, one lap down. Truex finished 25th. (Dick Conway)

Winston Racin

LEFT: As he climbs from his car following the Coors 200 at South Boston July 15, Rob Moroso restrains an angry Steve Bird. The crew chief was upset with L.D. Ottinger for making contact with his driver. Ottinger finished fourth to Moroso's fifth. (Dick Conway)

ABOVE: Robert Pressley (59) and Tommy Ellis (99) race hard for the lead at Orange County August 12. Ellis scraped the wall on lap 196, allowing Tommy Houston (6) to finish second. After the race, those close by witnessed the diminutive Ellis confront Pressley's car owner, seven-foot NBA all-star Brad Daugherty. (Dick Conway)

OPPOSITE: Tommy Houston handed this picture to a visitor and said, "This is what ended it." After missing the drivers' meeting prior to the All Pro Auto Parts 300 at Charlotte October 7, Houston had to start from the rear of the field. He was then involved in an early crash that sent a piece of debris through the nose of his car centered below the grille, causing his engine to blow. Moroso won the race and rose from third place in the standings to lead Houston by nine points with just two races to go. (David Chobat)

31-car field due to an accident with Max Prestwood and Billy Standridge on lap 197.

"Billy Standridge should not be allowed on the race track," Moroso fumed. "He was holding [Prestwood] up, and [Prestwood] tapped him to let him know he was wanting by. Then Standridge tried to spin him and barely caught him and spun himself. He came down and turned me straight into the wall."

Ingram held a three-point lead over Houston entering the August 12 event at Orange County, but finished 28th after a crash that also involved Moroso and Chuck Bown. Robert Pressley and Ellis got together racing for the lead on the 196th of 200 laps, which slammed Ellis into the wall. Houston took advantage of the melee to finish second and take the lead in the title chase.

The next few races were nearly devastating to Moroso. Lackluster runs and crashes dropped him to fourth in points following the September 23 race at Richmond, where Ellis finished second to take a nine-point lead over Houston. Moroso then dropped to fifth with a 23rd-place finish September 16 at Dover, 127 points behind Ellis.

Moroso's youthful, devil-may-care attitude might have contributed to the team's midseason decline. Moroso was a hard-headed kid who did things his way.

"I think some of it was because Robbie was so young and successful," Bird said. "I guess me and [engine builder Bob] Rinaldi were like second dads. We just had to help him and talk him through. Anybody young and successful sometimes gets out of control. I wouldn't say he was totally out of control, but he was close."

Houston's win September 23 at Martinsville, together with Ellis's blown engine, gave Houston a 92-point lead in the standings. Moroso came home second, moving him to third in the championship hunt, 125 points behind Houston and 33 behind Ellis. He vaulted past both by winning at Charlotte on October 7.

Only one other driver—Mark Martin in 1995 and '96—has won three of the division's races in a row at Charlotte.

"When we came to this race, I thought we were the only Busch team with a chance to win all three of the

remaining races," Moroso said. "I thought if we could do well at all three, we could pull out the championship. We won today, so we're right there."

Both Houston and Ellis had had their share of trouble that afternoon. An overflow of oil forced Ellis to the pits on the fourth lap, and he later crashed. Houston had to start from the rear of the field after he missed the drivers' meeting, and when Ed Berrier's engine blew about five laps into the race, a piece of his block went through Houston's radiator.

Houston completed only 24 laps at Charlotte and finished 39th. He trailed Moroso by nine points, but when Moroso finished 12th after being black-flagged October 21 at Rockingham, Houston regained the top spot in the standings with a fifth-place finish. With one race to go, Houston led Moroso by 19 points.

At Rockingham, Moroso had thought he was the last car on the lead circuit and took a lap-172 restart in front of Bobby Hillin. Patty Moise spun to bring out another caution one lap later, but Moroso was listed by NASCAR as the leader. Moroso passed the pace car

on his way to what he thought was his correct position, resulting in a two-lap penalty.

"NASCAR never told us we were the leader, and I honestly don't think we were," said Dick Moroso, Rob's father and team owner. "They said they didn't have time to check on it, but that they'd get it straightened out. Then something happened, and out came the caution. We never got the chance to slow Rob down."

Leading Moroso in the home stretch, Houston looked forward to Martinsville's October 29 season finale.

"I was thinking we were in pretty good shape if something didn't happen," Houston said. "If the thing didn't blow up or get caught in a wreck, I felt we were gonna be OK."

But Houston wasn't OK at Martinsville. A broken valve spring ended his best chance at winning a championship. Moroso finished third and beat Houston for the title by 55 points. Ellis wound up just one point behind Houston in third.

"Tommy was heartbroken, but after the race was over, we were sitting out there in the van," recalled Martha, Houston's wife. "Rob and Eileen [Moroso's girlfriend] got in the van with us, and we watched and talked through the whole Modified race that followed our race."

Added Tommy, with a smile: "Rob said since he'd won the Busch championship, he'd like to go on and win the Winston Cup championship. Then, he'd kind of like to be a professional bowler."

"Rob was like one of the kids," Martha Houston concluded. "Marty [the middle of the Houstons' three sons] spent the night with him in Charlotte. He came back and said, 'You won't believe this. He's got his Charlotte trophy in the closet, and he hangs sweaters on it.'"

But less than a year later, after moving to the Winston Cup circuit, Moroso would be dead.

On September 30, 1990, just four days after his 22nd birthday, Moroso and the driver of a second vehicle were killed in an accident in Mooresville, N.C. It was later discovered that Moroso had been driving under the influence of alcohol.

"Dick Moroso called me that night, about 2 o'clock in the morning," said Bird, who joined Steve Grissom's Busch Grand National team after Moroso clinched the title. "It was like losing a son. We were still close after I left. It's hard for me to explain . . . "

Bird's words trailed off. A rough-and-tumble bear of a man, tears filled the corners of his eyes.

"We'd be riding on the lake in my boat, and Robbie would be sitting on this big deck over the motor," said Bird, the memory, a good one, coming back. "We'd be running 50 mph, and he'd just fall off into the water just for the hell of it. Robbie wanted to have fun and enjoy life. He did, in the short life that he had."

LEFT: The dance of a champion, on top of his car after clinching the title. Tommy Houston said that Rob Moroso told him after the race that he had two more goals in life—to win the Winston Cup championship, and to be a professional bowler. (Dick Conway)
OPPOSITE: Rob Moroso celebrates at Martinsville with his father, Dick. Less than a year later, Moroso was killed in an automobile accident in Mooresville, N.C., hours after competing in a Winston Cup event at North Wilkesboro. The elder Moroso fielded Winston Cup and Busch Grand National teams for a few more years. He died in 1999 of brain cancer. (Dick Conway)

LEFT: Michael Waltrip miraculously walked away from this crash at Bristol on April 7, 1990. Most consider it the worst looking wreck they've ever seen. (Ray Shough) RIGHT: Although Chuck Bown (63) drove for the uncle and cousin of Jimmy Hensley (25), both drivers insist the family factor never played into their battle for the 1990 championship. Hensley said the biggest factor in Bown's title was that he drove a car that was on "rails" every week. (Dick Conway)

1990
A Family Feud

The tiny hamlets of Ridgeway and Horsepasture are right next to each other in the foothills of Virginia, just a stone's throw from Martinsville. Not much goes on in the small towns other than a little good-natured bench racing now and then.

In 1990, folks in the area had plenty to talk about.

Chuck Bown was driving for Ridgeway car owner Hubert Hensley and his son, Jeff,

Labonte, in his first full year on the tour, took an early lead in the standings and was out front in the title chase on April 7, when Winston Cup regular Michael Waltrip was involved in one of the most hideous accidents imaginable.

Waltrip, who'd spun a few laps earlier, got together with Robert Pressley as they came off turn two on lap 171. Waltrip's car shot up the track and scraped a guard-rail, which gave way, sending it into the end of the backstretch wall. The Pontiac completely disintegrated, leaving nothing even faintly resembling a race car.

Bystanders rushed to the wreckage, fearing the worst. Waltrip, however, was uninjured and directed his extraction from the debris.

"There was this rollbar that came around my head, and [former NASCAR official] Harold Kinder's got this jaws-of-life thing getting ready to clamp down on this sucker," said Waltrip, whose legs were lying on the pavement in the accident. "I said, 'Harold, if you snap that thing, it's gonna hit me upside the head. I can crawl right out through there.' Well, right out through there was where the motor had been. But never one time did I think about this being strange."

Waltrip was checked in the infield care center and then taken to a nearby hospital for observation. He was released the following morning and raced in Bristol's Winston Cup event that afternoon as if nothing had happened.

"I remember riding on a golf cart down the front straightaway to get into the helicopter to go to the hospital, and I saw Robert Pressley," Waltrip said. "I thought, 'I ought to get off this golf cart and kick his ass.'

"He might've beat me up. I don't know. But I would've been a winner either way, because if I'd gone over there to fight him and he whipped me, I could've just said, 'Well, I've been in a bad wreck.' That's the only thing I regret, because he deserved it."

competing against Jimmy Hensley, Horsepasture's home-town hero, for the Busch Grand National championship. Throw in a little rivalry between relatives—Jimmy was Hubert's nephew—and the war was on.

"It was pretty tough, because it was almost like a community divided," said Jeff Hensley, Bown's crew chief. "It never came between me and Jimmy or Daddy and Jimmy, but everybody in Ridgeway, Horsepasture, and Martinsville had their favorite."

Said Jimmy Hensley: "They were competitors like everybody else. They were the team to beat. It could've been Jack Ingram or Tommy Houston. I never tried to focus on it being kin people. They were up front every week, and that's where I was gonna be every week, too."

A switch during the off season from Chevrolet to Buick V-6 engines gave Bown and the Hensleys the reliability they'd missed in 1989. Despite the new-found strength under the hood, Bown's season got off to a bad start at Daytona on February 17, when he was caught up in a multi-car pileup in turn four on the 14th lap.

When the smoke cleared, 23 cars had been damaged.

"It was a mega-wreck," Bown recalled. "We made repairs, and we were terrible, banged up all to heck, but most of them couldn't get back out at all."

Dale Earnhardt captured the first of five consecutive Busch Grand National wins at Daytona. Bobby

---

ABOVE: Moments after Michael Waltrip's crash, his older brother, three-time Winston Cup champion Darrell Waltrip, stands over the wreckage, sobbing. The elder Waltrip is being restrained by his then-crew chief, Jeff Hammond, and a NASCAR official. (Dick Conway) OPPOSITE: Without a doubt, this is the most violent impact that a driver has ever walked away from. More than 10 years after the incident, people simply refer to it as "The Crash". Notice at bottom left how close Waltrip's wreckage comes to getting run over by Kenny Wallace (36) and Dana Patten (86). (Ray Shough)

L. D. Ottinger, who would eventually win the race, remembers sitting with Earnhardt during the red flag that followed Waltrip's accident.

"Dale went to check on Michael, and he came back through there shaking his head. I thought, 'Well, he's been killed,' " Ottinger said. "Dale said, 'You ain't gonna believe it. That crazy son-of-a-bitch ain't hurt.' I thought he was joking."

Bown led all 200 laps at Lanier Raceway on April 28, and then won again the next week at South Boston. Hensley finished fourth and Labonte 12th, leaving the two tied in the championship battle, and Bown trailed them by only five points. Hensley took a brief lead with a win on May 12 at Nazareth, but Bown won for the third time in four races on May 19 at Hickory. The victory gave Bown an advantage in the standings he would keep for the rest of the year.

Testing for the Hickory race helped determine which chassis to use. "We were one of the first teams to really implement testing," said Jeff Hensley. "We wore South Boston out testing for different places. Other teams would go test at Charlotte or Daytona, but we tested somewhere every week. That was before they had a limit. We'd go practice races, make pit stops, and run 250 laps straight."

"At Hickory, we used a different chassis than we'd used at South Boston," Bown said. "We tested with two cars and couldn't make up our minds about which one to use. The suspensions under the two were quite a bit different. We were having such success with the first one, but this new one seemed so good. We gave it a shot, sat on the pole, and won the race."

Bown won for the fourth time in 1990 on June 9 at Orange County, and he said that as the season progressed, NASCAR officials began taking a much closer look at his car.

"Things were going so good, they started tearing us down unbelievably in post-race inspection," Bown recalled. "They would dismantle the motor. They would pull the rear end out. They were measuring the suspension components. They would even dismount our tires. They really thought we were cheating, and I think some of the competition did, too. But we weren't. We just had our stuff together."

Short tracks were Bown's forte, and on July 8 he conquered one of the sport's toughest bullrings—the one third of a mile Oxford Plains. Forty-three cars from all over the country started the event, and about that many more failed to qualify. Somehow, Bown managed to lead twice for 220 of the race's 306 laps, including the final 192.

That was a major accomplishment at Oxford.

"Winning that race probably meant more to me than actually winning the championship," said Jeff Hensley. "Not that we didn't beat good people to win the championship, but we beat the best people in short-track racing. Midwest guys were there. Busch North guys were there, and we were there. And we kicked their ass."

OPPOSITE: Kenny Wallace is framed in smoke after the engine in his Pontiac blew at Orange County June 9. Wallace completed 122 of the event's 200 laps, and was credited with a 27th-place finish in the 29-car field. The problem knocked Wallace from fourth to sixth in the Busch Grand National standings. (Ray Shough) BELOW LEFT: Bobby Moon (85), Kenny Wallace, and Dick Trickle (33) pull off the near-impossible by going three wide without crashing at Dover June 2. Dana Patten and Jeff Burton (12) are right behind the battle. Michael Waltrip won the race, less than two months after his incredible Bristol accident. (Ray Shough) BELOW RIGHT: Bobby Labonte's car slides down New Hampshire's backstretch on its roof during the track's inaugural Busch Grand National event July 15. Also involved in the incident were Dale Jarrett (with the word "Crunch" appropriately emblazoned on his rear bumper), Jimmy Hensley, Morgan Shepherd (9) and Ricky Craven (spinning blue car, right). (Ray Shough)

Bown had learned a lot racing on the Busch North tour before joining the Hensleys. Comprised at the time exclusively of short tracks like Oxford, racing in that division was simply this: survival of the fittest.

"The high-point guys always had to start at the back, and that was a tremendous lesson in how to be patient and yet race hard enough to get from the back to the front in 100 laps," Bown said. "You wise up with time, and learn that you've got to finish to win. Anybody can take you out at any time and you've just got to be aware of that."

Steve Grissom, a former Alabama high school football star then driving family-owned equipment, gave Bown a reminder of just how tough short track racing could be when they got together racing for the lead July 28 at Pulaski County. Grissom booted Bown out of the way shortly after a restart, and went on to collect the first win of his career.

"Chuck took it real easy going into turn one, because there was a bunch of oil-dry down," said Jeff Hensley. "Grissom ran down on the flat part of the race track and just body-slammed us. Chuck got back up beside him going into [turn] three, and he run us into the inside pit wall.

"That was a race we clearly should've won. If Grissom

ABOVE: Michael Waltrip came back to Bristol April 24 for the track's night race, but was caught up in another wreck. Here, he's racing Ward Burton (5) and Bobby Labonte for position. Labonte was the best of the three that night. He started from the pole and finished 15th. (Ray Shough)

hadn't been going for his first win, it was gonna be a hell of a wreck. That was the only reason [Bown] didn't go on and crash him out."

After winning August 11 at Orange County, Bown and the Hensleys hit a dry spell.

"We got to where we couldn't do nothing right," Jeff Hensley said. "We'd be leading the race and blow an engine. It looked like Jimmy was gonna come back and win the championship. But every time we'd have trouble, Jimmy would have trouble. We tried everything we could for the last eight races to give it to him, and he wouldn't take it."

At one race—neither Jimmy nor Jeff can remember where it was—the window net on Jimmy's car fell down and he had to drive one handed until catching a caution to correct the problem. It was minor, but irritating problems like these helped seal the championship for Bown.

"We just never could close the gap on them," Jimmy said. "Every time they'd have something go wrong, we'd have something go wrong. I remember having my window net fall down. It wasn't major stuff. Stuff just happened where I didn't finish as good as I could have."

Although Bown spun on pit road while trying to make a green-flag pit stop, his 18th-place finish October 20 at Rockingham put him over the top in the title chase. Looking back on a career that had seen its share of hardships made the championship that much sweeter.

"I paid my dues. I started out in Oregon, moved to North Carolina, to New Hampshire, and back to Virginia," Bown said. "It was a very big deal to me, because I know championships don't come very often. You might win three in a row or might never win another one."

"We never looked up until it was over," added Jeff Hensley. "And sometimes I regret that, because I never enjoyed winning the championship. To this day, I've never enjoyed one minute of it, because as soon as were crowned champions, we went to work on '91. I never took the time to let it really sink in that we had actually won the championship. I couldn't see the forest for the trees."

The 1991 campaign again would be a family affair in the Busch Grand National division, but it wouldn't be between the Hensleys. It would come down to the younger brothers of former Winston Cup champions.

Winston Classic

Congratulations!
CHUCK BOWN
and
HENSLEY RACING

1990 BUSCH GRAND NATIONAL CHAMPION

ABOVE: Chuck Bown and his crew celebrate the 1990 championship at Martinsville, about 15 miles from the team's shop in Ridgeway, Va. Bown is pictured on the bottom row in the Nescafe driver's uniform, with his wife, Debbie. Jeff Hensley, a former Busch Grand National driver and Bown's crew chief, is just to the right of Bown. (Ray Shough)
RIGHT: After the season finale, drivers Elton Sawyer and Patty Moise were married in her hometown of Jacksonville, Fla. They're the only husband and wife duo to have competed against each other in a major motorsports division. (Ray Shough)

1991
My Kid Brother Can Beat Your Kid Brother

The early racing careers of Bobby Labonte and Kenny Wallace are remarkably similar. Both paid their dues as crew members for various teams in the mid-1980s. Both raced whatever they could get their hands on.

And both had older brothers who had won Winston Cup championships. Labonte owned his own team, but always sought advice from Terry, who'd won the Winston Cup in 1984. Wallace's operation was fielded by Rusty, the 1989 champ.

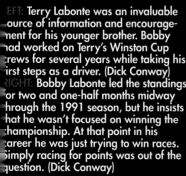

LEFT: Terry Labonte was an invaluable source of information and encouragement for his younger brother. Bobby had worked on Terry's Winston Cup crews for several years while taking his first steps as a driver. (Dick Conway) RIGHT: Bobby Labonte led the standings for two and one-half months midway through the 1991 season, but he insists that he wasn't focused on winning the championship. At that point in his career he was just trying to win races. Simply racing for points was out of the question. (Dick Conway)

The family connection was evident as the 1991 Busch Grand National season began at Daytona. Bobby Labonte wrecked his primary car during the final practice session, but quickly struck a deal to start the car Terry had qualified 11th.

"It was real windy Friday afternoon. They'd closed the airport down because of the high winds," Labonte said. "We were fast, but I went into turn three and was like, 'OK, I'm not comfortable here. I'm gonna come in.' But some guys were behind me, and when

they went by, it took the air off the spoiler, lifted it up, and I went around."

Unfortunately for the Labontes, the February 16 Goody's 300 didn't turn out any better than "Happy Hour" had. On the first lap between turns three and four, Labonte spun and began a melee that collected at least 16 other cars, eight of which couldn't continue.

"That was definitely not the start we wanted to the season," Labonte said dryly.

The bad luck wasn't over for Labonte. He led much of the March 2 event at Rockingham, but spun in turn two while trying to retake the lead from Dale Jarrett four laps from the end. On flat tires, Labonte limped to a sixth-place finish.

"It was inexperience on my part trying to pass at the wrong place at the wrong time on older tires," Labonte said. "I should've let him go and finished second, but of course, that wasn't in my vocabulary at the time. I was definitely hungry."

Wallace, meanwhile, finished 10th, third, and sec-

ond in the season's first three races. In the fourth, on March 10 at Martinsville, he used a third-place finish to go to the front of the line in the championship chase.

Two weeks later, Wallace captured his first Busch Grand National win at Volusia County, Fla.

"When we got to Charlotte, Rusty was sitting there in his pickup truck waiting on me," Wallace said. "I got off the plane with the trophy, and he grabbed that thing and still has it to this day."

Wallace's lead vanished on March 31 at Hickory, where he crashed after contact with Tommy Ellis. Wallace's mishap dropped him to 20th in the final rundown, and his slide continued over the next few races.

"Back then, they laid a bumper to you in a heartbeat. That was the way of racing," said a diplomatic Wallace of his run-in with Ellis.

Labonte finished second April 6 at Darlington, again getting passed late in the race by Jarrett. It was tough coming so close to victory lane, only to have it snatched away. On April 13 at Bristol, Labonte finally made it to racing's Promised Land. Who Labonte passed for the win made that victory even more special.

"Dale Earnhardt had a left rear tire going down," Labonte said. "I was running behind him and thought, 'Man, I'll never catch him.' Sure enough, I got by him in turns three and four. He rubbed me all the way through the corner. I got by him and thought, 'Hot diggidy dog! This could be the day.' "

Labonte cut Wallace's lead in the standings to just five points April 27 at Lanier. A week later, on May 4 at South Boston, Labonte gained the upper hand in the championship battle for the first time by finishing sixth to Wallace's 15th.

But wins and championships didn't seem to matter much in the wake of the South Boston event. After Gary Neice's car veered toward the turn-three wall and crashed on lap 201, he had to be cut from the car. The 36-year-old Candler, N.C., native was taken to Halifax/South Boston Community Hospital, where he was pronounced dead at 6 p.m., about 35 minutes after the accident.

According to a May 7 report released by Virginia state medical examiners, Neice had died of "acute coronary insufficiency"—basically, a heart attack.

Labonte was atop the standings for the next two and a half months, his lead over Wallace reaching a high of 111 points after the June 1 event at Dover. A

LEFT: Kenny Wallace (left) presented Bobby Labonte with his biggest challenge for the 1991 championship. The two exchanged the lead in the standings almost every week. Surprisingly, Labonte now says he was probably too young to realize what winning the title meant. (Dick Conway) ABOVE: Bobby Labonte's crew goes to work at Orange County June 8. Racing on bullring short tracks like Orange County was always close, as evidenced by the damage to the rear of Labonte's Oldsmobile. Despite the crunched bodywork and starting 29th in the 31-car field, he was able to finish sixth. (Dick Conway) OPPOSITE: Bobby Labonte climbs into older brother Terry's car for the start of the Goody's 300 February 16. Labonte had wrecked his primary car during practice the day before. Then, during the first lap of the race, he spun and started a multicar accident, destroying a second car in as many days. It was a disappointing start to the season. (Dick Conway)

RIGHT: Watkins Glen held its first Busch Grand National event on June 29. Terry Labonte won the Fay's 150, while Bobby Labonte finished 16th. Here, Bobby leads Jimmy Hensley through the uphill esses. Hensley finished 21st, one lap down. (Dick Conway)

BELOW: Bobby Labonte's father, Bob (right), served as his crew chief. As calm and reserved as his sons are, Bob Labonte has never been afraid to speak his mind at any time and at any place. He still isn't. (Dick Conway)

OPPOSITE: Bobby Labonte has always been a driver who concentrates on the task at hand without a lot of unnecessary pretense. (Dick Conway)

blown engine and a pit-road collision with Jeff Gordon cost Labonte dearly on July 14 at New Hampshire. Wallace's win jumped him from 77 points behind Labonte to 51 ahead.

"After that race, I flew home with Davey Allison on his airplane," Wallace said. "I'll never forget Davey's words. He said, 'Man, I wish I could win a Busch race.' At that time, he was a superstar. I said, 'Davey, I'd cut off one of my fingers to accomplish what you've accomplished.' He wanted to win a Busch race so bad. He tried and tried and tried and couldn't win one. That day was a really neat day."

Almost two years later to the day, Allison died from injuries he sustained in a helicopter crash shortly after competing in New Hampshire's inaugural Winston Cup race. He never won a Busch Grand National race.

The championship battle swung in Wallace's favor during the July 27 event at Pulaski County, where he finished second and Labonte was 25th. In just six races, Labonte had gone from 111 points ahead of Wallace to trailing his rival by 173.

Labonte had brake problems at Pulaski County that required time behind the wall to fix, and when he made it back onto the track, he was almost immediately involved in an accident. Still, Labonte and his crew refused to give up.

"There wasn't a panic," Labonte said. "We just kept plugging along. We knew we were running good. We just needed to have the breaks go our way and not make as many mistakes."

A late yellow flag on August 3 at IRP erased Chuck Bown's seven-second lead over Labonte. Bown's safety harnesses came unhooked during the caution, and with 11 laps to go, he stopped in turn two to refasten them.

"I didn't want people to read about me getting killed because I didn't have my belts on," Bown said. "That would've been pretty stupid. With 10 to go and leading the race, I knew if anybody could get a piece of me, they were going to."

Wallace was involved in a wreck with Ward Burton at IRP, so Labonte's victory erased more than half his deficit in the standings. But competition again took a back seat after the race, when tragedy struck the circuit for the second time in 1991.

A little more than a month before Jack Ingram's planned retirement from driving, his son and crew chief, Robbie, suffered serious injuries when he fell asleep while driving the team's transporter back from to North Carolina from IRP. The younger Ingram died August 5 at the University of Kentucky Medical Center in Lexington, Ky.

Ingram canceled plans to compete in the August 10 event at Orange County.

"That overshadowed anything that had ever happened to me in my whole life," said Ingram, who finished ninth at IRP. "Racing gave me a lot. Sometimes, it took a little away from me."

After the August 23 event at Bristol, Wallace led Labonte by 72 points. Eight days later at Darlington, Labonte took a one-point lead. After each of the next four races, the two would exchange the top spot in the standings by a few points either way. Going back and forth like that might have been tough for many drivers, but not these two.

"Heck, I was probably too new, young and not thinking about it to be nervous about it," Labonte said. "I probably didn't realize what it meant at the time. I probably took it for granted that we were there. At the same time, it was kind of fun, because Kenny and I have a good relationship. It was always me against him every weekend. Neither one of us could get ahead."

On October 5 at Charlotte, Earnhardt nudged Phil Parsons into a spin coming off the fourth turn on lap 21, an accident that also collected Labonte. NASCAR

officials deemed Earnhardt's actions rough driving and parked him for the rest of the day.

Of course, that didn't mean much to Labonte, whose car was badly damaged. Labonte's crew, and a few extras, made patchwork repairs to get him back on the track. He finished 19th, 25 laps down.

"I remember thinking, 'We're done for now. This has ruined our chances [to win the championship].'"

Labonte said. "I was sitting there on pit road, and Steve Hmiel [then the crew chief for Mark Martin's Winston Cup effort], who I'd worked with at Billy Hagan's shop for many years, looked in the right side window and said, 'Don't give up.'

"I didn't expect Steve to be there. He just stepped right in and was helping tape it up to make sure pieces weren't gonna fall off so we could try to get back out there and get as many points as we could."

Wallace led Labonte by 33 points after Charlotte, but his hopes of capturing the championship were dashed for good on October 13 at New Hampshire. Wallace slammed into the third-turn wall on lap 208 and suffered a concussion, three broken ribs, and positional vertigo.

"That's where it ended," said Wallace, who trailed Labonte by 42 points after the race. "The rear end wasn't welded real good, and it broke out from underneath the car. I went flying into that wall, and I thought, 'Oh, my God.' I hit so hard it cracked three of my ribs on the right side.

"I got out of the car under pure adrenaline. The next thing I know, I felt like I was at home, sleeping really, really sound. I was so at peace. Then, I opened my eyes and realized I was laying on the race track. That was probably the scariest moment in my whole career."

Wallace started his car October 19 at Rockingham, but turned it over to Rusty, who took it to a third-place finish. Labonte stuck right with the Wallaces and came home eighth. There'd been some controversy about Rusty taking over for Kenny at Rockingham, but in the end, Bobby admits Terry would've done the same thing for him.

"What's fair for one is fair for another," Labonte said.

The injuries were still bothering Wallace as the tour headed to Martinsville for its October 27 season finale. He qualified well off the pace, and the race had barely started before he experienced brake trouble.

"It was over when we got to Martinsville," Wallace concluded. "I wasn't cocky. I'd had the crap knocked out of me two weeks before that. I felt like somebody had knocked me upside the head with a two-by-four."

Labonte rode his fifth-place finish in the event all the way to the championship. Coming up the hard way and owning his own equipment meant the world to the young Texan.

"There was satisfaction, because the team was all mine," Labonte said. "There wasn't a silent partner. I rented a shop from my brother. It meant a lot, just for the fact that it was my stuff. I worked hard at it.

"I started working on race cars seven or eight years before that, not knowing much about them. I was sweeping floors, running Late Models. When you set a goal and achieve it, it's pretty exciting."

The battle for the 1992 crown would be even closer than it had been between Labonte and Wallace. But just as it had in 1991, tragedy would strike the Busch Grand National Series.

ABOVE: Kenny Wallace's name is over the window of the No. 36 car at Rockingham October 19, but it's 1989 Winston Cup champion Rusty Wallace behind the wheel. The younger Wallace had sustained broken ribs and a concussion the week before at New Hampshire. After starting the ACDelco 200, Kenny turned his car over to Rusty, who took it to a third-place finish. As a result, Bobby Labonte's lead in the standings was cut to 19 points going into the last race of the year. (Graham Niven)

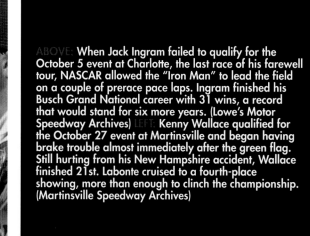

ABOVE: When Jack Ingram failed to qualify for the October 5 event at Charlotte, the last race of his farewell tour, NASCAR allowed the "Iron Man" to lead the field on a couple of prerace pace laps. Ingram finished his Busch Grand National career with 31 wins, a record that would stand for six more years. (Lowe's Motor Speedway Archives) LEFT: Kenny Wallace qualified for the October 27 event at Martinsville and began having brake trouble almost immediately after the green flag. Still hurting from his New Hampshire accident, Wallace finished 21st. Labonte cruised to a fourth-place showing, more than enough to clinch the championship. (Martinsville Speedway Archives)

1992
High Times
And Heartbreak

The 1992 Busch Grand National season was one of the division's most exciting, but at the same time one of its most heartbreaking.

Three drivers—Joe Nemechek, Bobby Labonte, and Todd Bodine—were in contention for the championship until the final laps of the year, and the margin of victory was the slimmest ever. But on a muggy August day, Clifford Allison lost his life while practicing for the tour's inaugural race at Michigan Speedway.

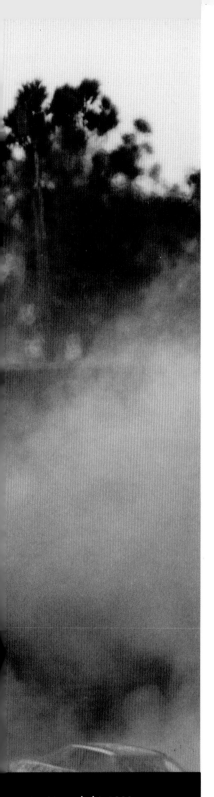

LEFT: Joe Nemechek's 1992 season got off to a horrifying start at Daytona February 15. After colliding with Jimmy Spencer on lap 76, Nemechek's car bursts into flames in turn two. Also involved are Chuck Bown (pinched between Nemechek and the wall); Todd Bodine (34); Tom Peck (19); and Bobby Labonte (Slim Jim-sponsored car). Nemechek's car slides to the apron in a ball of flames as Peck drives by. (Martha Nemechek Collection) RIGHT: Jeff Gordon had a busy year in 1992. He won Atlanta's inaugural Busch Grand National race March 14, and was signed by Winston Cup car owner Rick Hendrick. That ignited a firestorm of controversy concerning Chevrolet's luring Gordon from the Ford camp. (Bryan Hallman)

The season was very memorable for the best reasons—and the worst. The February 15 opener at Daytona well might have been a sign of things to come. Nemechek spun between turns one and two on lap 76, and his car was quickly engulfed in a horrifying ball of flames. Bodine and Labonte, also caught up in the accident, scurried out of their crumpled machines to help Nemechek.

"I got bad loose after a pit stop, and I hit the wall pretty hard," Nemechek said. "I knew the car was full of gas, and that was bad. All of a sudden, gas started coming through the car. It was on fire and burning. I just kind of tucked up and was along for the ride."

A new sternum strap kept Nemechek in the car, even after he'd unfastened the rest of his safety harnesses.

"About that time, I had to take a breath, because I couldn't hold my breath any longer," Nemechek continued. "It was pretty nasty. That's when I started kind of going wild. I was thinking, 'I'm gonna burn up in this thing.'"

Bodine could barely see Nemechek inside his car because of the smoke.

"He kind of gave up," Bodine said. "His arms flopped down, and his head kind of went down. He was done. His energy was gone. So I reached in, got the sternum strap undone, and pulled him out."

Nemechek's buttocks were burned when he sat on the door frame. Bodine remembers the car being so hot that it already had melted the door's paint away. Still, Nemechek's problems weren't over. A safety worker fired a blast of fire extinguisher chemicals in Nemechek's face once he was freed, preventing him from taking a breath of fresh air.

Bodine and Labonte finally got Nemechek to safety.

"We got him out, got him on the ground, and lifted his visor up to make sure he was breathing," Labonte said. "You don't sit there and say, 'Well, what should I do here?' You just do it."

Although Nemechek would claw his way into the top 10 in points just two races later, he said it took four or five months for his injuries to heal completely.

Kenny Wallace went on top of the standings with a second-place finish March 7 at Richmond. A Winston Cup ride for the 1992 season had gone away just before Daytona, and Wallace had to scramble to put together a Busch Grand National program with team owner Felix Sabates.

Something must have been working, because Wallace would be king of the hill for the next four months. And while the battle for the title had stabilized, spring would bring a couple of memorable moments.

On April 18 at Hickory, just two days after the death of his father, Oren, Tommy Houston overcame two spins and a record 26 cautions to capture the last win of his career, and, almost certainly, the most emotional. The night of the race, Houston and his family attended his father's visitation. The funeral was held the next day.

"I hadn't planned on racing that race," said Houston, who took a provisional to start last in the 30-car field. "Everybody said, 'There ain't nothing you can do. You might as well go on and race. He would've wanted you to.' I really felt proud to be able to win in that situation."

Two races later, a win was taken away from a competitor for the first time in the division's history. Jeff Burton beat Bobby Dotter to the finish line May 2 at New River Valley Speedway in Radford, Va., but inspectors found an unproved rear-end assembly in Burton's car. Dotter inherited the victory, the first of his career.

OPPOSITE AND ABOVE: **Joe Nemechek's car slides to the apron at Daytona in a ball of flames as Tom Peck drives by (opposite). Finally, Todd Bodine helps Nemechek out of his burning car, his helmet and uniform blackened by the flames (above). (Martha Nemechek Collection)**

"The part was not illegal," Burton said. "It was not approved, and that's a major difference. It may function properly, but NASCAR has never had the chance to review it for quality. It's not what won the race for us."

Added Dotter: "I would have liked to have had all the hoopla that goes along with the victory lane celebration, but on the other hand, I'm glad for the team. It was a long day and a half [until NASCAR's final decision was rendered]."

Wallace fell to third in the standings behind new leader Nemechek and Robert Pressley when he dropped a cylinder July 12 at New Hampshire, where his championship hopes had ended the year before. His fortunes would only spiral downward from there.

A few weeks later, a disagreement between Wallace and Steve Bird led to the crew chief's departure. It

was all downhill from there for Wallace's team.

"When 'Birdie' left, it was pretty much over," Wallace said. "Birdie carried me, and we led the points the first half of the year, ran real strong. Then, all of a sudden, we got in some type of little pissing match, and he quit."

Ernie Irvan won Talladega Superspeedway's first Busch Grand National event July 25, and then Nemechek scored his first win August 1 at IRP. Two weeks later, competitors prepared for the circuit's first stop at Michigan.

During practice on August 13, Clifford Allison, the son of Winston Cup legend Bobby Allison and younger brother of superstar Davey Allison, backed his car into the wall between turns three and four. Its right side then swung around and into the barrier before sliding to the apron.

Allison died about 1:30 p.m. while en route to W.A. Foote Memorial Hospital in Jackson, Mich. The cause of death was severe head injuries.

Two days later, Bodine held off a furious charge by eight Winston Cup regulars to win the race. He dedicated the victory to Allison and his family.

"[Allison's death] just took the wind out of everybody's sails. We didn't even really care to go racing," Bodine said.

Nemechek was the next highest-finishing Busch Grand National regular, in 10th place, and on August 23 at New Hampshire, he won for the second time in 1992.

The normally reticent Nemechek couldn't help but smile as he recalled battling with Dale Earnhardt as the New Hampshire race neared its close.

"Those last few laps, we just rubbed and banged," said Nemechek, who led Bodine by 103 points after the race. "Coming off turn two, I looked over one time, and all you could see was his black helmet, dark goggles, and his teeth, smiling. I was thinking, 'This is cool.'

"When I got to the next corner, he gave me a big ol' pop in the butt and sent me way up the track. I never let off the gas. I just held her down, and she did a major power slide all the way around the corner. I beat him by a fender."

An early wreck August 28 at Bristol cost Nemechek part of his advantage in the standings over Bodine, who won despite a heated battle with Jeff Burton. Burton spun 11 laps from the end and then angrily nudged his car into the right side of Bodine's after the race.

Bodine overtook Nemechek in the championship battle September 5 at Darlington, but just barely. Bodine led Nemechek by eight points and Labonte by 185. Nemechek and Bodine then exchanged the top spot after each of the next three races. Labonte, meanwhile, was fighting it out with Pressley for third place.

The competitive tension was only heightened by the rivals' contrasting personalities.

"Joe and Bobby are a little bit different. Let's put it that way," Bodine said. "Joe's pretty hard to talk to at the race track, because he's *all* business. He doesn't want to know nothing [about anybody else]. Bobby's kind of quiet, anyway, kind of keeps to himself."

OPPOSITE: Busch Grand National drivers gather for a team photo before a charity softball game against Camel GT competitors held in conjunction with the division's June 27 event at Watkins Glen. Pictured on the bottom row, from left to right, are Tom Peck, Ward Burton, Elton Sawyer, Kenny Wallace, Joe Nemechek, Ernie Irvan, Bobby Labonte, and NASCAR official Andy Hall. The back row includes Ricky Craven, Jeff Gordon, Richard Lasater (partially obscured by Gordon), Steve Grissom, Troy Beebe, Robert Pressley, Anheuser-Busch public relations representative Dennis Punch, Butch Miller, Jeff Burton, and Clifford Allison. (Ray Shough) BELOW LEFT: Todd Bodine gets position under Bobby Labonte at Orange County June 6. Labonte, however, would come back to finish third, while Bodine was sixth, the last car on the lead lap behind winner Robert Pressley. (Bryan Hallman) BELOW RIGHT: Although Todd Bodine was in the thick of the championship battle in 1992, he insists that it didn't affect him. "I'm not one to get nervous about that stuff," Bodine said. "My philosophy has always been to give 110 percent. That's all you can do." (Bryan Hallman)

On October 10 at Charlotte, Bodine finished 37th as a result of an early crash with Dale Jarrett. That gave Nemechek a 73-point lead in the standings, and Labonte used his third-place showing in the event to close to within 85 points of Nemechek. Bodine lost more ground October 18 at Martinsville when his transmission stripped its gears coming to the green flag.

"If it wasn't for those two races, we would've won the championship," Bodine said.

Labonte won at Martinsville and trailed Nemechek by 60 points with just two races to go. He moved even closer on October 24 at Rockingham in a race won by Mark Martin. Martin later was fined $5,000 because of an altered gasket in his carburetor. NASCAR ruled that while the part did not significantly enhance the car's performance, the intent to do so was there.

Entering the last race of the year, Nemechek led Labonte by 33 points. All Nemechek needed to do was finish sixth, and the championship would be his. But when the November 8 event at Hickory began, Nemechek encountered two major stumbling blocks. First, Labonte and his crew found the right chassis combination to make his car a virtual rocketship. And second, Nemechek's car was getting beat on at almost every turn.

"That was one of the best cars I've ever had on a race track," Labonte said. "That thing would fly. I had Nemechek lapped twice, at least, and I'd be like, 'I've got him now. If I can get him a lap down, I've got this thing won.' And, man, the yellow flag would come out and save him."

Cautions were about the only thing saving Nemechek.

"Jimmy Spencer was in that race, and for some reason, I got knocked around by him all day," Nemechek said of his foe that day, who eventually was parked by NASCAR for rough driving. "And by everybody else, I got knocked around all day. The nose was knocked off. The car was tore all to pieces. I had a bull's-eye on all four corners of my car."

On lap 284, Nemechek and Chuck Bown crossed under the last of 13 yellow flags virtually side by side. Officials ruled that Nemechek was due the sixth position, and that's where he finished to clinch the crown by three points over Labonte.

It's still the slimmest championship margin of victory in the history of the division.

"They threw everything at me they could," Nemechek said proudly. "Especially at that last race, it was like they were out to get me. I beat them."

ABOVE LEFT AND RIGHT: Jeff Burton slams into the rear of Joe Nemechek as Robert Pressley (59) slides by, and Tom Peck locks his brakes in the background. The multicar wreck snowballs with Tommy Ellis's Buick winding up on the hood of Ricky Craven's machine. Tracy Leslie (72) scoots by to the inside. (Bryan Hallman)

ABOVE: Joe Nemechek managed to finish sixth at Hickory—exactly where he needed to be to nail down the championship. He's joined in victory lane by his girlfriend (now wife) Andrea (to left of Nemechek); younger brother John (to right of Nemechek); and mother Martha. (Bryan Hallman)

LEFT: Steve Grissom (left) talks with crew member Dennis Adcock. Grissom said that signing a sponsor for the full 1993 Busch Series schedule was crucial to his championship hopes. He also felt a certain amount of satisfaction because his team was not considered a threat to win the championship prior to the season. (Martinsville Speedway Archives) RIGHT: At Myrtle Beach on June 12, Jerry Glanville (81), then head coach of the NFL's Atlanta Falcons, spins out and crashes. Glanville raced when his schedule as a head coach would permit. (Bryan Hallman)

1993
Grissom Grabs the Ring

Most Busch Series champions point to a specific race or string of on-track events as a turning point in their title run. Not Steve Grissom.

According to Grissom, his biggest break came when Channellock opted to sponsor him for the full 1993 campaign. The year before, Grissom's family-owned team had been sponsored in 15 races by Channellock and in another 15 by Roddenberry's, a food company. In another event, the left side of his car carried one sponsor's paint scheme, and the right side featured the other backer's colors. It was a strange and confusing mixture.

Grissom had been shut out of victory lane in 1992. But having one sponsor for 1993 meant spending more time under the hood and less time in the paint shop, swapping colors and decals. The new-found attention to detail would show in Grissom's performance.

"When the '93 season rolled around and all the gurus were making their picks about who was gonna be the one to beat for the championship, our name wasn't even mentioned," said Grissom, a noticeable hint of satisfaction in his voice. "We were just a bunch of guys that got together. Nobody was a genius.

"Nobody had a lot of championship experience in the Busch Series. We would sit around and laugh about people not even considering us, and yet here we were in position to compete for the championship."

Grissom's most serious challenger for the title came from another driver on the rebound, David Green. After a stellar rookie season in 1991, Green had been released from his ride with Filmar Racing. Green had spent 1992 on the sidelines, working for Labonte Racing and hoping for another shot.

Green made the most of the opportunity when Bobby Labonte moved to the Winston Cup circuit in 1993. After posting top-10 finishes in the first three races of the year, Green found himself atop the Busch Series standings for the first time in his career.

"We took [Labonte's] name off the roof and put my name on it," Green recalled. "Stuff like that happens in a lot of other situations, but there's other changes—a different crew, different sponsor. Nothing changed for us. It was strictly one decal coming off and another decal going on. We kept our consistency and focus."

A win by Grissom April 10 at Hickory and a third-place finish in the next race on the schedule, on May 1 at Orange County, gave Grissom enough momentum to overtake Green in the championship battle. Still, after the disappointing year he'd had in 1992, Grissom wasn't counting points. Not yet.

The next month and a half would be a roller coaster of emotions for Grissom. He maintained an advantage on Green May 8 at Martinsville and May 23 at Nazareth, but a blown engine May 29 at Charlotte and a broken rocker arm June 5 at Dover cost him dearly. Green regained the lead in the standings, and after Dover, led Grissom by 33 points.

"It sounds like we were having a lot of motor trouble, but actually we were probably having less than some of the other teams," said Grissom, who finished 17th on five cylinders at Dover. "That was just an inherent problem with the V-6s at that time. They had good power and ran well, but it wasn't uncommon to have blown motors."

Grissom was back in front with a less-than-stellar 13th-place finish June 26 at Watkins Glen in a race won by Winston Cup star Bill Elliott. Grissom grinned at the memory of his effort that afternoon—hopping curbs, going off course, turning left and right—and said simply, "I guess David just had worse luck than we had."

That bad luck seemed to have fallen on Grissom moments after the green flag waved July 4 at Milwaukee, in the division's first visit to the facility since 1985. Going into turn one on the first lap, Joe Nemechek turned into the left side of Grissom's Chevrolet while trying to avoid a pileup. The contact broke the valve stem off of Grissom's left front tire. The tire went flat, and four laps into the race, Grissom was a lap down.

Grissom and crew chief Bryant Frazier made the decision to pit approximately 140 laps into the race, and while it put them behind another lap, it gave them track position when others came in for service.

"When we came back out, we were right behind Larry Pearson, who was the leader," Grissom said. "On fresh tires, we went right by him. Larry kept running, waiting on a caution. Tires

ABOVE: Larry Pearson spins off turn four at Charlotte May 29, as Dale Jarrett looks for an opening to get by safely. The crash eliminated Pearson from the Champion Spark Plug 300. He finished 28th, while Jarrett was third. (Bryan Hallman) RIGHT: Dale Earnhardt tucks the nose of his Chevrolet under Steve Grissom's bumper at Dover June 5. Earnhardt finished 13th, three laps down to winner Todd Bodine. Grissom was 17th, four laps down. David Green maintained his lead over Grissom in the standings with an 11th-place finish. (Dover Downs International Speedway Archives) OPPOSITE: Early in Martinsville's May 8 event, Steve Grissom (31) tags the spinning car of Rodney Combs (1), as Roger Sawyer (05) also gets turned around. Grissom came back to finish eighth, while Combs took 10th, and Sawyer 14th. (Bryan Hallman)

RIGHT: A prankster put this sign on Jerry Glanville's pit box at Myrtle Beach during the Carolina Pride/Budweiser 250. Glanville made the prediction come true—he finished 27th after a crash. (Bryan Hallman)
BELOW: David Green (44) gets caught in a multicar accident at Myrtle Beach. Also involved are Clay Brown (15), Rodney Combs (1), and Troy Beebe (blue car, partially obscured by Combs). Green came back from the incident to finish eighth. After the race, Green had a 20-point lead over Steve Grissom. (Bryan Hallman)

TOP TEN REASON'S JERRY GLANVILLE WILL <u>HIT</u> THE WALL AT MYRTLE RACEWAY

10) NO PLACE FOR ELVIS TO SIT.

9) Because Deion isn't Driving

8) It's Becoming Habit

7) The Race Isn't In The Dome

6) Too Many HAMMER Moves while Driving

5) Can't Win ~~only~~ on THE Road

4) Bum PHillipS IS IN His PIT CREW!

3) Impossible To Race With Case of Milwaukee's Best In Front Seat

2) CAN'T Fit Cowboy HAt and BeltBuckle on Racing outfit!

1) Because David Letterman Is moving to CBS

meant enough at that time that we came around to where we're a lap and a half down.

"We opened up that much distance on him. Larry finally went in, and when he came back on the track, we were a half-lap down. He was gaining on us with his new tires, but then the caution came out, and we were still on the lead lap."

The race's final caution came out on lap 235, and Grissom cruised down pit road for two fresh tires. Although it dropped him to near the bottom of the top 10 with just a few laps to go, Grissom's fresh tires gave him the advantage. Meanwhile, Pearson got Green loose with a nudge on lap 246 and went back into the lead.

Pearson didn't keep the point for long. Grissom got by him two laps from the end to score his second victory of the season.

"We went back out after the last caution, and when they dropped the green, we drove by them like they weren't even there," Grissom said. "We lined up eighth or ninth on the restart, and Larry had gotten away. But we mowed him down and went by him."

Grissom had another encounter with Pearson two races later, on July 31 at IRP. Todd Bodine and Robert Pressley, running first and second, wrecked while trying to lap Troy Beebe on lap 172. Grissom plowed into the accident, then was collected by Pearson.

"I got whoaed down, but here came Larry Pearson," Grissom said. "The track was blocked. He hit me in the back end and knocked me from the track plumb up on a dirt mound around a light pole. Right place, wrong time."

Grissom's problem at IRP gave Green a slim, four-point cushion. It wouldn't last.

On August 14 at Michigan, Grissom was credited with a fourth-place finish after runner-up Dale Earnhardt was disqualified for using an illegal carburetor. Holes had been drilled in the metering blocks of Earnhardt's carburetor, allowing for more fuel to be pushed through, giving him more horsepower. That dropped Earnhardt from second to 44th in the field, and moved everybody else up a notch.

"I only run 12 races a year as a hobby, so we don't have the facilities, the capabilities, the time, or the

money to build our own stuff," Earnhardt said. "So we buy it in good faith, and we put it on our cars. I assure you absolutely no one on this team knew about this until NASCAR showed it to us after the race."

Green logged a lackluster 18th place finish at Michigan and fell to 47 points behind Grissom. He wouldn't see first place again in 1993. Three races later, after

ABOVE: The rear of Ernie Irvan's Chevrolet lifts into the air after a wild last-lap scramble for the win at Talladega July 24. Irvan was tapped into the spin by Tracy Leslie (72), which allowed Dale Earnhardt (3) to take the win. Irvan finished in 17th place. It was the division's first visit to the mammoth 2.66-mile superspeedway. (Bryan Hallman)

Grissom finished fifth and Green 12th on September 4 at Darlington, Grissom had a fairly comfortable 167-point lead over his rival. The gap closed, however, during the next four events.

Businessman Gary Bechtel had signed Grissom to drive the Diamond Ridge Motorsports Winston Cup entry in 1994. Bechtel wanted Grissom to run 1993's fall Winston Cup event at Charlotte as a warm-up, but the driver, concerned with winning the Busch Series title, balked.

"I did not want to run that race. I told Gary that we were in the hunt for the championship," Grissom said. "Bryant and my crew guys had worked night and day. They were the reason we were in the position we were in. I wasn't going to let that Winston Cup deal get in the way of what these guys had worked for all year long."

In hindsight, it didn't do Grissom much good to skip Charlotte's Winston Cup race. More engine trouble doomed his Busch Series effort to a dismal 28th-place finish, allowing Green to close back to within 45 points.

"We blew up the motor in a practice before qualifying," Grissom said. "We put another motor in and qualified, just had to throw it in at the last minute. We went out the next morning in practice and blew up again.

"Ben Barnes, who was doing our engines at the time, had to finish up another brand-new motor and bring it to us Saturday morning before the race. We ran 134 laps of that race and blew that thing sky high."

Tempers flared October 17 at Martinsville between Grissom and Green, who made contact racing for second behind Chuck Bown on lap 275. Green looped his car, but came back to finish sixth to Grissom's second. Angry, Green backed into Grissom's car on pit road after the race, and a staredown between drivers and crews ensued.

Bob Labonte, the burly, brusque father of Bobby and Terry, restored order.

"As quick as I pulled in behind David on pit road after the race, he cranked his car up, threw it in reverse, and backed up on the hood of our car," Grissom recalled. "Everybody came a-runnin'. Man, was David forevermore hot. I wasn't so worried about David being mad as I was Bob Labonte.

"Bob comes walking down there, and me and David were yelling and the crews were yelling. Bob was the last one to get there, but when he came, it was just like E.F. Hutton walking up. Everybody was yelling and then it was—shh—dead silence. Everybody went

quiet. I was thinking, 'What's fixin' to happen?' Bob said, 'Good job,' turned around, and walked off. That was the end of it. David went his way and we went our way."

A broken crankshaft October 23 at Rockingham cost Green nearly 100 points, and possibly the championship. Grissom clinched the crown with a ninth-place finish November 7 at Hickory, a race won by upstart Johnny Rumley. Green's slim hopes were dashed for good when he crashed trying to chase down his boss, Bobby Labonte.

"I was trying my durndest to catch him," Green said. "I probably just tried a little too hard. I should've been a little more patient. Chasing after the leader, whoever it might've been, I just got a little too anxious too quick."

With the championship firmly in his grasp, Grissom tried to reflect on his accomplishments. It took a while, but what he'd done finally sank in after the division's annual awards banquet in Charlotte.

"It started to set in, the people who had won the championship in the past and now me," Grissom said. "To be mentioned with people like Jack Ingram and Sam Ard, those guys are real racers. Man, I'll never forget when I first came into the Busch Series. When you'd go to all those short tracks, you were going into Jack Ingram's, Tommy Ellis's, L. D. Ottinger's backyards. They had run there forever."

BELOW LEFT: At the Food City 250 August 27 at Bristol, Grissom finished seventh and David Green was 29th. That gave Grissom a healthy 139-point lead. (Phil Cavali) **BELOW RIGHT:** Johnny Rumley (00) won at Hickory November 7, in just his seventh start on the tour—the quickest any driver has ever made it to victory lane. Steve Grissom's ninth-place finish in the event gave him an insurmountable 188-point lead over David Green going into the last race of the year. (Chad Fletcher)

David Green spins at Martinsville October 17 after making contact with Steve Grissom as they raced for second behind Chuck Bown. A confrontation between the two after the race was averted by Bob Labonte, Green's crew chief. (Bryan Hallman)

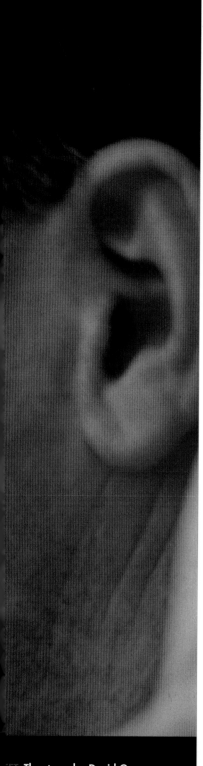

LEFT: The struggles David Green faced earlier in his career made winning the 1994 Busch Series championship that much sweeter. After winning a race in his rookie year, Green was released by his team. He sat out the 1992 campaign but worked for Bobby Labonte. His patience paid off when Labonte moved to the Winston Cup circuit. (Phil Cavali) RIGHT: Prior to the Busch Light 300 at Atlanta March 12, Joe Nemechek congratulates Shawna Robinson on becoming the first female to capture the pole for any major NASCAR event. Her 174.330-mph effort edged Nemechek for the top spot. (Phil Cavali)

1994
No More Mistakes

David Green thought that mistakes had cost him the 1993 Busch Series championship, and he was determined not to go down that road again in 1994.

Losing the title to Steve Grissom made Green hungrier and more focused on logging top-five finishes week in and week out.

"When the awards banquet was over in '93, I was so hurt within myself, because I felt I'd done some things because of a lack of experience," Green admitted.

"I was in a situation where I could win the championship, and I was disappointed in my on-track actions.

"I felt like I didn't fulfill my obligations to the team. When we headed into '94, I was gonna learn what I did wrong. I needed to do everything right and not make any mistakes. I had more fire than ever."

The season got off to a rocky start for both Green—who didn't post a top-10 finish until the fifth race—and Tommy Houston. Houston didn't have a sponsor, and for the first time in the division's history, failed to make the starting grid for the March 5 event at Richmond. The top 34 drivers made the field on their qualifying times, and Houston was 35th, missing the cut by a mere 14 thousandth of a second.

At least Houston was in good company. Dale Earnhardt, who two weeks before had captured his fifth straight Busch Series win at Daytona, also failed to qualify for the Hardee's Frisco 250.

"I had people come to me and say, 'Let's go talk to so-and-so. Let's see if you can start their car,' " said Houston, who'd started Rick Mast's car in September 1993 to keep his consecutive-start streak alive. "I told them no, that I'd already done that. I was kind of glad the streak was over with. I knew that eventually we were gonna miss one."

After Houston failed to qualify at Richmond, the next race on the schedule was also a significant one for the Busch Series. Shawna Robinson became the tour's first female driver to capture the pole position, turning in a then-track-record speed of 174.33 mph during qualifying for the March 12 event at Atlanta. The glow of the accomplishment faded on the first lap.

Mike Wallace dove low into the third turn, going three wide with Robinson and second-place starter Joe Nemechek. Robinson and Nemechek crashed and later sharply criticized Wallace on ESPN's telecast of the race.

Both claimed that Wallace had bragged before the race that he was going to get Robinson's car loose as soon as possible.

"He flat turned into my car," Robinson fumed. "There's a big dent on the right side to prove it. It just shows what kind of class somebody has out there. I'm working hard to get where I am. If somebody just can't take the fact that a woman's in racing, and he thinks he's gonna do something like that, I'm not walking away."

Wallace responded in a tense post-race interview: "I don't know what anybody's blaming me for. Sometimes, you've got to use a little common sense between your foot and your brain to say, 'Lift if I'm in a bad situation.' It appears somebody didn't lift and wanted to blame it on me. I didn't do anything wrong."

Nearly lost in the controversy was the fact that Harry Gant scored what would be the final win of his Busch Series career. Meanwhile, Green slowly began to creep back into the championship hunt. He was 20th in the standings after Atlanta, 11th after a runner-up showing March 20 at Martinsville, 10th after the March 26 race at Darlington, and sixth following a third-place run April 3 at Hickory in a race won by Ricky Craven.

Next, on April 9 at Bristol, came one of the most bizarre finishes anyone could remember.

Green was on Mark Martin's bumper pressing for the lead when Robert Pressley crashed in turn three on lap 246. The yellow flag came out, and Martin appeared headed for an uncontested victory. As the pace car was coming off turn four to bring the field to the checkered flag under caution, however, Martin pulled off the track and into the infield, apparently headed for victory lane.

There was only one small problem. The race wasn't over yet. Green stayed on the track and cruised to his first—and as it turned out, only—win of the year.

"That's the dumbest thing I've ever done in my life," Martin said.

Green was probably just as shocked as Martin. "Something looked out of place, and that was when Mark pulled off the race track and the pace car stayed out," Green said. "Not that I ever thought about following him, but I just thought, 'Something looks funny here.'

ABOVE: David Green starts on the outside of the front row at New Hampshire May 7, next to his boss, pole-sitter Bobby Labonte. Green finished sixth, but mechanical problems sent Labonte spiraling to 35th. (Phil Cavali) RIGHT: Shawna Robinson (46) and Joe Nemechek wait out the pace laps at Atlanta. In turn three of the first lap, Mike Wallace dove under Robinson, sending her up the track and into Nemechek. Both Robinson and Nemechek crashed, and afterward had harsh words for Wallace. (Bryan Hallman) OPPOSITE: Vermont native Kevin Lepage had a new sponsor at Hickory in April, the Vermont Teddy Bear Co. It wasn't the biggest sponsorship package in the sport, but it was certainly one of the most unusual. Lepage made 21 starts in 1994, with one top-10 finish. (Bryan Hallman)

ABOVE: In this accident at Charlotte May 28, Chad Little (at far right) was knocked unconscious and also sustained a broken leg and broken shoulder blade. He started the next two races, but turned his car over to relief drivers Derrike Cope at Dover and to Jeff Green at Myrtle Beach. (Phil Cavali) RIGHT: Ricky Craven's crew goes under the hood at South Boston to remedy an overheating problem. Craven finished 21st, 23 laps down to winner Dennis Setzer. The problem allowed David Green to move to first in the standings. (Chad Fletcher) OPPOSITE: David Green widened his lead over Ricky Craven in the second half of 1994 with consistency on all types of tracks. Green answered those who criticized his low win total by saying he did what he had to do to win the championship. (Bryan Hallman)

"It wasn't until I crossed the finish line that my crew realized what had happened, and maybe it was then I realized what had happened. It could've been just as embarrassing for me as it was for Mark Martin, but he handled it with such class that it really made it a lot easier for me to accept a gift from out of the sky."

The win moved Green to second in the standings behind Randy LaJoie, but then Green fell back to fifth after crashing April 30 at Orange County. Craven mounted a charge in the title chase with a win May 22 at Nazareth and an 11th-place effort May 28 at Charlotte. After that race, Craven trailed Kenny Wallace for the lead by just two points, and Green was only 11 points behind Craven.

Craven made it to the top of the heap with a fifth-place run June 4 at Dover, while Green came home 15th and Wallace 38th following an engine failure.

"In my opinion, we did more with less than anybody in racing that year," said Craven, who led Green by 48 points after Dover. "If you include the car we used at Daytona and Talladega, we had three cars and three engines. That's all we had for resources all year long. But what we did have, which was key, was a lot of enthusiasm from some young, energetic people."

It took a month, but Green clawed his way back into contention with top-five finishes at Watkins Glen, and Milwaukee. On July 16 at South Boston, which hadn't hosted a Busch Series race since 1991, Craven and Wallace banged into each other while racing for the lead on lap 212, sending Wallace hard into the frontstretch wall.

As soon as Wallace came back on the track on lap 252, during the event's 12th caution period, he slammed into Craven's car on the backstretch. As a result, Wallace was penalized five laps by NASCAR. Craven wound up finishing 21st.

"Both of us got a little excited and ended up wrecking," said Craven of the incident with Wallace. "It popped a hole in the radiator. I can look back now and laugh, but at the time . . .

"I almost think that we raced each other harder because we were good friends than we would've had we not known each other. We just wore each other out. We ran side by side, bumpin' and grindin'. All of a sudden, we just got carried away."

Craven's problems handed the lead in the standings to Green, who finished fourth behind winner Dennis Setzer. The wins weren't piling up for Green, but the top fives were.

"To finish first, first you've got to finish," Green said. "Working in the shop, Bob Sr. would make sure that I fixed whatever I tore up. We might not have had the greatest team and the fastest car each week, but Bobby and Terry Labonte had always shown that consistency counts. Naturally, we would've liked to have won races, but if we couldn't win, then we were gonna run as good as we could."

A blown engine July 23 at Talladega cost Craven second place in the standings, which he lost to Hermie Sadler. Craven lost more ground eight days later at Hickory, but he made it back to second with a sixth-place run August 5 at IRP.

After their final pit stops, Craven hit a tire left on pit road by one of Green's crew members.

"I was pretty upset that I had hit this tire. It hurt my race car, and we didn't finish as well as we should've," Craven said. "I had to go to somebody, and Bob Labonte's the boss. Bob was sitting on the wall after the race, so I sat down next to him and said as gentlemanly as I could, 'Bob, what are we going to do about these tires laying out on pit road?'

"He just stares straight into the grandstands, and 20 seconds later, he looks over at me and says, 'How about if you steer around them?' I said, 'OK,' got up, and walked away. I was madder than a hornet. Bob's reply wasn't exactly what I was looking for."

Green stayed ahead of the battle for second among Craven, Sadler, and Chad Little during the final two months of the season. Entering the last race, on October 22 at Rockingham, Green led Craven by 84 points and Little by 91. The fairly comfortable margin allowed Green to drive conservatively, and he finished 12th to nail down the championship.

Craven came home third and Little fifth at Rockingham, but the efforts came too late.

"By the end of the season, our stuff was just flat worn out. We only had two engines left, and after qualifying, one of them started smoking," Craven said. "We put the other engine in, and it was due to be rebuilt. It had 600 miles on it.

"I wasn't disappointed with losing the championship to David, but looking back on it now, what really sticks out are the races we gave away. We lost the championship by 46 points, and I can go back and recount so many situations where we could've retained those points. It's almost painful to think back about those races."

There weren't any big celebrations for Green after the season finale. He and girlfriend Diane Hollingsworth [now his wife] ate canned chili for dinner that night, and the next day, he was back at the track for a few more media interviews.

Dale Earnhardt, who was to clinch his seventh Winston Cup championship later that afternoon, congratulated Green on his accomplishment.

"I'll never forget Earnhardt coming by and saying, 'Hey, it feels good, doesn't it?' " Green recalled, a smile coming to his face. But the next day, it was back to work at the team's shop in Trinity, N.C. On Tuesday after the Rockingham race, Green and a couple of crew members were in the shop's break room a few minutes after lunch was supposed to have ended.

Bob Labonte put an end to that foolishness, championship or no championship.

"Bob stuck his head in there and said, 'Hey, guys, the party's over. We need to get back to work here,'" Green said. "Here it is, a couple of days after winning the championship, and we have no other races until Daytona in February, but Bob's as focused as ever. When he walked out, we all sat there and said, 'We must've missed that party, because we ain't been to one yet.'"

OPPOSITE: Ernie Irvan was critically injured during a Winston Cup practice session at Michigan August 20. Six days later, friend Mark Martin drove Irvan's car to a 10th-place finish at Bristol. Irvan's name remained over the window, while Martin placed his underneath. (Chad Fletcher) BELOW LEFT: Ricky Craven stops for tires at IRP August 5. Seconds later, he struck a tire left on pit road by David Green's crew. Angry that his car had been damaged and his race affected by the crew's error, Craven tried to confront Bob Labonte, Green's crew-chief, after the race. (Chad Fletcher) BELOW RIGHT: David Green's title gave Labonte Racing two championships in four years. Bobby Labonte became the first person to win as both a driver and car owner. (Phil Cavali)

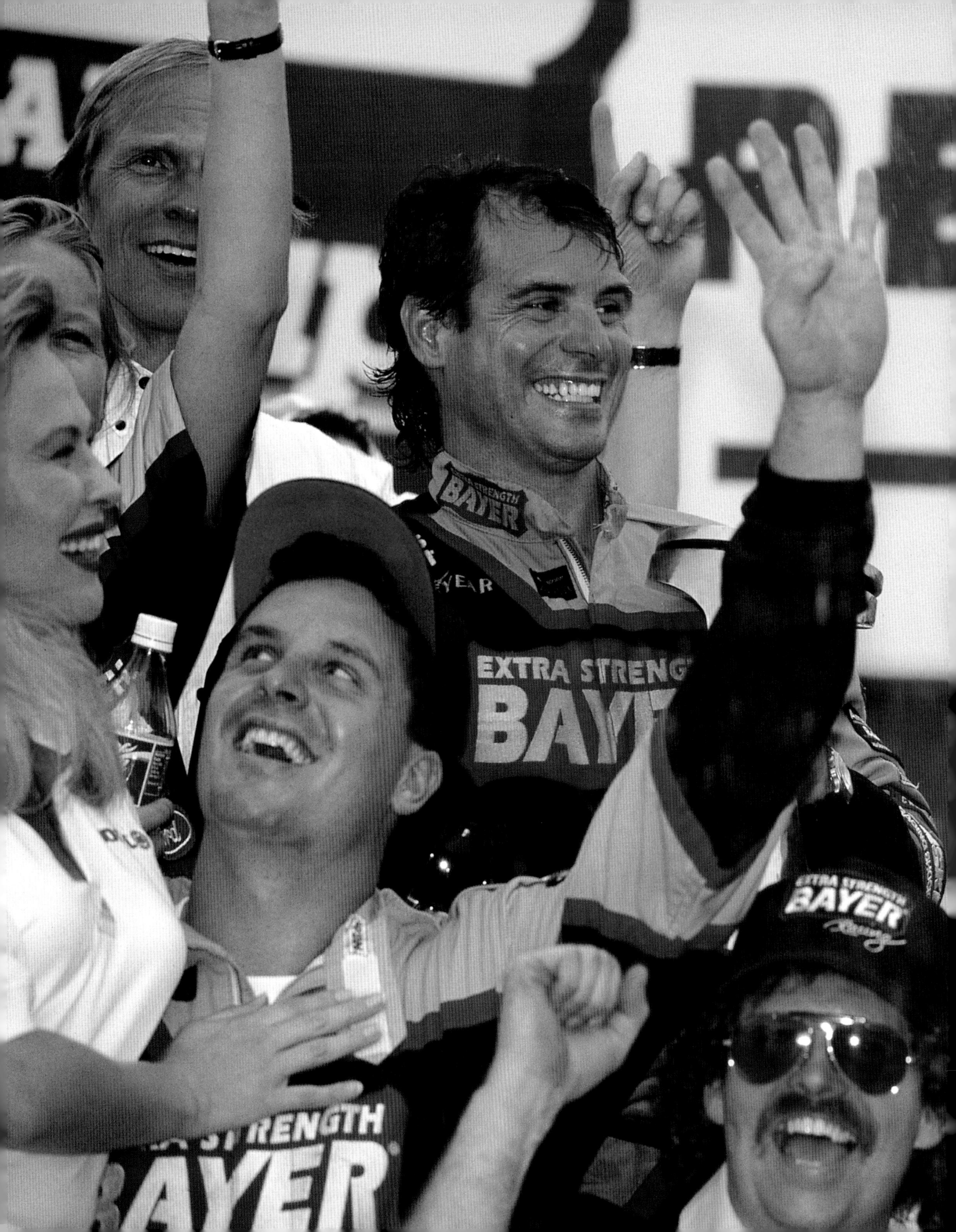
EXTRA STRENGTH BAYER
EXTRA STRENGTH BAYER Racing

LEFT: While Johnny Benson had a rough May afternoon at Charlotte in 1995, Chad Little had an extremely good one. His win was especially satisfying because he'd been seriously hurt in Charlotte's spring event the year before. Here, Little's wife, Donna, sprays champagne into the air in a raucous victory lane celebration. (Lowe's Motor Speedway Archives) RIGHT: Johnny Benson didn't win as many races as Chad Little in 1995, but his consistency earned him the Busch Series championship. That's not to say Benson was driving conservatively. "The only time you can really points race is when you start getting a comfortable lead, and then you want to make sure you don't make any mistakes," Benson said. (Phil Cavali)

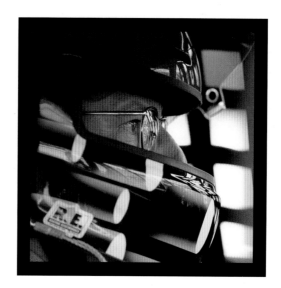

1995
From Top Rookie To Champion

It would have been easy for Johnny Benson to panic when Chad Little won the first two races of the 1995 Busch Series season, but Benson is a stoic sort, not given to many emotional highs and lows.

The Michigan native went about the business of driving Bill Baumgardner's BACE Motorsports Chevrolet the same way he had in 1994, when he captured Rookie of the Year honors. As a result, Benson was on top of the Busch Series standings four races into the schedule.

As great a year as Little had, Benson's turned out better.

"We didn't think we were gonna go in there and lead the points from the beginning of the year," Benson said. "The goal was to go win the championship, and the only race that counts is the last one. After the first couple of races, Chad was on a roll, but we didn't let that bother us."

Gone in 1995 was the roaring beehive of V-6 engines. The division reverted back to the deeper pitched, eight-cylinder powerplants because that's the way the passenger vehicle industry was headed. After teams checked into Daytona for the February 18 opener, it appeared the new engines had Little befuddled.

Little took the last provisional available to a Busch Series regular to start 42nd (three additional spots were used by Busch North competitors). During the final practice session, Little's team put a different carburetor under the hood for the third time that week.

"The difference was like night and day," Little said. "All of a sudden, I'm three miles an hour faster at any given point on the race track."

During the race, Little didn't make it to the top five until just after the final restart. He worked his way from seventh on the lap 109 green flag to second on the 118th of the event's 120 laps. Then, after a wild multi-car crash in turn four, he was first.

"I was behind Steve Grissom, and he was extremely loose," Little said. "I got up close enough to take some wind away from him. He got real loose and slid up the track. When he did, he got into Mark Martin, and, boy, there was a melee right behind me. Boom—the race ends under caution."

In addition to marking the first win of Little's career, the victory proved historic for many reasons. It was the first Ford series win at Daytona and the first win by a tour regular at the track since the division's launch in 1982. Little was also the first driver in the 1990s to win a Busch Series race at the facility other than Dale Earnhardt, who "retired" from competition in the division at the end of the 1994 campaign. Finally, no driver ever had started from as far back in the field and gone on to win.

After Daytona, Little headed to Rockingham, where he completely dominated the February 25 event. Little led all but 20 laps, losing the top spot only when he pitted under cautions. Said Little: "It was one of those races where I could drive high, low, aggressively and still feel confident that I wasn't doing anything stupid."

Engine failure March 4 at Richmond dropped Little to third in the standings, one spot behind Benson, who'd quietly put together finishes of 10th, fourth, and third in the first three races. One week later, Little led 88 laps at Atlanta before another blown engine knocked him out of the running.

Benson took the lead from Ken Schrader with eight laps to go and led the rest of the way for his first win of the year. The victory also moved Benson to the top of the standings.

BELOW LEFT: On February 18, Chad Little became the first Busch Series regular to win at Daytona since the division was formed in 1982. Little made the field by using the last provisional available to a Busch Series competitor. Here he's joined in Daytona's victory lane by his team co-owner and then-Washington Redskins quarterback, Mark Rypien. (Phil Cavali) **BELOW RIGHT:** Johnny Benson claims he wasn't worried when Chad Little got off to such a good start in 1995. "We felt that the speedways weren't going to be our top tracks, but we knew that the short-track season was going to be really good for us, and it was. Starting off that way was fine. It set out a challenge for us." (Bryan Hallman)

ABOVE: Charlotte wasn't kind to Johnny Benson in 1995. Contact early in the race with Rick Wilson triggered this melee on May 27, which also involved Kenny Wallace (8) and Dennis Setzer (59). Benson limped to a 30th-place finish in the event. (Phil Cavali)

RIGHT: Chad Little was on his way to victory at Hickory April 15, but collided with the lapped car of Kevin Lepage (71) with 11 laps to go. Benson weaved past Little's spinning car to inherit the win. Years later, Little still gets a bit miffed at the mention of this incident. (Bryan Hallman)

RIGHT: Chad Little and crew member Harold Holly talk prior to the June 10 event at Myrtle Beach. It was a tough race for Little, who had a spark-plug wire come loose early in the race. He pitted under a caution and his crew corrected the problem. Little was involved in a crash on the restart moments later. (Chad Fletcher)

BELOW: Jimmy Spencer (20) gets a run on Chad Little as the green flag comes out for the final time with one lap to go at Talladega July 22. Little wasn't sure if either of them would make it back to the finish line. (Chad Fletcher)

OPPOSITE: Chad Little briefly regained the lead in the standings with his South Boston win, but battery problems at IRP August 4, dropped him behind Johnny Benson in the battle for the championship. The alternator in Little's car hadn't been checked before the race. "It was a mental mistake on our crew's part. The alternator went out, and that's what caused the battery to go dead," Little said. (Chad Fletcher)

"Winning at any race track is big," Benson said. "It was late in the race before we got the lead, but it's the last lap that counts."

Little was again the class of the field on April 15 at Hickory, leading twice for 167 of the race's 300 laps. But when the field streamed into turn three moments after a lap-289 restart, however, Little got bumped by Kevin Lepage's lapped car. The contact sent Little spinning into the wall—and out of contention for his third win of the year. Benson, running second at the time of the incident, inherited the victory.

"I've never really forgiven Kevin Lepage for that. I tease him about it today," said Little. "I was mad as heck at NASCAR, because I thought they should've waited one more lap so we could have a single-file restart.

"Whether I came down too low or Kevin pushed up a little bit, we made contact. My contention's always been that I was leading and he was a lap down. He certainly wasn't going to win the race."

An April 29 event at Orange County was dropped from the schedule when the facility was sold, resulting in a break of nearly a month. When the tour hit the track again May 13 at New Hampshire, Little won. But then Little was involved in a crash eight days later at Nazareth, dropping him to 231 points behind Benson.

At Charlotte on May 27, Benson was tagged by Rick Wilson as they headed down the frontstretch, triggering a multi-car pileup. Little won again to move within 124 points of the lead.

"Next to Daytona, that was probably the most special win of the year for me because it was the place where just the year before, I'd gotten hurt," said Little.

Little finished second and Benson seventh behind winner Terry Labonte in a June 25 event at Watkins Glen televised by CBS, the first Busch Series race carried live by a national noncable TV network. On July 2 in Milwaukee, Little put together an eighth-place run while Benson was involved in a lap-160 crash with Patty Moise. That allowed Little to cut Benson's advantage in the standings to 76 points, and at the following race it got even closer.

Fourteen different drivers exchanged the lead 29 times at Talladega on July 22, with Little coming out on top. Ward Burton and Randy LaJoie flipped their cars in separate incidents, and Robbie Reiser sustained a severe concussion in yet another accident. Finally, Little led Jimmy Spencer to a restart with just one lap to go.

"I remember thinking, 'Well, more than likely, I'm not going to win this, but neither is he. I'm not going to let him pass me. We're going to wreck,'" Little said. "I got a really good restart, and luckily, he wasn't able to get up close enough to make a challenge."

Moise came home seventh, the best-ever finish for a woman in the Busch Series. Then Mike Wallace drove into the side of Little's car on the cool-down lap, angry over a mishap earlier in the race. Wallace later was fined $2,000.

Despite finishing fifth at Talladega, Benson saw his advantage over Little shrink to just 51 points. Little backed up his win on the circuit's biggest track by capturing another victory July 29 on one of its smallest, South Boston. For the first time since late February, Little was back on top of the Busch Series standings, leading Benson by 14 points.

"We were leading the points, and I was thinking, 'Doggone, I've really got a shot at winning this championship,'" Little recalled. "That was probably my mistake, because right after that, we really started having some problems."

The problems began at the next race, on August 4 at IRP, where a dead battery dropped Little to a 20th-place finish. Benson's 13th-place showing wasn't great, but it was good enough to put him back in first place in the standings. He kept the spot for the rest of the year.

On August 19 at Michigan, NASCAR took a driver's win away for only the second time in the division's history. Dale Jarrett was dropped from first to last place for an illegally modified intake manifold, which handed the victory to Mark Martin. Jarrett's carburetor sat on a pad that had been raised about three-eighths of an inch, allowing for enhanced air-fuel flow into the cylinders.

"Something like an intake is sitting right there in plain view of everybody," Jarrett said. "If they [NASCAR inspectors] are doing their job, that's something that should have been talked about before the race started."

Countered Busch Series Director Ray Hill: "Just because you got away with something once doesn't mean it's legal when we do find it."

An early wreck September 2 at Darlington, a scrape with Jeff Green on the last lap September 8 in Richmond and a 13th-place finish September 16 at Dover all but ended Little's hopes of being crowned champion. Benson used finishes of second, third, and ninth in those same events to pull away. And despite crashing October 7 at Charlotte, Benson still gained ground on Little, who was caught up in a separate incident.

Benson could have clinched the title at Charlotte, but a collision with Spencer delayed the celebration for a couple of weeks.

"I was running third, racing Jimmy Spencer pretty hard," Benson said. "I lost the back of the car, hit Jimmy, and we both crashed. I was still trying to race for the win. That's what got me in trouble."

The October 21 event at Rockingham came down to one of the most exciting finishes anyone could remember. Benson was busily racing Mike Wallace for the lead, when coming off turn four on the last lap, Todd Bodine dove under both to take the win.

"Mike Wallace was using the mirror extremely heavy on every competitor that was coming up to challenge him," Benson said. "I'd seen him run Mark Martin off the race track and two or three other guys. I was thinking, 'Man, this is going to be an interesting last lap or two.'

"I kept trying to get underneath him, knowing that on the last lap, I was gonna run through turns three and four on the top. When I went down into turn three on the last lap, I went in there harder than I had all day long. I got alongside Mike and, of course, he decided to run me up toward the wall.

"When he did that, it ended up hurting both of us. Then Todd came down on the inside and beat us to the line. I think we had a pretty good shot at winning that race had Mike not run us up the track."

Although Benson wound up third, it was more than enough to seal the championship. Little won some high-profile races in 1995, but in the end, Benson's consistency was the deciding factor.

"Chad had tremendous horsepower for the big tracks, and to race against that is tough to do," Benson said. "That was their strong spot, and they took advantage of it. That's how they approached their bid for the championship. We approached it by trying to be consistent, but trying to still win races."

With Benson on his way to the Winston Cup tour, BACE Motorsports had to find a replacement. The driver Baumgardner signed would have some big shoes to fill.

OPPOSITE: **Chad Little had trouble in October at Charlotte when he clashed with Greg Sacks, and crew chief Gary Cogswell leads repairs after the incident. Rival teams started catching up to Little as they figured out his early-season setup secrets. The team also switched engine programs midway through the year, which might have contributed to Little's second-half decline. (Chad Fletcher)**
BELOW: **One of the Busch Series' most memorable finishes took place at Rockingham October 21, when Todd Bodine (72) went to the inside of Mike Wallace (90) and Johnny Benson in turn four on the last lap. They crossed the finish line three wide, with Bodine scoring the win by an estimated six inches. Benson's third-place finish gave him the 1995 title. (Bryan Hallman)**

LEFT: Crew chief Steve Bird (standing), directs repairs to Randy LaJoie's car after the driver was involved in an early accident at Homestead November 3, 1996. LaJoie lost a lap in the scramble, but later made it up. He clinched the championship with a 10th-place finish. (Chad Fletcher) RIGHT: Like Randy LaJoie, David Green was also driving for a new team in 1996. Here, Green is on the outside of the front row at Rockingham February 24, a race in which he finished sixth. A week later he moved to the top of the Busch Series standings, where he stayed for almost seven months. (Phil Cavali)

1996
A Long Time
in Coming

Randy LaJoie has a helmet on a shelf in his office, one of several in his collection that he's worn through the years. It has a three-inch gash on the back.

The mark was put there by a guardrail that came through his car in a terrifying tumble during a qualifying race for the 1984 Daytona 500. LaJoie could have been seriously injured by the debris, but he walked away from the wreckage to race another day.

LaJoie hands the helmet to a visitor, and says simply, "It wasn't my time."

It took 12 more years of hardship to gain a solid foothold in the sport, but LaJoie finally found a home with BACE Motorsports in 1996. LaJoie had been fired from Bill Davis's Winston Cup team the year before, and he was replacing a champion. That didn't seem to matter. He had nothing to lose.

After the season's third race, a March 2 event at Richmond won by Jeff Purvis, LaJoie and David Green were tied for the lead in the championship chase. Green finished second to Terry Labonte March 9 at Atlanta, while LaJoie dropped out early with engine failure. It would be more than seven months before LaJoie would catch Green, who also was driving for a new team owner, Buz McCall.

Green won his first race of the year April 6 at Hickory, while LaJoie came in third. Although Green was able to capture the victory, his American Equipment Racing team experienced the first of several slip-ups in the pits. Shoddy pit work would be a problem that plagued the effort all year.

"After our pit stop where we got behind, as I came back up through there, I had to pass Randy," Green said. "We made a little contact—nothing intentional—just Hickory. The very next lap, he returned the favor. He didn't spin me out. He just kind of said, 'OK, here's how that feels,' and off we went."

LaJoie came back with a victory of his own May 19 at Nazareth, the first of his career. LaJoie was on his way.

"My dad always taught me that the first win's the hardest one," LaJoie said, his eyes beaming. "Success breeds success. It pumped everybody up. The teams that do the little things best are the ones that are gonna win, and when you win, it makes you do the little things."

LaJoie cut into Green's margin in each of the next three races. On May 25 at Charlotte, LaJoie was fifth, while a tire left loose during a pit stop dropped Green to 19th. LaJoie won again June 1 at Dover, with Green fourth. LaJoie led four times for 196 laps June 8 at South Boston, but a scrape with Hermie Sadler dropped him out of contention for the victory. LaJoie came back to finish fifth, while a hung throttle led to a wreck and a 20th-place finish for Green.

Green and younger brother Jeff were the only two leaders June 22 at Myrtle Beach, with the older Green eventually coming out on top. A third Green brother, Mark, the middle sibling, finished 10th after having started on the outside of David on the front row.

LaJoie limped to an 18th-place finish, two laps down.

"My car was better for 50 or 60 laps, and after 60 laps, Jeff's car was better than mine," said David, who again had to come back from problems in the pits. "We got a long run going, and he passed me. There was a caution with 40 laps to go, and we made our pit stops.

"He beat me out of the pits, but I was able to use my muscle. It was a short enough race at the end to where I could hold him off. To me, there's such a calm about racing with your brothers. If I'd run second and he'd beat me, I might not have been so calm."

LaJoie finished 30th June 30 at Watkins Glen because of a faulty rear end, dropping him to 188 points behind Green, who sat on the pole and finished fifth. Green's advantage never again would be as big as it was after the division's only road course race.

"We weren't agreeing on a lot of things within our team before that race," admitted Green, who was often at odds with others about the direction of the team and its sometimes sloppy pit stops. "We were just trying to work through some growing pains. Buz McCall had given me the opportunity when I joined this team to use my experience to help it grow.

"I think sometimes the guys might've thought I'd fell over and hit my head.

ABOVE: Although his path appears blocked, Randy LaJoie somehow manages to drive through this crash involving Mike McLaughlin (34) and Joe Nemechek (87) at Daytona February 17. LaJoie finished seventh in his first race as Johnny Benson's replacement at BACE Motorsports. (Phil Cavali) OPPOSITE: Randy LaJoie's battered Chevrolet limps around the Nashville track March 17. LaJoie was involved in a couple of mishaps, but completed enough laps to finish 21st in the 40-car field. David Green finished second in the event behind his former team owner, Bobby Labonte. (Elmer Kappell)

ABOVE: Dale Earnhardt Jr. (31) made the first start of his Busch Series career at Myrtle Beach June 22, qualifying seventh and finishing 14th. Here he slips past a spinning Bobby Dotter as Tim Fedewa (40) goes by on the outside. (Bonnie Hallman)

LEFT: A broken rear-end gear dropped Randy LaJoie to 30th at Watkins Glen June 30, costing him more ground on David Green in the championship chase. LaJoie was driving a backup car in the race after wrecking his primary machine during qualifying. (Phil Cavali) OPPOSITE: Todd Bodine goes for a wild ride down the backstretch at Talladega July 27. Bodine got blocked going for the lead, and when he momentarily let off the throttle, third-place Randy LaJoie bumped him into the spin. (Bryan Hallman)

Sometimes maybe I felt like that about them. But after Watkins Glen, we really got it turned around a little bit. That was a big key for us."

Still, the momentum was short-lived. Green got mixed up with Curtis Markham July 7 at Milwaukee, then got tagged from behind by LaJoie in the turn-four melee. All were able to continue without bringing out a caution, but minutes later Green slammed into the turn-two wall.

LaJoie was able to finish third, but Green fell to 32nd in the 42-car field. Green's lead in the standings dwindled from 188 to 90 points.

Another win awaited LaJoie July 12 at New Hampshire, and he somehow managed to put together a third-place run July 27 at Talladega, where fumes in his car nearly caused him to pass out during the race.

"The wood [blocks] in the chassis caught on fire, and I was inhaling the smoke," LaJoie said. "I got carbon monoxide poisoning. I remember spinning Todd Bodine out. After the race, I had to go to the infield care center, because I pretty much didn't know where I was at. I was lucky to finish where I did."

Just how does a driver compete so strongly in such a dire condition?

"That, I don't know," LaJoie continued. "That's where the racing gods must take over. I remember parking it, getting out, and pretty much falling over. Carbon monoxide poisoning is not a good thing. It messed me up for two or three weeks after that."

Luck favored LaJoie August 2 at IRP when leaders Chad Little and Hermie Sadler ran into a multi-car accident on lap 183. LaJoie weaved his way through the mess to score his fourth win of the season.

"About halfway down the backstretch, my spotter said, 'Trouble going into three,'" said LaJoie, who trailed Green by only 29 points after the race. "Hermie and Chad ran into the wreck wide open and wrecked each other. I'm not sure if they were racing back to the caution or if their spotters never said anything. One of their tires bounced off my hood. We had a dominant car, but I don't think I could've passed those two guys if it hadn't been for their own mistakes."

LaJoie, though, lost nearly 100 points in the next four races. Debris from Ricky Craven's August 23 wreck at Bristol shot under LaJoie's car and destroyed its steering. Green was fourth and LaJoie fifth August 31 at Darlington, and on September 8 at Richmond, Green finished second to LaJoie's eighth.

With four races to go, Green led LaJoie by 128 points.

"At Richmond, we announced that we were going Cup racing in '97," Green said. "The thing that I feared most was that it was going to be a distraction. It was [a distraction], because we didn't have the luxury of a whole separate group of people working on Cup stuff.

"I said to the race team, 'You guys have one year of Busch racing under your belt. I think I'm ready for Winston Cup, but we really need more experience on our race team. Just one year of Busch racing isn't gonna cut it in Winston Cup.'"

The beginning of the end for Green came September 14 at Dover, where LaJoie won again. Another wheel was left loose on a pit stop, costing Green a top-10 finish. He wound up 18th, but that wasn't as bad as it was going to be October 5 at Charlotte, where Green was knocked unconscious and hospitalized overnight after slamming into first Darrell Lanigan and then Shane Hall in a crash on the 65th circuit.

The accident allowed LaJoie to take the top spot in the standings for the first time.

"David, I think, was in a conservative mode," LaJoie said. "That bites you. He shouldn't have been where he was at. If he would've been running more aggressively, he would never have got wrecked."

Going into the last race of the season, Green trailed LaJoie by 33 points. Early in the November 3 finale at Homestead, it looked as if Green was going to capture the second title of his career. Thirty laps into the race, rookie David Hutto's car glanced off the wall between turns one and two and into the right side of LaJoie's Chevrolet.

Calmly, LaJoie's Steve Bird-led crew made repairs and sent him back out, but not before he lost a lap. LaJoie got back on the lead circuit on lap 74—coincidentally, also his car number—when Rodney Combs stalled on the backstretch. LaJoie then ran as high as fourth before fading to conserve fuel. He finished 10th, one spot behind Green, to clinch the championship.

"I thought the accident had totally chucked the rear end out of that race car, because I could look over and the door was caved in," LaJoie said. "What's amazing is the radial tire cap didn't get stuck on anything. Nine

times out of 10, when that comes off, it rips the brake line off and gets wadded up in the rear end, so you lose a half-dozen laps trying to get the tire off."

Green said several people told him Combs stopped on the track on purpose, an allegation that Bird adamantly denies.

"I still question why a certain car stopped on the track long enough for a caution to come out," Green said. "Then that car drove back in. I was told that there were some deals going on between Steve Bird and somebody on Combs's team. Whether it was true or false is yet to be seen. I just know what I hear, which made the sting a little bit stingier."

Whatever the causes, it finally had happened. After years of wondering whether he'd ever catch a break, the championship was LaJoie's.

"I'd been through a lot," LaJoie said. "Some of it might've been my own doing, but I knew I could drive. I'll guarantee not many people thought I could. Score one for the underdog. For all the non-believers, there it is. We got the championship, and you couldn't take it away from us."

BELOW LEFT: Tommy Houston comes in for a pit stop at Charlotte October 5, during the next-to-last race of his Busch Series career. Houston made the 400th start of his career earlier in the year at Atlanta, becoming the first competitor to reach that plateau. (Lowe's Motor Speedway Archives) **BELOW RIGHT:** David Green is extricated from his car after crashing in Charlotte's October event as Randy LaJoie passes by in the background. Green was knocked unconscious and hospitalized overnight after crashing with Darrell Lanigan and Shane Hall in turn four. LaJoie took the lead in the standings as a result of Green's accident. (Bryan Hallman)

ABOVE: A blown tire caused Todd Bodine all sorts of problems at Bristol August 23. Flames erupted from underneath the hood as he tried to make it to pit road, forcing him to stop and be helped from his car by safety workers. Bodine was credited with a 34th-place finish. (Bob Dudley) RIGHT: Randy LaJoie's third-place finish at Talladega was nothing short of a miracle, because after the race he collapsed from carbon monoxide poisoning. A piece of wood ballast in the car had caught fire, and LaJoie breathed the fumes for much of the race. (Chad Fletcher)

:FT: The Busch Series debuted west
f the Mississippi River at Las Vegas
1otor Speedway March 15, 1997.
eff Green made his first visit to
ictory lane in the event. It was his
00th start on the circuit. (Phil Cavali)
IGHT: Ignition problems at Las Vegas
elegated Randy LaJoie to a 29th-
lace finish, moving him to third in
1e standings behind leader Todd
odine and runner-up Phil Parsons.
aJoie was 99 points out of first place
>llowing the event. (Phil Cavali)

1997
What Hard Feelings?

What Randy LaJoie, Bill Baumgardner, and Steve Bird had built in 1996 was very nearly destroyed in the days and weeks leading into the 1997 campaign.

Their problems boiled down to money. Baumgardner rented a building owned by LaJoie to use as the team's shop in 1996, but the two disagreed over the price. LaJoie also believed his salary was at least $200,000 below market value and insisted on renegotiating after he clinched the title.

All was not well in the BACE Motorsports camp. LaJoie was hours away from agreeing to drive for Dennis Shoemaker in 1997, and Baumgardner said he had Tony Stewart lined up to drive his car. Yet in February, with LaJoie already in Daytona, Baumgardner and his driver came up with an 11th-hour agreement to settle their differences. Or at least smooth them over for the time being.

Remarkably, LaJoie went out and won February 15 at Daytona to become only the second Busch Series regular to win the season opener. He led twice for 56 of the event's 120 laps, more than any other driver.

"All week long, people were asking, 'What's going on with BACE Motorsports? Why are they cutting each other's throats, stabbing each other in the back?'" Baumgardner said. "The green flag dropped, and BACE Motorsports pulled together, went to the front, and won the race."

Added LaJoie: "It proved to me that we could put our differences aside and go race no matter what we were getting paid. We still had a job to do. That set the tone for the rest of the year. I think it put a lot of the fussin' out of the question. We were saying, 'OK, let's just shut up and race.'"

Todd Bodine finished second at Daytona, then took the lead in the standings with a sixth-place run March 8 at Atlanta. A week later, on March 16 at Las Vegas, the Busch Series made its first appearance west of the

Mississippi River, and Jeff Green made his first appearance in victory lane.

Green's win came in his 100th career start and in his first season with Diamond Ridge Motorsports. Following the race, Green was fourth in the standings, 115 points behind leader Bodine and 80 behind then-runner-up Phil Parsons, but he trailed third-place LaJoie by just 16.

LaJoie came back from subpar finishes at Atlanta and Las Vegas to wage a thrilling last-lap battle with Winston Cup regular Jeff Burton March 22 at Darlington. Burton, who'd dominated earlier in the day, got under LaJoie for the lead coming off turn two on the final lap. But when Burton's momentum carried him up the track in turn three, LaJoie dove back to his inside to regain the advantage.

It was the way racing was meant to be.

"Jeff was way better than I was, but I was able to hold him off until the white flag," said LaJoie with a smile. "He got a run coming out of turn two, and I couldn't block him. I'd already figured out halfway down the backstretch what I was going to do. I hit the brake, then floored the gas and turned left.

"If Burton would've tapped the brake, I would've taken us both out. He went up the hill, and my car turned and drove underneath him. All I had to do was keep it low enough coming out of turn four so he couldn't pass me. Being in victory lane at Darlington, with that last-lap pass, it couldn't have been any better."

Bodine finished out of the top 10 for the first time in 1997 when he got caught in a crash April 12 at Bristol. That gave LaJoie a 32-point cushion in the title chase. A couple of races later, LaJoie had the first of several heated confrontations with Buckshot Jones.

Jones thought LaJoie had spun him early in the

ABOVE: Jason Keller (57) and Jeff Burton (9) spin off the fourth turn on the final lap at Richmond March 1. The two made contact while racing for the lead, and their mishap allowed Burton's teammate, Mark Martin, to capture the victory. (Phil Cavali)
OPPOSITE: After a stormy offseason that nearly led to his departure from BACE Motorsports, Randy LaJoie beats Todd Bodine (36) to the checkered flag at Daytona February 15. The friction between LaJoie and team owner Bill Baumgardner notwithstanding, it was a great way to start off the season. (Darryl Graham)

RIGHT: Public relations representative Paula Pickette tries to cool BACE Motorsports tire changer Keith Bainbridge with wet towels during Gateway International Raceway's inaugural Busch Series event July 26. Temperatures soared into the high 90s in the St. Louis area, with near-100 percent humidity. The track surface crumbled in the turns, which led to 14 caution flags that ate up 81 laps. The fiasco, won by Elliott Sadler, took 3 hours, 48 minutes and 25 seconds to complete—the longest race in Busch Series history. (Chad Fletcher)

BELOW: Mark Martin drives under a crash involving, among others, Mike McLaughlin (34), and Dennis Setzer (43), at Talladega April 26. Buckshot Jones claimed the accident was triggered when he got hit from behind by Randy LaJoie, although LaJoie denied any contact was made. Martin posted the 31st win of his Busch Series career in the event, tying him with Jack Ingram for the most wins in the division's history. (Phil Cavali)

April 26 event at Talladega and triggered a multi-car accident. On the cool-down lap after the checkered flag, Jones rammed LaJoie's car in turn three in an incident that also collected Joe Bessey. For his actions, Jones later was fined $2,000.

Mark Martin captured his 31st career Busch Series victory at Talladega, tying him with Jack Ingram for most in the division's history. Martin broke Ingram's record with a win later in the year at Rockingham.

"I idolized Jack Ingram when I first started racing the Busch Series and even before," Martin said. "I didn't race in the Busch Series a lot back when he was winning all his races, but I sure knew what he was doing. Even if you didn't follow the Busch Series real close, you knew who was winning the majority of the races, and it was Jack during the 1980s."

Bodine took a slim nine-point lead over LaJoie in the standings May 24 at Charlotte, and Green was third, 164 back of Bodine. After the race, Diamond Ridge Motorsports owner Gary Bechtel folded Green's Busch Series team, and moved Green into his Winston Cup car, replacing Robert Pressley.

"We'll never know what could've happened," said Green. "I told [Bechtel] I wanted to stay in the Busch Series, but he pretty much said, 'We don't have a sponsor, and we can't afford it any more. You can run it, but we're not gonna give you 110 percent like we were.' By him saying that, it wasn't gonna be worthwhile to stay in the Busch Series."

LaJoie wasn't exactly sorry to see Green leave.

"I thought it was going to be a three-man race, and then Jeff went Winston Cup racing," LaJoie said. "They'd just started to click. Then they pulled the rug out from under the Busch program. That was a sigh of relief for me, and I'm sure it was for Todd, too, because then we only had to worry about beating one car instead of two."

It would've been tough to top Darlington's tremendous finish, but LaJoie and Dale Shaw came close June 13 at South Boston. For several laps at the end of the race, the two cars were virtually welded together, trading paint while dicing for the victory. LaJoie beat Shaw to the finish line by forty-eight thousandths of a second for his third win of the season. After LaJoie shoved Shaw out of the way in a Busch North Series race the year before, Shaw had vowed revenge. And LaJoie remembered it.

"Here we are at South Boston, and he's got four

fresh tires—soakers, probably—and he's coming in a hurry," LaJoie said. "All I can remember was him yelling at me at the gas pump [following the Busch North race the year before]. I was thinking, 'This is not good.'"

LaJoie settled in for a tough fight with Shaw, and that's exactly what he got. "I had two handfuls of steering wheel, harder than I've ever had in my life," LaJoie said. "But he tried so hard not to get into me that he ended up breaking his car loose, which was enough for me to beat him by a foot. Obviously, he forgot what he told me a year earlier."

Bodine finished second June 29 at Watkins Glen, while late-race mechanical problems dropped LaJoie

to a 21st-place finish. That put Bodine atop the standings for the last time, by 18 points over LaJoie.

Both drivers identified the next race on the schedule, the July 6 event at Milwaukee, as the season's turning point. Contact with Dick Trickle sent Kevin Lepage crashing between turns three and four with two laps to go. Second-place Bodine tried racing LaJoie back to the caution flag for the win, but got tangled up with the lapped car driven by Chris Diamond. Bodine fell from second to 11th and dropped 32 points behind LaJoie in the title chase.

ABOVE: Mike McLaughlin and Todd Bodine take their cool-down lap together at Watkins Glen June 29. They'd finished first and second, respectively. The outcome was special in several ways: The drivers are good friends and rode their motorcycles to the race together; both are New York natives; and they were teammates at Cicci-Welliver Racing at the time. (Charles Berch)

The crowd went nuts, and some immediately took up a collection to help pay the fine that was surely coming Jones's way. It proved to be a stiff one: Jones was fined $5,000 and docked 50 points.

"He gave me a shot and moved me out of the way, so I returned the favor and he wrecked," LaJoie said. "After the Talladega deal, I knew what he was gonna do, so I tried to hide. I tried to pull up alongside Robert Pressley going down the backstretch because I saw [Jones] waiting for me.

"I knew what he was gonna do, but Robert wouldn't let me up on the outside. He thought I was trying to pass him. Once I heard his motor go, I had to jump on mine. He just caught me and drove straight into the wall. I could not believe the noise from the crowd. I heard that, and it was incredible."

"I had Randy. I had him cold. I had Randy passed for the win coming to get the white and yellow flags," Bodine insisted. "He went high around the wreck, and I went below the wreck. When I went low, Chris was there. I started going under him, and he just turned left and came all the way to the bottom of the track. I jumped his wheel and started sliding backwards."

LaJoie's advantage grew slowly, but steadily, during the next few weeks. Despite another battle with Jones August 22 at Bristol, LaJoie's lead in the standings grew to 130 points over Bodine. While their Talladega confrontation was seen by relatively few, Jones and LaJoie wiped each other out in full view of thousands at Bristol and a million or so more on television.

Jones got LaJoie out of shape as they raced for position in turn two with less than 20 laps to go, and the next time around LaJoie responded by punting his nemesis into the turn-one wall. Jones limped his battered car to the backstretch, where he waited for LaJoie to come by under caution. Once Jones saw LaJoie's red-white-and-blue machine, he gunned his engine and drove up the track in turn three. He barely clipped LaJoie's left rear quarter panel.

Bodine earned his only victory of the year in the division's debut at the California Speedway, but it came too late to catch LaJoie, who clinched the championship the next week. When Bodine was involved in a wreck October 25 at Rockingham, it was all over. LaJoie's 20th-place finish was good enough.

Only three other drivers had won two Busch Series championships, and only two had done it in consecutive seasons. LaJoie also became the first driver to collect $1 million in winnings in a single season. His career winnings topped Tommy Houston for first on the division's all-time money list.

What's more, Baumgardner had fielded three championship teams in a row, something that had never been done by any other car owner.

"I just couldn't believe it," LaJoie said. "You read the record books, and it was quite an accomplishment. We were on top of our ball game. That really pumped me up to become the first driver to win the championship three years in a row. I really wanted that. Cale Yarborough had done it in Winston Cup. That was my goal through the winter."

OPPOSITE: Joe Nemechek climbs from his car after scoring an emotional win at Homestead November 9. Nemechek's younger brother, John, sustained fatal injuries in a Craftsman Truck Series event at the track nearly eight months earlier. (Phil Cavali) ABOVE: Randy LaJoie celebrates his second straight Busch Series title with a series off smoky burnouts on Homestead's fronstretch. LaJoie's runner-up finish in the event was his 15th top-five finish of the season. In 1997, LaJoie became the first Busch Series driver to earn more than $1 million in winnings in a single season. (Phil Cavali)

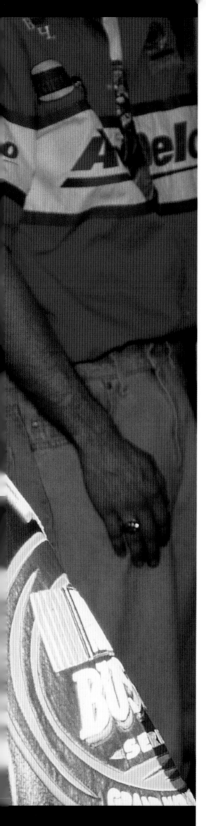

FT: When Dale Earnhardt Jr.
arted the race at Homestead
ovember 15, 1998, it gave him
ough points to be crowned
ampion. The title was the ninth for
e Earnhardt family in NASCAR
mpetition, and it wouldn't be the
st. Here, "Big E" congratulates
ittle E" on his accomplishment.
hil Cavali) RIGHT: Dale Earnhardt
began his first full-time Busch
ries season with this tumble down
aytona's backstretch on February
, 1998. The son of the seven-time
inston Cup champion completed
of the event's 120 laps, and
ished 37th. (Jay Jageler)

1998
The New Kid In Town

Dale Earnhardt Jr.'s first full season of Busch Series competition began with a somersault at Daytona and ended with a blown engine at Homestead. Sandwiched in between was a stellar performance that left him a champion. Just like his father—the one with seven Winston Cup trophies.

Earnhardt Jr., however, didn't go unchallenged in 1998. Mike McLaughlin led the standings for several weeks early in the year, and then Matt Kenseth matched "Little E" almost step for step the rest of the way.

The year got off to a spectacular, if somewhat bumpy, start for Earnhardt. He got together with Dick Trickle late in the February 14 season opener at Daytona and spun off the back straightaway before launching into a grinding series of barrel rolls.

"It was pretty exciting going down the backstretch like that, but I didn't want to be in that predicament," said Earnhardt, who finished 37th.

And the very next week, on February 21 at Rockingham, Kenseth nudged Tony Stewart out of the way in the fourth turn of the final lap to score his first Busch Series win. The battle for the championship was on.

"I had a real good run off turn four, and the air got him a little bit loose," Kenseth said. "He came back down, and I just barely nudged him. I really didn't need to bump him to win the race. I thought I could have won the race one on one, but we got caught up with some lapped traffic, and that's just the way it turned out."

Stewart wasn't thrilled to finish second.

"That was the only way he could get by us," Stewart fumed. "He got us loose to where I had to get out of the gas for a second, and that was enough for him to get by. I was on the gas as hard as I could go, and evidently it wasn't hard enough for him. I wouldn't have taken him out."

Earnhardt showed a flash of brilliance by running second to Jimmy Spencer February 28 at Las Vegas. He could have given Spencer a move-over bump in turn two on the last lap, but didn't. Why?

"I knew it would be heck to pay getting back through [turns] three and four if he ever got back to me," Earnhardt said. "He's *baaaad* to get you back."

After getting caught in two multi-car crashes March 21 at Darlington, Earnhardt dropped to fifth in the standings behind leader McLaughlin and fourth-place Kenseth. He began a comeback with a second-place finish March 28 at Bristol. Junior then finished one spot better the next week at Texas, April 4.

Earnhardt laid a fender to Joe Nemechek on the next-to-last lap in the Lone Star State, and went on to capture his first win. With that, he was out front in the title chase for the first time.

ABOVE: Tim Fedewa's car comes to rest on its roof following a crash during a March 14 practice session for the next day's BellSouth Mobility/Opryland 320 at Nashville. Mike McLaughlin's car (to the left of Fedewa's) was also destroyed. McLaughlin won the event in a backup machine. (Chad Fletcher) OPPOSITE: Kevin Grubb's car slams into Brewco Motorsports' unprotected pit stall at Hickory April 11. Brewco's Todd Wilkerson can be seen jumping from the team's pit box. Busch Series officials and track safety personnel later attend to Wilkerson, who broke his left wrist and elbow in the accident. Ed Berrier won the event in his 208th start on the tour, ending the division's longest winless streak. Due to expansion into new markets and NASCAR's rising purse requirements, the Galaxy Food Centers 300 was Hickory's last Busch Series race. (Chad Fletcher)

"Winning in front of my father and him being at the race track, that just overshadows everything," Earnhardt said. "I'm proud of my father and my grandfather [the late Ralph Earnhardt, who won NASCAR's Sportsman championship in 1956] and what they've done. I'm just glad I'm able to be successful at it, too. Growing up all those years, I wondered if I had what it took."

Thirty-four of the 43 starters at Talladega April 25 were damaged to varying degrees, including Kenseth, who finished eighth, and Earnhardt, who was 32nd. That put Kenseth atop the standings, but McLaughlin then regained the advantage and held it throughout the month of May.

Earnhardt, meanwhile, was having major problems. After leading the first 61 laps May 17 at Nazareth, he missed the entrance to an access road leading to pit road during a caution. He dove from the track across a grassy strip to the access road and, as a result, was dropped by NASCAR to the rear of the longest line of traffic on the restart. A subsequent accident dropped Earnhardt to a 28th-place finish.

"When they told us pit road was open, I'd passed it," Earnhardt said. "What advantage did I gain by going across the grass? I was just trying to get into the pits. They put us in the rear, back where everybody wrecks."

Another crash May 23 at Charlotte left Earnhardt

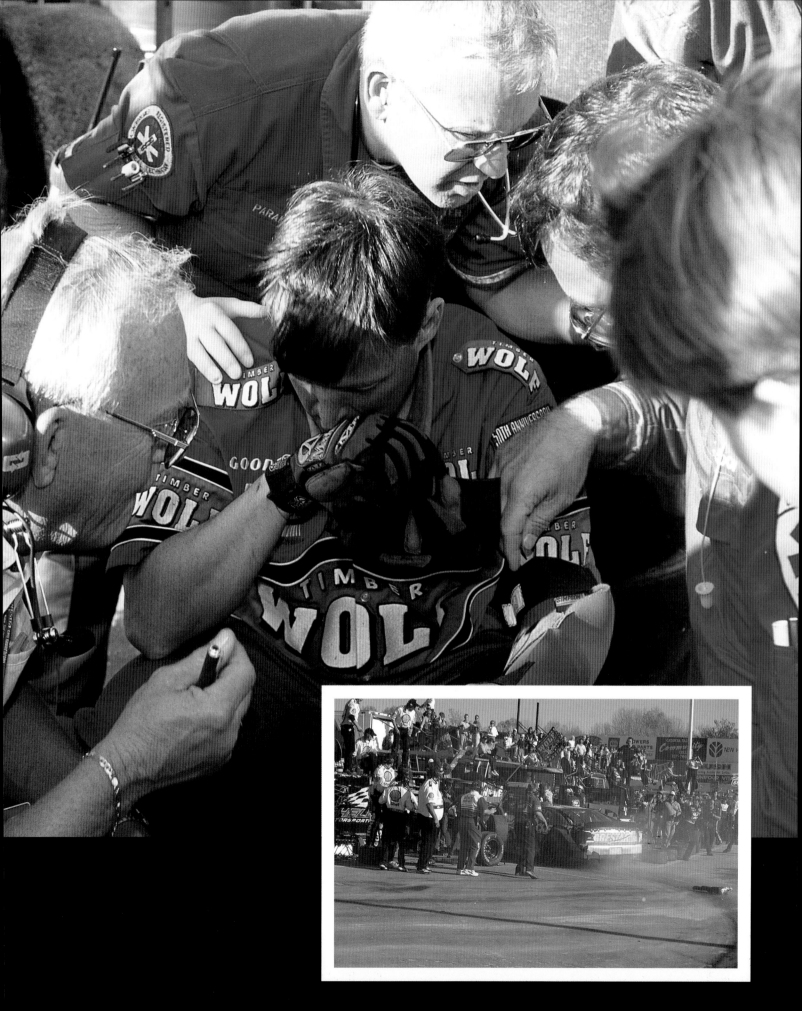

ABOVE: Dale Earnhardt Jr. spins at the entrance to pit road while trying to make a midrace pit stop at Dover May 30. Earnhardt had to go around the track again before getting serviced, but he came back to win the event. It was his second victory of the year. (Larry McTighe) LEFT: Moments after spinning between turns three and four an angry Jeff Purvis drives into the side of Mark Green's car at South Boston July 25. A fight broke out between their crews, leading to a $10,000 fine and four-race suspension for Purvis, as well as fines, probations, and suspensions for several crew members. (Chad Fletcher) OPPOSITE: Todd Bodine congratulates Mike McLaughlin on his win at Charlotte October 3. McLaughlin ran the last 94 laps without stopping for fuel to beat second-place Matt Kenseth to the finish line by more than 24 seconds. (Phil Cavali)

trailing McLaughlin by 189 points and Kenseth by 188.

As he had at Las Vegas earlier in the year, Earnhardt showed his patient, calculating side May 30 at Dover when he looped his car at the entrance to pit road while trying to make a mid-race, green-flag pit stop. Rather than panic, he came around again and pitted without another incident.

With Kenseth out of the way after a blown tire sent him crashing into the first-turn wall, Earnhardt captured his second victory of the season. He still trailed McLaughlin by 164 points after the race.

Kenseth won again June 14 in the division's debut at Pikes Peak International Raceway in Colorado, and reclaimed the lead in the standings. McLaughlin traded paint with Ron Hornaday during the race, and their crews exchanged shoves in the garage afterward.

Earnhardt slapped the wall between turns one and two on lap 225 after contact with Stewart, and a lap later, Stewart's car was smoking from another scrap with Earnhardt. The fireworks weren't over.

A brief scuffle broke out in NASCAR's mobile office after the race, leading to fines for Earnhardt ($5,000); crew chief Tony Eury Sr. ($2,500); Stewart's crew chief, Bryant Frazier ($1,000), and a 90-day probation for all.

"[Stewart] got into me pretty hard and beat the tires up," Earnhardt said after the race. "I was gonna let that go, and then after the race, him and his little crew chief buddy talked a bunch of crap up there in the NASCAR hauler. So we ain't gonna let that go.

"They [NASCAR officials] are pretty upset about our actions today. I'll have to go home and think about it, but I feel like I stood up for what I thought was right and did the right thing. We had a race car to win the race."

Earnhardt dominated the July 5 event at Milwaukee, leading 208 of 250 laps and beating Elton Sawyer to the finish line by five and one half seconds. Randy LaJoie then won his final race for BACE Motorsports on July 11 at Myrtle Beach.

LaJoie ultimately would finish fourth in the Busch Series standings in 1998, a tremendous season for most, but sorely disappointing for LaJoie and Baumgardner. LaJoie left the team at the end of the year.

"We couldn't afford to stay on top of technology," LaJoie said. "We couldn't beat Little E and Kenseth because they were on a mission, and we weren't. We had been on a mission for two years, and it seemed like the mission was over for some of us. When 10 guys are just working and five guys are on a mission, that doesn't cut it. Little E and Kenseth had 15 guys on a mission. They waxed our butt."

McLaughlin finished third at Myrtle Beach, with Earnhardt fifth and Kenseth sixth. McLaughlin led Kenseth by three points in the championship battle and Earnhardt by 12. McLaughlin, however, faded over the final months of the season due to turnover in his team, bad racing luck that led to accidents that weren't his fault, and mechanical failures.

Earnhardt scorched the field July 19 at California by leading all but nine of the race's 150 laps, giving him a lead in the standings he hadn't seen since mid-April and one he wouldn't give up the rest of the year. Earnhardt, though, wasn't counting his championship money just yet.

"Things happen that set you back into reality and put you back in your place," Earnhardt said after the race. "Never again will I think that I'm any better at this than anybody else. After Myrtle Beach [where he'd struggled with the handling on his car before finishing fifth], that proved to me that I'm nothing you can't find at any Saturday-night bullring."

NASCAR officials were kept busy handing out penalties during and after the July 25 race at South Boston. Jeff Purvis and Mark Green made contact on the 142nd lap, sending Purvis crashing into the wall between turns three and four. As both entered pit road, which had no inside wall to separate crews from cars whizzing by, Purvis steered his Chevrolet into Green's. Fistfights raged between their crews.

Purvis was suspended for four races, and following a July 30 appeal at IRP, his fine was doubled to $10,000 by the National Stock Car Racing Commission. Johnny Allen, Purvis's crew chief, was fined $250, less than the others because although he wasn't actually involved in the fight, he was still considered ultimately responsible for the actions of his crew. Phoenix Racing crew member Jason Taylor was fined $2,500, suspended for the rest of the year, and later fired by the team, and Kenneth Campbell, Green's crew chief, was fined $2,500.

Earnhardt led the first 245 laps at South Boston, but was black flagged and sent to the pits for one lap for spinning Joe Bessey's slower car. Tim Fedewa inherited the win.

"We were leading the race and getting a little pressure from behind, so I had to do something," Earnhardt said. "It's a shame. I understand where NASCAR's coming from. They don't want to put up with too much rootin' and gougin'.

"We run behind [Bessey] for about 10 or 15 laps trying to lap him. It's real hard to lap people, especially on this tight track, without pushing and shoving a little bit. If he ain't gonna move over, that's what he's gonna get."

Earnhardt won at IRP July 31, again at Richmond September 11, and for the final time in 1998 at Gateway on October 17. While Kenseth and McLaughlin also scored wins late in the year, Earnhardt slowly pulled away with the points lead. He finished second November 7 at Atlanta in a race that had been rained out and postponed earlier in the year, to all but clinch the title.

"I guess it will sink in once I see the look in my daddy's eyes next week," Earnhardt said after the Atlanta event. When he took the checkered flag at November 15 at Homestead, that put Earnhardt over the top. He finished 42nd in the 43-car field due to a blown engine, but it didn't matter. The championship was his.

"I really had no idea what to expect, how to win a championship, how to be consistent," Earnhardt said, acknowledging that his crew "kind of pointed me in the right direction. When I got out of line, they'd knock me around and send me back on my way."

For 1999, Earnhardt would be back on his way to another season-long battle with Kenseth and Jeff Green.

ABOVE LEFT: Joe Bessey slams into the wall between turns three and four on lap 243 at South Boston after making contact with Dale Earnhardt Jr. Earnhardt, who had led the entire race to that point, was penalized a lap for his role in the incident, which handed the victory to Tim Fedewa (33). (Don Kelly) ABOVE RIGHT: Robert Pressley's blazing car slows to a stop against the fourth-turn wall at Bristol August 21. Several other cars were involved in the accident and NASCAR officials brought out the red flag to ensure a race to the finish. After the restart, Kevin Lepage passed Dale Jarrett with two laps to go to claim the victory. (Phil Cavali)

ABOVE: St. Louis Cardinals baseball slugger Mark McGwire became a part-owner in Bobby Hillin's Busch Series team early in the year. In October at Gateway, the driver's helmet paid tribute to McGwire's historic 70-homer season. (Chad Fletcher)

RIGHT: Dale Earnhardt Jr. and Matt Kenseth share a laugh during pre-race ceremonies at Gateway. The season-long battle for the championship between the two brought a lot of attention to the division. (Chad Fletcher)

LEFT: Dale Earnhardt Jr. was a budding superstar in 1999. He was besieged by fans, media, and sponsor representatives, from the time he arrived in the garage until he left. He vowed to continue being his own man though the pressure on him was enormous. (Chad Fletcher)
RIGHT: Matt Kenseth was back with team owner Robbie Reiser (background) in 1999, and both were determined to beat Dale Earnhardt Jr. to the title. Both drivers faced many distractions, but again, they fought each other for the championship all year. (Phil Cavali)

1999
A Superstar Is Born

If the 1998 season had taught Dale Earnhardt Jr. how to drive a race car to a championship, in 1999 he would learn how to be a superstar.

It was hard enough to deal with being the son of Dale Earnhardt. But once those expectations were backed up with legitimate success on the race track, the demands on the younger Earnhardt became heavier than on any other champion in the division's history.

With a circus atmosphere surrounding his limited Winston Cup schedule in 2000, in addition to his pursuit of a second Busch Series championship, Earnhardt's season nearly spun out of control.

"I couldn't think at all at the race track," Earnhardt said. "There was nowhere I could go. The trailer was packed full of people. The lounge was packed full of people. There were lines standing outside the trailer. There's people crowded around the race car. I want to be a good spokesman for our sponsor, but if we don't win on the race track, they ain't gonna be around too damn long."

Randy LaJoie won the February 13 opener at Daytona in a wild finish that saw young Casey Atwood take a tumbling, upside-down ride under the white flag. Earnhardt had wrecked earlier in the race, and then was involved in another accident February 20 at Rockingham. Another title contender, Matt Kenseth, led 108 of 200 laps and finished third at Rockingham in a race won by Winston Cup regular Jeff Burton.

But some of the biggest news of the weekend came from a driver who didn't make the field. Jeff Green, after Winston Cup rides with Diamond Ridge Motorsports and Team Sabco fell through, joined Progressive Motorsports for the 1999 campaign.

Rain washed out the only round of time trials scheduled at Rockingham. Green's brand-new team had no car owner's points from the previous year to fall back on, so after being one of the fastest in practice, it was forced to load up and go home.

"I went to several car owners and asked them to let Jeff start the race," said team owner Greg Pollex. "They all turned me down. That's one thing I'll not forget. I'll do anything for anybody, but when you stiff me, don't come back to me and ask for anything."

Winston Cup drivers competing in the Busch Series had always been an issue, but leading up to the March 6 event at Las Vegas, the controversy reached a boiling point. Seventeen Winston Cup drivers made the race, forcing several top Busch Series teams to miss the race. Mark Martin won the event, and seven of the top-10 finishers were Winston Cup regulars.

"It's a punch in the gut when they send a guy home that was fifth or sixth in points," said Earnhardt, who was the event's highest-finishing Busch Series regular in sixth. "It's difficult, because those guys lack a lot of experience. The only way they're gonna get it is to get on the race track."

Another dominant performance went by the wayside for Kenseth March 27 at Texas. He led twice for 127 laps in the rain-shortened event, but went a lap down when he pitted under green. Several cars wrecked in turn four shortly thereafter, and Kenseth spun trying to race leader Green back to the caution flag. Embarrassed, Kenseth finished 18th. Meanwhile, Earnhardt fell to sixth in the standings after a 10th-place finish at Texas. It was there that Earnhardt and his handlers reached an impasse on his schedule.

Earnhardt made it abundantly clear that he was tired of being pulled in every direction. He was given some breathing room. The transporter was cleared. Junior got a motorcoach. Public relations representatives had "Dale Jr. Days" inserted into their calendars, days on which the driver was not to be scheduled for appearances, interviews, or anything else.

The redirection worked. Three races later, Earnhardt was leading the standings. From then on, only he and Kenseth would find themselves atop the Busch Series heap.

Kenseth regained the lead with a third-place finish May 14 at Richmond, then solidified it with a rousing victory May 23 at Nazareth. The race was delayed five hours by rain, but the weather certainly didn't dampen the competition once the green flag fell.

LEFT: Mike Skinner's victory in Atlanta's March 13 Yellow Freight 300 was initially taken away by NASCAR when inspectors found modified intake ports in the engine of his Emerald Performance Group Chevrolet. Team owner David Ridling vehemently denied any wrongdoing, and an appeal four days later returned the win. Still, the team was fined nearly $19,000. (Phil Cavali) BELOW: Dale Earnhardt Jr. suffered his second wreck in as many races when he got together in turn four with Jason Keller (57) at Rockingham February 20. The crash led to a dismal 35th-place finish for Earnhardt, who completed only 128 of the event's 197 laps. (Bryan Hallman) OPPOSITE: At Daytona February 13, Casey Atwood came off the fourth turn on the next-to-last lap running second to Randy LaJoie, but slid under the white flag on his roof after getting hit from behind by Andy Hillenburg (18). While LaJoie kept the lead, Atwood finished 17th. (Larry McTighe)

It took Dale Earnhardt Jr. until June 5 at Dover to reach victory
lane in 1999. The win moved him past Matt Kenseth to the top of
the Busch Series standings, and it began a roll that wouldn't stop
for three more weeks. (Phil Cavali)

Green led 102 of the first 109 laps, but failed to pit with the rest of the leaders during a caution period because of miscommunication between himself, his spotter, and NASCAR. He wound up 28th on the re-start and never made it back to first place.

Seconds after clearing an accident on lap 140, Tim Fedewa dove under Earnhardt for the lead. The move miffed Earnhardt, who then passed Todd Bodine for second place coming to another caution flag on lap 154.

It was Bodine's turn to be angry. He nailed Earnhardt's car during the caution, but the contact seriously damaged Bodine's car.

"You race 'Ironhead Jr.,' and that's what happens," Bodine fumed. "He just didn't think. There's three guys sitting across the race track in danger, and he wants to race back to the yellow. It's pretty stupid. That's how people get hurt."

With darkness quickly descending, Kenseth roared to the inside of both Earnhardt and Fedewa in turn three on lap 151. When the race was called 17 laps later because of poor visibility, Kenseth won.

"I got a really good run," Kenseth said. "[Earnhardt] was spinning the tires a little bit. You never like to go three wide at a track like that, but I made sure we had good brakes to slow down and keep it on the white line."

Earnhardt won his first race of the year June 5 at Dover, while Kenseth was caught up in a couple of acci-dents. That pushed Earnhardt to the top of the standings again, and the following week, at South Boston, he held off a hard-charging Green for another victory.

A third consecutive win was in store for Earnhardt June 27 at Watkins Glen. Canadian road-racing ace Ron Fellows had won the Craftsman Truck Series event from the pole the day before, and he started first in the Lysol 200 Busch Series race as well. Fel-lows led 52 of the race's 82 laps, but Earnhardt passed

him going into turn one of the last lap.

Amazingly, Earnhardt drove the last 20 laps with one hand, while using the other to keep his faltering transmission in gear.

"It's difficult to drive that place with two hands, but with one hand, it's *real* hard," Earnhardt quipped.

On July 4 at Milwaukee, Casey Atwood, at the age of 18 years and 10 months, became the youngest Busch Se-ries winner ever. He nudged Green out of the racing groove between turns three and four on the last lap. Even before the big finish, it had been an eventful weekend.

Earnhardt suffered a broken right shoulder blade the day before in a crash during practice. Later that afternoon, Jeff Krogh was critically injured in the fi-nal warm-up for the next day's race and never raced again on the tour. Earnhardt overcame his injury to finish third and maintain a 139-point lead over Kenseth, who finished fifth.

"When I needed to drive hard, I couldn't lean in the seat," Earnhardt said. "Most of the day, I could hold myself up in my seat with my left hand, but that got hard after a while. It was just wearing me out."

At Myrtle Beach July 17, Jason Keller's strong run was ended with a cut tire after he tangled with Phil Par-sons with less than five laps to go. That handed the win to Green, Keller's Progressive Motorsports teammate.

BELOW LEFT: Dale Earnhardt Jr. captured his third consecutive win of the season at Watkins Glen June 27, by passing road-racing specialist Ron Fellows going into turn one on the last lap. Earnhardt drove the last 20 laps with one hand holding the steering wheel and the other on the shift lever to keep the car in gear. (Charles Berch)
BELOW RIGHT: A crash during a practice session at Milwaukee July 3 broke Dale Earnhardt Jr.'s right shoulder blade, but he fared much better than Jeff Krogh. The Idaho native sustained severe, life-threatening head injuries during the final practice and never raced on the tour again. Earnhardt came back to finish third in the next day's DieHard 250. (Steve Benesh)

Kenseth finished third and halved Earnhardt's lead in the standings after the defending champion spun twice en route to a 25th-place finish.

"We had a terrible handling race car from the start," said Earnhardt, who started from the pole. "We went from the front to the back and got lapped. I got our lap back and then got to beatin' and bangin' in the back with those guys and knocked the toe-in out. I spun the car out, got that fixed. I had the flat spot on the tire, blew the tire out, spun on the grass. It was a horrible night."

The situation went from bad to worse for Earnhardt at Pikes Peak July 24. Bodine made contact with Earnhardt while racing for fourth on lap 240, sending Earnhardt's Chevrolet into the wall between turns one and two. After the incident, Earnhardt called the balding Bodine a "cueball-headed fool."

Kenseth finished seventh behind race winner Andy Santerre to go from 62 points behind Earnhardt to 24 points ahead in the title chase. The lead was brief. Earnhardt won July 31 at Gateway, reclaiming a lead he would keep the rest of the year.

At IRP on August 6, Kenseth finished fourth and Earnhardt fifth. Earnhardt's lead was just one point, but it widened again when he won at Michigan August 21 and Kenseth finished 22nd with a sick engine.

Kenseth's win at Bristol August 27 narrowed the gap, and on August 4 at Darlington, it got even closer. Kenseth finished third, while Earnhardt was 12th. Earnhardt had tried to make a green-flag stop, but came in too fast and nearly lost control. He had to make another lap before stopping, which cost him precious track position.

But problems in three of the next four races helped seal Kenseth's fate in the championship battle. Earnhardt won September 10 at Richmond by passing Martin seven laps from the end, while Kenseth struggled to a 20th-place showing. And then on September 25 at Dover, in another race won by Atwood, Earnhardt and Kenseth got together on lap 120 while racing for the lead.

Both drivers crashed. Earnhardt wound up finishing 33rd and Kenseth 38th, and Kenseth subsequently trailed his rival by 113 points.

"I was probably running too hard for that point of the race," Earnhardt admitted. "Matt definitely had a faster car than I did. Every once in a while, I'd see him get loose, and I'd try to make a charge to get by him and lead some laps. I got up underneath him going into turn one, and up off of turn two, I got loose, overcorrected, turned into him, and took us both out."

Countered Kenseth: "The damage was terrible. We had another brand-new car, and it cost [team owners] Robbie [Reiser] and his dad [John] a whole bunch of money. We had that race won, pretty much. I didn't feel like anybody had a car that could've beat ours."

Green won the division's October 31 debut at Memphis Motorsports Park in Tennessee, with Earnhardt running second. Kenseth, however, dropped off the pace with another engine problem. He finished 21st and dropped 156 points behind Earnhardt with just two races to go.

"It just went all at once," Kenseth said. "We were getting ready for a restart, stood on the gas, and something broke. It had us on seven cylinders, but it didn't hurt enough to blow up."

Earnhardt clinched the championship November 6 at Phoenix by finishing second to Jeff Gordon.

"When we won the championship in 1998, there wasn't a lot of pressure to win because we were rookies," Earnhardt said. "So if we'd lost, that was our excuse. When you win a championship, people expect you to run like champions every year."

At Homestead on November 13, Kenseth fell to third in the championship standings behind Earnhardt and Green when he was caught in an accident on the first lap.

Green refused to speculate on what might have been had he not missed the spring Rockingham event. Even if he'd won the race, he still would have finished second in the standings behind Earnhardt. But if the team had been able to avoid other mishaps, things indeed might have turned out differently.

"At Watkins Glen, I was in the top 10 and broke a transmission late in the race. At Bristol, I was leading and had a bad pit stop," Green said. "At Richmond, we were running fourth or fifth with 30 laps to go and broke an axle. Michigan, we just didn't run good."

The following year Green would have the chance to change his luck.

ABOVE: Dale Earnhardt Jr. and Matt Kenseth scrap on lap 120 at Dover September 25. A somewhat embarrassed Earnhardt accepted blame for the incident, but it took Kenseth quite a while to forgive his rival. (Jim Smith) RIGHT: Although Jeff Green missed Rockingham's spring event, he came on strong late in the season to take second place in the final standings. Here, Green celebrates his victory at Memphis October 31. The win was emotional because it came just a few days after the death of Amy Campbell, the wife of Progressive Motorsports co-owner Bob Campbell. She was killed in an automobile accident. (Chad Fletcher) OPPOSITE: Casey Atwood runs up on Jeff Green's bumper between turns three and four of the final lap at Milwaukee. Contact between the two moved Green up the track, allowing Atwood to become the Busch Series' youngest winner at the age of 18 years, 10 months. (Steve Benesh)

FT: The field sits ready for action at Myrtle Beach June 17, 2000, a race at would be won by Jeff Green. Myrtle Beach and South Boston, here Green had also won a week arlier, each held their final Busch eries events in 2000. (Bambi Mattila) GHT: Harold Holly (right), Green's ew chief, is as tough a competitor as ny driver and is considered one of e mechanical genuises in the sport. aid Green of Holly: "Second is no ood for him." (Phil Cavali)

2000
Complete Control

Most observers figured Jeff Green would have a decent season in 2000, but nobody could have forseen what actually occurred.

Green won six races, posted 25 top-five finishes in 32 starts and beat ppc Racing teammate Jason Keller for the championship by an astounding 616 points. When Green's top fives and point margin broke records Sam Ard had held for 16 years, it seemed like the future of the sport was meeting its past.

"Sam Ard and Jack Ingram, I didn't have a chance to race against those guys, but they're legends, no doubt about it," Green said. "Their names are household names, and they will be always. We'll be in the record books forever as champions."

Technically, the organization for which Green won the title was different from the one that had backed him a year earlier. Michigan businessman John Bender joined Greg Pollex and Bob Campbell to form ppc Racing for the 2000 season. But several key Progressive Motorsports elements were still in place, including Green, Keller, and their respective crew chiefs, Harold Holly and Steve Addington.

The organizational change had little impact on Green's performance. But just as Dale Earnhardt Jr. had two years earlier, Green rolled his Chevrolet in the first race of the year. Unintentional contact with Bobby Hamilton Jr. sent Green flying through the air just past the starter's stand on lap 14 February 19 at Daytona, and he finished 42nd.

"It was totally my fault," said Green, who was uninjured in the mishap. "I thought I had enough room to get down there, and I didn't. Those guys were driving like it's the last lap. We had a pretty good car, but you have to have all four tires on the ground before you can win these things."

A second-place finish a week later at Rockingham got things headed in the right direction for Green, but he would have to wait to visit victory lane. Mark Martin, who the year before had announced that 2000 would be his last year of Busch Series competition, won four of his first five starts on the tour. He was also well on his way to victory March 4 at Las Vegas when he

had to check up with just a couple of laps remaining to avoid Jack Sprague's spinning car.

The Las Vegas win went to Martin's Roush Racing teammate, Jeff Burton. With Winston Cup stars Matt Kenseth and Sterling Marlin making their marks in the Busch Series win column as well, it took eight races for a tour regular to make it into victory lane. That event, though, was a doozy.

Green got into the back of then-leader Chad Chaffin on lap 243 April 8 at Nashville, beginning a chain reaction that damaged several top-10 cars. Randy LaJoie was eighth as the accident unfolded, but somehow managed to squirt through the almost completely blocked track in turn four to post his first, and as it turned out, only, win of the year.

Those involved in the start of the multi-car mishap were quick to point fingers.

"That's typical Jeff Green," said Chaffin, who, like Green, raced at Nashville in the Late Model Stock ranks. "I've run with him a long time, and it's not the first time he's turned me around. You see a lot of guys get into a quarter panel trying to pass, but that was grille to rear bumper. I don't know how you justify that."

On the other hand, Green thought the pileup could have been avoided had third-place finisher Todd Bodine been more patient. After the race, Bodine led LaJoie by eight points and Green by 43.

"I can't blame it all on [Bodine], because I turned the 77 [Chaffin] a little bit," Green said. "But if he would have just given me a little more room, everybody would have been able to save it and we would have been OK."

A week later, after a fifth-place finish at Talladega, Green had clawed his way to the top of the Busch Series standings. The charge had begun, and it gathered momentum when Green captured his first victory of the year at Richmond May 5.

But then on May 12, during a practice session at New Hampshire, Adam Petty, the fourth-generation driver from racing's most famous family, was killed when his throttle stuck going into the third turn.

ABOVE: Jack Sprague spins in turn four with a little more than two laps to go in the Sam's Town 300 at Las Vegas March 4. Mark Martin (60) checks up to avoid Sprague, erasing a lead he'd held for much of the race. Jeff Burton (9), Martin's Roush Racing teammate, took the victory. (Bryan Hallman) RIGHT: Jeff Green spins to the inside as several more cars continue to pile up behind him April 8 at Nashville. The incident began with contact between Green and Chad Chaffin (not pictured). Randy LaJoie snaked his way through the smoke and debris to score his only win of the year. (Elmer Kappell) OPPOSITE: Jeff Green started the 2000 season upside down at Daytona February 19, but ended the season on top of the division. He said this incident, along with a couple of others, forced him to be more patient behind the wheel. (Mark Hawkins)

It was the Busch Series' first on-track fatality since Clifford Allison was killed nearly eight years earlier. About 120 people attended a memorial service in Petty's memory hours after the accident, and the following morning, several in the garage had spears of broccoli—Petty's favorite food—pinned to their shirts or credential lanyards.

"Part of my function as a series director is to work with, mold, teach, and do everything that I possibly can to help a young driver's career progress," said Busch Series Director John Darby. "When a career comes to a sudden stop like it did in this case, it's like sticking a knife in my chest. It's like he was one of my own. It hurts real bad."

Sadly, Petty's was not the only NASCAR-related death in 2000. Christain Lovendahl, Mark Martin's nephew and the crew chief for Emerald Performance Group and driver P. J. Jones, was killed in a traffic accident near Mooresville, N.C., just six days before Petty's mishap. Winston Cup driver Kenny Irwin lost his life two months later at New Hampshire when his car struck the wall in almost the exact spot as Petty's had. Finally, Tony Roper, who began the year in the Busch Series as the driver for Washington Erving Motorsports, was killed during an October 13 Craftsman Truck Series event at Texas.

With Green rarely slipping on the race track,

Bodine and Keller fought it out for second place in the standings. Keller got by Martin for the June 3 win at Dover, while Bodine slipped to 13th, one lap down.

"To beat Mark Martin was something," Keller said. "I know a lot of people say that your last win is your most memorable, but for me, that one will probably always be one of my most memorable because of who I beat and how I beat him. He didn't have problems. We just were able to beat him."

Green then won back-to-back races at South Boston and Myrtle Beach, traditional bullring short tracks that would be dropped from the Busch Series schedule in 2001. South Boston had hosted the tour in its early years when fewer tracks wanted dates, but in the end, NASCAR's expansion into bigger markets took its toll on the Virginia track.

While Green was busy building his lead in the standings, Bodine's run of horrible luck continued. Five laps into the July 1 Econo Lodge 200 at Nazareth, Bodine got turned from behind by rookie Kevin Harvick on a restart. The incident dropped Bodine's Cicci-Welliver Racing Chevrolet to 40th in the running order.

"I guess I'm just not destined to win [a championship]," said a dejected Bodine after the Nazareth event.

Keller's third-place finish at Nazareth moved him to second in the standings. For Keller, that was the good news. The bad news was that he trailed Green by an incredible 499 points. This was a championship that was all but decided with three months to go in the season.

That's not to say that there wasn't any excitement left. Green and his older brother David went at each other with little mercy July 22 at Pikes Peak. Jeff came out on top to post his fifth win of the year.

"Hopefully, Mom didn't have a heart attack watching the race," David quipped.

Keller finished second behind Harvick August 25 at Bristol, but not without a helping hand from Jeff Green. The transmission in Keller's car got stuck between gears during a late red flag, and he had to get a push from Green afterward to get going again. His efforts moved Keller back to second in the standings,

ABOVE: Kyle Petty made an emotional return to racing at Dover three weeks after the death of his son. The elder Petty finished 26th in the event, and concentrated on running Adam's No. 45 Busch Series car for most of the remainder of the year. (Phil Cavali)

OPPOSITE: Adam Petty takes to the track during practice at New Hampshire May 12. Within minutes, the throttle in Petty's Chevrolet hung wide open, sending him violently into the third-turn wall. The fourth-generation driver was pronounced dead hours later. (Bambi Mattila)

where he settled for the rest of the year.

"Jeff wrapped the championship up a lot earlier than I wrapped second up," Keller said. "We kind of work as one team, although he has his team members and I have my team members. [Being 1-2] was very gratifying, just because it was a goal we had set."

Green finished out of the top five only three times in the 24 races following his Nashville debacle in April. He was 10th June 25 at Watkins Glen, 14th because of an ill-handling car August 19 at Michigan, and 42nd September 23 at Dover. Green qualified second for the Dover event, but demolished his car when he cut a tire with about five minutes remaining in the final practice session September 22.

It got worse for Green early in the Dover race. He and Jimmy Spencer had just cleared a wreck between turns one and two when they made contact that sent Green's backup car hard into the inside wall on the backstretch. A livid Green threw his arms up in disgust as Spencer passed by under the ensuing caution.

"Spencer run over me," Green fumed. "I don't know if he was trying to beat me back to the caution or what, but he don't have no room to talk about anybody else and how they drive. He flat run over me. He's not out there to do anything—just to make money."

A similar setback might have been disastrous for drivers in closer points races, but Green probably didn't lose a lot of sleep after Dover. Although Keller gained 133 points on his ppc Racing teammate, Green still had an extremely comfortable 516-point cushion. Green then nailed down his sixth and final win of the year with a thrilling last-lap pass of Jeff Burton October 21 at Rockingham.

Eight days later at Memphis, Green officially clinched the title just by taking the green flag. There were still two races remaining in 2000.

"We did it in style. That's what I'm happy about," Green said. "We didn't run second a couple of times and just finish every race to win this championship. We won races. We had 25 top fives. That's dominating."

Late in the year, ppc Racing announced plans to switch from Chevrolets to Fords in 2001. Some wondered why an organization that had finished 1-2 in the standings, that had been so completely successful, would tinker with what seemed to be perfection.

Green said it was just a sign of the times.

"The performance level has to go up from year to year to win these races," Green said. "We'll get stagnant if we keep staying the same. Harold [Holly, crew chief] and myself feel the [Ford] body's better than a Chevrolet. I think they've got more horsepower. When you've got a better body and more horsepower, you're gonna run faster."

The 2001 campaign is the 20th year of Busch Series competition. The future of the Busch Series is bright, thanks to the tradition established by such early drivers as Jack Ingram and Sam Ard, and continued by Larry Pearson, Mike Alexander, Tommy Ellis, Bobby Labonte, Joe Nemechek, and Jeff Green. The Winston Cup circuit will most assuredly always be cast in the spotlight, but for the Busch Series, its competition, heart, and soul will always remain second to none.

BELOW: Jason Keller leads ppc Racing teammate Jeff Green at Bristol August 25. They would ultimately finish second and third in the event, respectively. Although Keller's 616-point deficit was the largest in the division's history, his second-place finish in the 2000 Busch Series standings was the best of his career. (Phil Cavali) OPPOSITE: Kevin Harvick enjoyed one of the best seasons ever for a Busch Series rookie, winning three races and finishing third in the standings. Part of the Richard Childress Racing organization, Harvick was pegged as one of the sport's future superstars. (Phil Cavali)

These are the drivers who made it to the top of their sport, from the inaugural years of what has become the Busch Series, to the threshold of its 20th season of competition. From left to right on the front row are Joe Nemechek, Dale Earnhardt Jr., Bobby Labonte and David Green. Chuck Bown, Jack Ingram, Larry Pearson and Randy LaJoie make up the second row, while Sam Ard, Steve Grissom, and Johnny Benson are on the back row. Jeff Green, the 2000 Busch Series champion, is shown in the inset photograph. (Phil Cavali)

Acknowledgments

First, to my Lord and Savior, Jesus Christ. Without Him, none of this would be possible.

This book also would not have happened without the support of three very special families. Joe, Sandi, Jennifer, and Joe Estep Jr. introduced me to this sport and sustained me many times with their chili and Shoney's coupons. Fred, Judy, Lee Ann, and Joe Knight gave me room and board, and most importantly, love, during the darkest months of my life. Jamie, James, Lib, and Amy Reynolds provided a safety net as I chased a dream. I consider it an honor to call each member of these families a lifelong friend.

I have a deep appreciation for David Bull and Skylar Browning, whose belief in this project made it happen. Designers Tom Morgan and Liz McGhee have produced a beautiful book that brings my words to life.

Dick Conway and Dennis Punch have served various Busch Series teams and sponsors as public relations representatives since the early 1980s and also have been instrumental in putting this book together. Conway provided encouragement and some tremendous photography, and Punch allowed me to make copies of every Busch Series race report from 1982 through 1995. They are mentors in every sense of the word.

I will be forever thankful to Deb Williams and Steve Waid for taking a chance on an unknown reporter from a small-town community newspaper. Sometimes I still wonder how I possibly can get paid for doing something I love so much. Thanks also goes to the rest of the staff at *NASCAR Winston Cup Scene*, both past and present: Tom Jensen, Jeff Owens, Mark Ashenfelter, Art Weinstein, Ben White, Scott Greig, Susanne Corrado, David Green, and Tom Stinson.

We also have the best photographers in the motorsports world at *Scene*. Phil Cavali is an incredible artist, and this project wouldn't be complete without his work. Bambi Mattila, Chad Fletcher, Bryan Hallman, Ray Shough, Don Kelly, Jay Jageler, Jim Smith, Darryl Graham, Elmer Kappel, Steve Benesh, Charles Berch, and Gary Shook are awesome as well. Thanks also goes to Harold "Wow!" Hinson for allowing the use of several shots from Lowe's Motor Speedway's treasure trove of photos.

The members of the Busch Series community—the drivers, officials, team owners, crew members and public relations representatives—make mine the best job in the world. Busch Series Director John Darby is a tough, by-the-book official, but he's also one of the truly "good guys" in the sport. And, John, if that pace car job ever becomes available, I'm your man.

There are also a handful of people who should be mentioned for the roles they've played in my life, including the 1992-94 staff of *The Alleghany News*, Ron Brown, Lynn Worth, Jule Hubbard, Paula Hampton, Darlene Wyatt, and Lynn Barnes; as well as Jerry Lankford; Mike Evans; Deborah Evans Price; Liz Cavanaugh; Kevin Kirk; Bob Kribbs; Rev. Freddie Braswell, and everybody at Maplewood Baptist Church in Yadkinville, N.C.; Joy Johnson; Phil Baxter; Adrian York; Mark "Second String" Hayes; Dick Gordon; Dr. Jerry Punch; Tom and Jean Reavis, and Charlene Hubbard. In many indirect ways, these folks have helped make this project a reality.

My thanks go to those already mentioned, but my heart belongs to my family, beginning with my father, Sidney, and brother, Doug. Doug, I know you prefer being called Douglas, but, hey, it's my book. I'm blessed in having a wife, Jeanie, who is also my very best friend. Jeanie came up with the title for this project, *Second To None*, but the other 39,997 words are mine. Jeanie, our twin sons Adam and Jesse, and Richard, my son from a previous marriage, are my reasons for being.

Rick Houston
Hamptonville, N.C.
February 2001

Tommy Houston pits during the season finale at Martinsville October 29, 1989. A broken valve spring caused Houston to finish 24th, handing the championship to Rob Moroso. This was the closest the legendary driver would ever come to winning the championship. (Dick Conway)

MW01056815

Daniel & Revelation
Secrets of Bible Prophecy

Copyright © by Pacific Press Publishing
Association, Nampa, Idaho, USA. This
edition by Amazing Facts Publishing is
published under a licensing agreement
with the copyright owner. All international
rights reserved.

All original digital illustrations and
artwork are the property of Amazing Facts.
P.O. Box 1058, Roseville, CA 95678
All rights reserved.

All Scripture quotations, unless otherwise
indicated, are taken from the New King
James Version. Copyright ©1979, 1980,
1982 by Thomas Nelson, Inc. Used by
permission. All rights reserved.

Creative Director   Writer:
& Managing Editor: David C. Jarnes
Sam Godfrey

                           Editors:
Layout: Marvin Moore
Eric Smalling   Anthony Lester
Erin Engle

                           Other Contributing
Illustrations   Writers & Editors:
& Front Cover: Curtis Rittenour
Phil Mckay   Laurie Lyons

Printed in the USA.

DANIEL & REVELATION Secrets of Prophecy

Contents

A Portrait of Earth's History and Future 6

The major Bible books of Daniel and Revelation are our keys to understanding the past, present, and future—and both contain a window of hope revealing our place in prophecy today.

COME.
EXPLORE.
LEARN.

Thousands of Bible resources right at your fingertips!

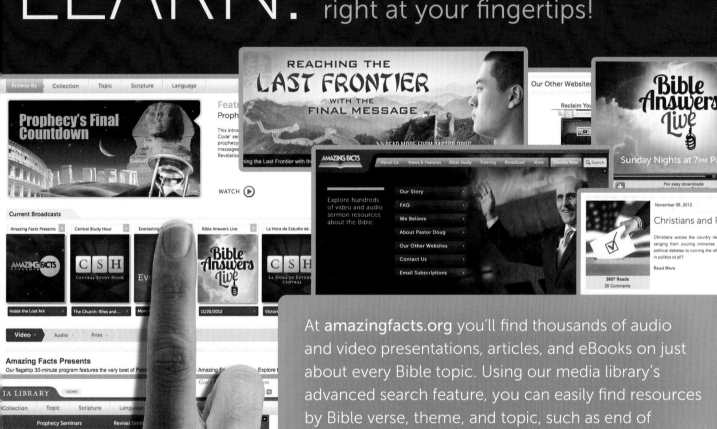

At **amazingfacts.org** you'll find thousands of audio and video presentations, articles, and eBooks on just about every Bible topic. Using our media library's advanced search feature, you can easily find resources by Bible verse, theme, and topic, such as end of the world, hell, the seven last plagues, forgiveness, salvation, and, of course, Bible prophecy!

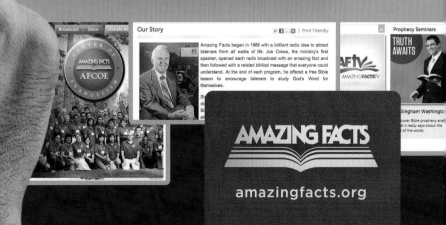

AMAZING FACTS

amazingfacts.org

A Portrait of Earth's History and Future

MODERN NUCLEAR SUBMARINES ARE AMONG THE MOST SOPHISTICATED ENGINEERING WONDERS OF THE WORLD. IN MANY WAYS THEY ARE EQUIVALENT TO A TIGHTLY PACKED, SELF-CONTAINED CITY IN WHICH A CREW OF 140 SHARES SPACE ABOUT THE SIZE OF A THREE-BEDROOM HOUSE.

Each submarine is powered by a nuclear reactor, which provides the energy that is converted to electricity. This amazing dynamo can run for more than 30 years and can carry the sub at least 400,000 miles without refueling. This power is also used to convert seawater to fresh water, purify the air, and turn the propeller that sends the submarine silently through the water—sometimes as deep as 800 feet!

Beneath the vast dark ocean, nuclear submarines manage to navigate using sonar and internal gyros. But as technologically advanced as this equipment is, nuclear submarines, of course, have no windows and still occasionally collide with a reef or another vessel. The only "window" to visually confirm their position while submerged is to draw near the surface and raise the periscope.

Have you ever wondered where our world is going? Is there a trustworthy way for us to peer into the future and get our bearings?

Many of us look at the moral decay in society—the crime, terrorism, wars, environmental disasters—and wonder, "Where are we heading? Something must give. Our world cannot continue spiraling downward much longer before imploding." To address this very issue, the Bible contains two major prophecy books that speak of the past, present, and future ... and they both contain a window of hope showing us our position in time today. They constitute a 360-degree periscope, showing us where our world is heading and revealing how we can have a secure future.

The Old Testament book of Daniel and the New Testament book of Revelation are powerful Bible periscopes. Together they provide us a broad panorama of yesterday, today, and tomorrow—a snapshot of world history from the time of Daniel while he was a captive in the country of Babylon in around 605 B.C. ... all the way down to the time when Christ will come again and beyond!

The book of Daniel was written by a Jewish young man who was taken captive by a foreign king and educated to be a statesmen in ancient Babylon. God revealed through dreams and visions to Daniel a great sweep of history that is confirmed by historians to be an accurate outline of world events. Daniel was a remarkably intelligent man who, despite threats of death, was also faithful to God. His book closes with the admonition that some things he wrote were to be locked up and revealed only later in time.

The book of Revelation was written by a follower of Jesus Christ whose name was John. During a time of persecution after the young church was making great progress, John was captured and then banished to a lonely island in order to be silenced—just at a time when he was most needed by the church. But God's plan was to speak deep things to this faithful follower, prophetic pictures of the future that would unlock truths from Daniel's book and carry them forward with an even clearer message.

Both Daniel and Revelation are books of prophecy that are filled with strange symbols about the past and the future. The average reader, unfamiliar with this special type of literature, might be confused by the beasts and the numbers, the idols and the mark of the beast. Do not be discouraged if you feel you cannot unlock every single verse in these two amazing books on your own. The God who opened the hearts of Daniel and John is the same God who will unlock these books in order to give you, a diligent searcher for truth, a taste of heavenly things.

> **"The Bible contains two major prophecy books that speak of the past, present, and future ... and they both contain a window of hope showing us our position in time today."**

This special magazine on Daniel and Revelation has been created to provide you with a quick introduction to some of the most fascinating scenes revealed to mankind. It opens a window in our suffocating world and lets us know that there is life beyond the baking temperatures of doom that are rising around us. If you need a key (or a hammer) to open a door to what God has in store for you, then take a refreshing breath as you open the pages before you.

Statue of Assyrian
King Ashurbanipal,
from Nimrud, Iraq,
875-860 B.C.

[Right] Ancient
Persian wall carving
in Iran. Possibly
from the time of
King Darius.

THE BOOK of DANIEL

Introduction to the Book of Daniel

> ## " "
> *The greatness of the kingdoms under the whole heaven shall be given to the people ... of the Most High.*
> —DANIEL 7:27

What You'll Learn

Who was Daniel the prophet?

Why is the book of Daniel a part of the Bible?

How does the book of Daniel apply to you today?

A WINGED LION, A FOUR-HEADED LEOPARD, A DRAGON-LIKE BEAST, A HORN THAT TALKS! STRANGE IMAGES FILL THE BOOK OF DANIEL, AN ANCIENT BOOK OF THE BIBLE FILLED WITH MYSTERIOUS SYMBOLS.

Who Was Daniel?

Daniel was probably a young member of Jerusalem's upper class. When King Nebuchadnezzar, founder and ruler of the Babylonian Empire, conquered the nation of Judah, he took some of its most prominent and promising citizens back to his land. Daniel was among these captives.

He was soon positioned as an advisor and administrator in the local government and developed such a good reputation that when the Persians later overthrew Babylon, they retained him as one of their top officials.

While Daniel held important positions in the service of the pagan kings of Babylon and Persia, he was foremost a servant of God. His main concerns were to see God's will done on earth and to see his people, the Hebrew nation, flourish.

Daniel lived at a time of great distress for the Jews. In fact, their nation no longer existed; it had been swallowed up by Babylon. So Daniel wrote to sustain them during those difficult times. His book gave an honest picture of what lay ahead for the Jews—and it was not very pretty. For the most part, the future held more of the same: Empire would succeed empire ... and through it all, God's people would be persecuted.

But Daniel's book held out hope. It spoke of a Messiah to come—actually specifying the time of His appearing. And its central theme was judgment. That might not sound very positive, but the coming of the judgment is actually good news to God's people.

The story of Daniel begins around 605 B.C.

The historical portions of this book provide Daniel's credentials as a faithful servant of God, modeling the way the Lord wants people to handle the temptations that stressful times can bring. They also build faith in God's rulership and goodness. These stories are uplifting and powerful, so please take the time to read them!

As Daniel makes clear, judgment means the end of evil and the establishment of God's kingdom. For God's people, it means resurrection and everlasting life.

In Babylon, Daniel received a new name —Belteshazzar.

Apocalyptic Prophecies

Daniel's book contains a mix of history and prophecy. Both are important. For the purpose of our study, however, we're going to focus on the chapters that look at God's prophetic revelations to Daniel, offering you interpretations that apply to events that have already passed and to events that are still to occur.

The prophecies in Daniel differ from most others found in the Old Testament.

Other prophets—such as Isaiah and Jeremiah, Hosea and Malachi—wrote what biblical scholars call "classical prophecy." Daniel's prophecy is of the type known as "apocalyptic."

While each kind of prophecy occasionally contains elements of the other, the following generalizations are helpful ...

CLASSICAL PROPHECY most resembles sermons. It points out the sins of God's people, tells them the consequences of continuing unfaithfulness, and calls them to repentance.

APOCALYPTIC PROPHECY often avoids commentary about sin and repentance, seeing the world through the lens of the final judgment—when people are either with God or against Him and there is no middle ground. It means to point out the important issues and show the big picture of God's plan through history. These prophecies were originally intended for God's people who were being persecuted, but they are valuable to all people.

Interpreting Daniel

Many of Daniel's prophecies contain strange and confusing symbolism. But the principle for understanding Daniel is quite simple—let the Bible be its own interpreter. In other words, look first to Scripture itself for clues as to how to understand those parts that seem obscure.

The book of Daniel is of particular help here, because its individual prophecies parallel one another—each adding to a picture previously portrayed. You can often clear up difficult parts of one prophecy by looking at the corresponding prophecy of another section.

Likewise, the book of Revelation is built on Daniel's prophecies, and the Gospels reveal references Jesus made to them, so these books also add to our understanding of Daniel. Since Daniel's prophecies deal with history, often in detail, knowledge of history is important too.

All the signs in the world around us indicate that we're living in the last days of earth's history—in the feet and toes of a statue that Nebuchadnezzar saw in his dream (see the next section). Where can we find God's plan for us in these last days? Where can we receive the motivation, commitment, and faith to get through them? The prophecies God gave Daniel point the way ... **D**

Daniel 2: A Great Image

God Reveals the Future

> He changes the times and the seasons;
> He removes kings and raises up kings; ...
> He reveals deep and secret things;
> He knows what is in the darkness,
> And light dwells with Him.
> —DANIEL 2:21–23

DANIEL 2 HAS BEEN CALLED THE FOUNDATION OF BIBLE PROPHECY. IN FACT, MANY OTHER PROPHECIES IN DANIEL AND REVELATION PROVIDE MORE DETAILS ON DANIEL 2. IF YOU UNDERSTAND THIS PROPHECY, YOU ARE WELL ON YOUR WAY TO MASTERING THE BIG PICTURE OF BIBLE PROPHECY.

Daniel 2 begins with a story about King Nebuchadnezzar.

The monarch had a vivid dream that greatly impressed him. He knew it was important, but when he woke, he couldn't remember the particulars of the dream ... never mind trying to figure out what it meant. He called in the best of his advisors, but they couldn't tell him what he had dreamed—even on threat of death. They had to admit that "there is no other who can tell it to the king except the gods, whose dwelling is not with flesh" (verse 11).

When Daniel heard about this situation, he knew that God was the only hope of an answer. So he and his friends prayed, and God answered their prayers by revealing "the secret" (v. 19) to Daniel in a vision at night.

Daniel succeeded where the wisest men of Babylon failed because of his connection to "the God in heaven who reveals secrets" (v. 28). Nebuchadnezzar's later endorsement (see vs. 46–49) of Daniel helps establish the credibility of the rest of what Daniel wrote in the book. The God who "gives wisdom to the wise" gave Daniel "wisdom and might" (vs. 21, 23).

What You'll Learn

How God revealed the political future of the world through a dream

Where that dream has been verified by history

What will be the last kingdom to rule before the end of the world

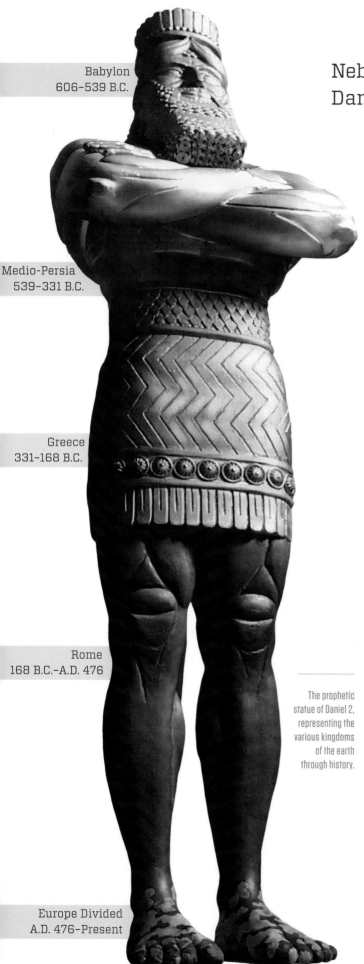

Babylon
606–539 B.C.

Medio-Persia
539–331 B.C.

Greece
331–168 B.C.

Rome
168 B.C.–A.D. 476

Europe Divided
A.D. 476–Present

The prophetic statue of Daniel 2, representing the various kingdoms of the earth through history.

Nebuchadnezzar's dream described in Daniel 2 occurred around 603 B.C.

Nebuchadnezzar's Question

Daniel introduced the dream itself and the prophecy it contained by telling us the question that was on King Nebuchadnezzar's mind when he went to bed that night:

> "As for you, O King, thoughts came to your mind while on your bed, about *what would come to pass after this;* and He who reveals secrets [God] has made known to you what will be" (v. 29, emphasis supplied).

The previous verse puts it this way: The "God in heaven ... has made known to King Nebuchadnezzar *what will be in the latter days*" (emphasis supplied). The primary concern of this prophecy, in other words, is how this world will end.

Nebuchadnezzar, Daniel said, dreamed of a great image—a statue. This statue was made up of five parts:

• A head made of gold
• Chest and arms of silver
• A belly and thighs of bronze
• Legs of iron
• Feet partly of iron and partly of clay.

Nebuchadnezzar then saw a stone cut out "without hands." The stone struck the statue on its feet and ground it into dust, which the wind blew away. Then the stone grew until it filled the whole earth (vs. 32–35).

What did this dream of an awesome statue reveal about the future? We don't have to guess, because God gave Daniel a full explanation for the king.

Daniel began his interpretation of the dream by telling Nebuchadnezzar what the head of gold represented: Nebuchadnezzar himself and, more broadly, the kingdom he ruled (v. 38; compare Daniel 7:17, 23). Each section of the image below

Why Kingdoms? *Nebuchadnezzar's interest lay in politics, the realm of nations and armies and rulers. So that's what this prophecy covers—the political history of the world from Nebuchadnezzar's time right down to the end of the world. Of course, God is interested in much more than political history: He's concerned about the religious realm on earth, because that determines people's eternal destiny. And that's really what the rest of the prophecies in Daniel's book are about; Daniel 2 lays the foundation of history on which the other prophecies are built.*

the head, in turn, represented a kingdom that would displace the one that preceded it:

"After you shall a rise another kingdom, inferior to yours; then another, a third kingdom. ... And the fourth kingdom ... will break in pieces and crush all the others" (vs. 39, 40).

In a later chapter, Daniel specifically names the two kingdoms that would succeed Babylon: Media/Persia (the Persian Empire, also known as Medo-Persia) and Greece (see Daniel 8:20, 21).

An Unexpected Turn

After describing four world empires that rise and fall, the prophecy takes an unexpected turn. Each of the first three kingdoms was displaced by a more powerful one; some ruler of another country would defeat the current ruling kingdom. But with the fourth kingdom, the pattern was broken. Rather than being defeated by some single, superior power, this "kingdom shall be divided ... just as you saw the iron mixed with ceramic clay" (v. 41).

In other words, the fourth kingdom was to be broken up into a number of smaller powers, some strong and some weak.

Daniel then described efforts to bind these powers into a single empire—even to the extent of mixing "with one another in marriage" (v. 23 NRSV). But these efforts would fail: "They will not adhere to one another, just as iron does not mix with clay" (v. 43).

History confirms the accuracy of the prophetic picture Daniel painted. The empire of Babylon was followed by those of Persia, Greece, and Rome. But then, rather than falling to some more powerful kingdom, the Roman Empire disintegrated into pieces—the nations that now make up much of Europe, the Middle East, and North Africa.

Since then, many rulers—among them, Charlemagne, Charles V of Spain, Napoleon, and Hitler—have tried to merge the pieces of Europe back together to form another empire. They've tried political and military approaches and even, as Daniel pointed out, intermarriage. But no one has been successful, just as prophecy foretold.

> **The kingdom that was divided was Rome.**

Some Bible scholars say it would take more than a united Europe to prove this prophecy wrong. The world God spoke of through Daniel's prophecy comprises the part of the globe where His people lived. Since Christians today are found throughout the world, only a kingdom that unites all the earth's nations into one political entity would falsify this prophecy.

> By the 19th century, attempts to unite the nations of Europe by intermarriage among the royal families had made these families nearly all interrelated.

The Prophecy's Climax

In the last verses of Daniel 2, his interpretation of the dream reaches its climax.

There will come one final world empire—but not built by human effort; this kingdom will be made "without hands" (v. 45). It will, in fact, obliterate and entirely replace all human kingdoms (see vs. 35, 44). God Himself will establish this kingdom that "shall never be destroyed," but "shall stand forever" (v. 44).

In these words, God told Nebuchadnezzar, and us, the true focus and end of earth's history. Human empires may for a moment have a degree of power and influence. But from the perspective of heaven, they are temporary, transitory. Ultimately, God's kingdom will triumph.

The point—only implied here but specifically stated later in Daniel's prophecies—is that God's people might be downtrodden for now. They might for the moment be subject to the powers of earth. But in the end they will share in God's triumph, His rule—the kingdom that will "stand forever." Would you like to be a part of God's kingdom? ▯

What About the Rest of the World?

In what sense do Daniel's prophecies foretell the "history of the world" if they don't even mention such world powers as China or America? The answer lies in God's purpose for prophecy. The Lord did not intend to provide us an unabridged history of the world, but rather a roadmap to eternal life by focusing on those people who were called to be His representatives on earth. The "world" of Bible prophecy is really the world of God's people. In Old Testament times, that meant Israel and the nations that had an impact on it. However, since New Testament times, Christianity has spread its influence worldwide. So in prophecies that extend into the New Testament era, the "world" encompasses the entire globe.

Babylonian Empire 606–539 B.C.

JERUSALEM
SYRIA
NINEVEH
ASSYRIA
MEDITERRANEAN SEA
PHOENICIA
BABYLON
JUDAH
MESOPOTAMIA
TAIMA
PERSIAN GULF
EGYPT
RED SEA
ARABIA

Medo-Persian Empire 539–331 B.C.

BYZANTIUM
GREECE
BLACK SEA
BACTRIA
LYDIA
TYRE
HARAN
JERUSALEM
SIDON
MEDIA
PARTHIA
MEDITERRANEAN SEA
BABYLON
LIBYA
PERSEPOLIS
EGYPT
ARABIA
PERSIS
PERSIAN GULF
RED SEA
ARABIAN SEA

Greek Empire 331–168 B.C.

BLACK SEA
GREECE
ANCYRA
CASPIAN SEA
SACAE
ATHENS
PHRYGIA
ARMENIA
NINEVEH
DAMASCUS
MEDIA
ARIANA
JERUSALEM
BABYLON
ALEXANDRIA
ASSYRIA
ARACHOSIA
MEDITERRANEAN SEA
PERSEPOLIS
INDIA
LIBYA
ARABIA
PERSIA
GEDROCIA
PATALA
EGYPT
PERSIAN GULF
RED SEA

Roman Empire 168 B.C.—A.D. 476

LONDON
BRITAIN
GERMANIA
BELGICA
GAUL
NORICUM
ATLANTIC OCEAN
LUSITANIA
ROME
DALMATIA
BYZANTIUM
ITALY
BLACK SEA
TARENTUM
PERGAMUM
LUSITANIA
MACEDONIA
PONTUS
BAETICA
SYRACUSE
ATHENS
GALATIA
CARTHAGE
CAPPADOCIA
ACHAEA
MAURITANIA
NUMIDIA
SYRIA
PARTHIAN EMPIRE
MEDITERRANEAN SEA
JERUSALEM
BABYLON
CYRENE
ALEXANDRIA
JUDEA
AFRICA
CYRENE
EGYPT

Daniel 7: Four Beasts and a Little Horn
Trial and Triumph

""

Jesus said to him, "It is as you said. Nevertheless, I say to you, hereafter you will see the Son of Man sitting at the right hand of the Power, and coming on the clouds of heaven."
—MATTHEW 26:64

What You'll Learn

How God revealed the future of the world through a dream

Where that dream has been verified by history

What religious power would rule the world

DANIEL 2 TELLS HOW GOD REVEALED THE FUTURE THROUGH A DREAM HE GAVE KING NEBUCHADNEZZAR. IN DANIEL 7, THE NEXT MAJOR PROPHECY, GOD REVEALS MORE OF THE FUTURE—BUT THIS TIME, DANIEL HIMSELF HAS THE DREAM.

When God sent a dream to Nebuchadnezzar in Daniel 2, He revealed the political history of the world. In chapter 7, God also speaks to Daniel, the prophet of His people, through a dream. It reveals the history of the world and the story of the people who were to preserve and share His good news of salvation.

Like the prophecy of Daniel 2, the prophecy of Daniel 7 comes in two parts: First a dream, and second, the interpretation. While Nebuchadnezzar's dream was relatively benign, Daniel saw stormy seas from which arose "four great beasts," all of which were fierce predators. Fascinated and probably horrified by the fourth beast, Daniel watched as three of its ten horns were plucked up, and another horn, "a little one," took their place.

Daniel's dream ended with a courtroom scene. Someone he called "the Ancient

of Days" was seated as judge, books were opened, and the beasts were condemned and their dominion taken away (vs. 9–13). Then Daniel saw the Ancient of Days give "One like the Son of Man ... dominion and glory and a kingdom that all peoples, nations, and languages should serve Him" (vs. 13, 14).

In the New Testament, Jesus calls Himself the "Son of man" more than 40 times, and in Matthew 26:64, He indirectly indicates that He is the Son of man of Daniel 7.

A Familiar Story
After reading Daniel 2, Daniel 7 should seem somewhat familiar to you. God used different images in the vision of Daniel 7 to tell the same basic story of the vision found

The fourth beast of Daniel 7.

in Daniel 2, while adding more details and a different perspective.

The four beasts in Daniel correspond to the four divisions of the statue in Daniel 2, representing four kingdoms (see vs. 17, 23). The **WINGED LION** of chapter 7 corresponds with the head of gold, which represented Babylon, in chapter 2.

The **BEAR** represented the next empire, Medo-Persia. The three ribs in its mouth stood for the three kingdoms this coalition defeated in its rise to power: Babylon, Lydia, and Egypt. It was "raised up on one side," which symbolized the Persians' eventual dominance over the Medes.

The **LEOPARD WITH FOUR WINGS**—what could be faster?—served as a fitting depiction of the speed of Alexander the Great's conquests as he established the Greek Empire. The leopard's four heads represented the parts into which that empire was divided upon Alexander's death.

The **FOURTH BEAST**, with its "**HUGE IRON TEETH**," represented the Roman Empire, which followed Greece as the major power in the Western world. And just as the iron empire in Daniel 2 fragmented into feet of iron and clay, so the fourth beast here divides into a group of horns. The ten horns symbolized the nations that grew out of the Roman

Empire as it aged, and invading Germanic tribes melded into it (see v. 24).

Daniel 7 has one final and crucial similarity to Daniel 2. That earlier chapter ends with dominion being taken from all the earthly powers and being given "forever" to the kingdom that God establishes. Likewise, the vision of Daniel 7 concludes with the assurance that the kingdom God establishes will be "an everlasting dominion, which shall not pass away, and His kingdom the one which shall not be destroyed" (v. 14).

The Angel's Assurance

Perhaps you've noticed that all the beasts in Daniel 7 are carnivorous. Daniel was concerned about the threat they represented, as he asked one of those "standing by" (probably an angel) the meaning of what he was seeing. That person answered with a two-sentence summary of the point of this whole chapter:

> "Those great beasts, which are four, are four kings which arise out of the earth. But the saints of the Most High shall receive the kingdom, and possess the kingdom forever, even forever and ever" (vs. 17, 18).

In other words, believers will face some difficult times, but in the end, God will accomplish His purposes. He will establish His kingdom, and His people will share in His victory.

Daniel obviously appreciated that reassurance, but he was still curious about that fourth nondescript beast and

In the Bible, the term saints simply means "God's people, believers." It doesn't refer only to a few ultra-righteous individuals.

its horns—particularly the "little horn" that had eyes and a mouth and that "was making war against the saints, and prevailing against them" (v. 21).

Just who or what did this horn represent? Daniel tells us several things about this entity that help us identify it:

1. Chronologically, it rose to power in the time of the 10 kings or nations—that is, sometime after the demise of the Roman Empire.

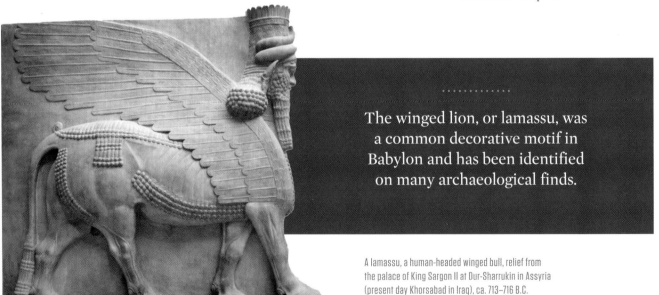

The winged lion, or lamassu, was a common decorative motif in Babylon and has been identified on many archaeological finds.

A lamassu, a human-headed winged bull, relief from the palace of King Sargon II at Dur-Sharrukin in Assyria (present day Khorsabad in Iraq), ca. 713–716 B.C. Department of Oriental Antiquities, Richelieu.

The winged lion and the bear with three ribs in its mouth.

2. Daniel saw that three of the horns were "plucked out by the roots," or subdued, to make way for this little horn, whose appearance was to become "greater than his fellows" (vs. 8, 20, 24).

3. The angel who interpreted the dream for Daniel said the little horn would be "different" from the first horns, probably in that it would have eyes and a mouth speaking "pompous words against the Most High"—against God, in other words.

4. The horn would also "persecute the saints of the Most High, and shall intend to change times and law." Obviously, the fact that human laws change isn't noteworthy; humans change

human laws all the time. These "times and law," however, are ones established by God and are untouchable to humans.

5. And finally, the interpreter gave Daniel a specific time period during which this horn would hold sway: "a time and times and half a time" (vs. 8, 24, 25).

The fact that it was a horn, like the other horns, suggests that it was a political power. But the fact that this horn was "different" from the others suggests that it was something more than a political entity. Its difference had to do with religion, since this horn practices blasphemy, persecution of God's people, and the changing of God's law.

The Horn's Identity

How might we identify this little horn power? Consider the following questions: What religious-political power arose during the decline of the Roman Empire?

THE MEDIEVAL CHRISTIAN CHURCH, PAPAL ROME, which through nearly all its existence has claimed to be a political state as well as a church.

How certain can we be?

WERE THREE OF THE GERMANIC TRIBES THAT DISPLACED THE ROMAN EMPIRE "UPROOTED" SO THIS CHURCH COULD FLOURISH? Yes. The Heruls, the Vandals, and the Ostrogoths—all of which professed Arianism, a form of Christianity that was competing with the Roman Church for supremacy in Western Europe—were overrun.

Though this section focuses on the church of the West, we must not forget that there was also apostasy and persecution of the church of the East.

DID THE MEDIEVAL ROMAN CHURCH PERSECUTE? Yes. More believers died for their religious convictions under persecutions, such as the Inquisition and the massacre in France on St. Bartholomew's Day, under the papal Roman Empire than by any other religious hand.

WHAT ABOUT THE "POMPOUS WORDS AGAINST THE MOST HIGH"? The leaders of this institution didn't attack God directly; in fact, they claimed to be serving Him. But they did usurp God's authority by claiming it for themselves. At the Fifth Lateran Council (1512), for instance, it was declared concerning the pope, "Thou art another God on earth." In the encyclical letter "On the Chief Duties of Christians as Citizens," dated January 10, 1890, Pope Leo VIII declared, "The supreme teacher in the Church is the Roman Pontiff. Union of minds therefore, requires ... complete submission ... to the Church and to the Roman Pontiff, as to God Himself." And on June 20, 1894, in "The Reunion of Christendom," the same pope claimed, "We hold upon this earth the place of God Almighty."

DID THIS CHURCH POWER ATTEMPT TO CHANGE GOD'S "TIMES AND LAW"? Yes. Petrus de Ancharano, for example, asserted: "'The pope can modify divine law, since his power is not of man, but of God, and he acts in the place of God upon earth'" (In Council. 373, no. 3 verso- see Lucius Ferraris, "Papa," art. 2, Prompta Bibliotheca, Venice: Gaspar Storti, 1772, 6:29).

The church went beyond simply claiming this power; it attempted to use it. The fourth of the Ten Commandments, God's law, specifies the seventh day of the week as the Sabbath—the day on which God's people are to refrain from work, the day on which they are to worship. Notice what, according to its own tenants, the church claims:

"Had she not such power, she could not have done that in which all modern religionists agree with her—she could not have substituted the observance of Sunday the first day of the week, for the observance of Saturday the seventh day, a change for which there is no Scriptural authority" (Stephen Keenan, *A Doctrinal Catechism,* 3rd American ed, New York: P.J. Kenedy, 1876, pg. 174).

In other words, this religious-political power openly admits it has attempted to change the very part of God's law that has to do with time.

The final identifying mark of the little-horn power is the "time and times and half a time" that Daniel 7 specifies for its period of dominance. The chart at the top of the next page shows the fulfillment of this part of the prophecy, confirming the identity of the little-horn power.

The book of Revelation indicates that after a brief hiatus, this power also figures prominently in last-day events.

Leopard with four heads and four wings.

> ## *"Then the saints shall be given into his hand for a time and times and half a time." —Daniel 7:25*

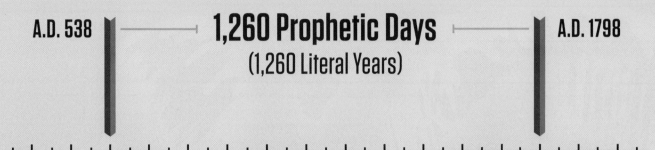

A.D. 538 ⊢———————⊣ **1,260 Prophetic Days** (1,260 Literal Years) ⊢———————⊣ **A.D. 1798**

Revelation 12:6, 14 makes it clear that Daniel's "time and times and half a time" is 1,260 symbolic days (each "time" is a 360-day year). And in the Bible, a symbolic day is a literal year (see Ezekiel 4:5, 6, and the sidebar "Daniel 9 Confirms Daniel 8," p. 33).

As for the starting and ending dates of this prophecy: The emperor of the eastern remnant of the Roman Empire decreed the bishop of Rome head of all Christian churches. This decree became effective in A.D. 538 with the defeat of the last of the Arian powers that had ruled much of the western remnants of the empire (including Italy). This 1,260-year time span saw most of the persecution that Christians have endured throughout history. It ended in 1798, when Napoleon's general Berthier took the pope prisoner and proclaimed his political rule at an end.

Like Daniel 2, chapter 7 foretells the history of the world. We see the four empires and their ultimate destruction by God's eternal kingdom. But Daniel 7 focuses on spiritual, rather than political, history. In it we see the rise of a religious-political power that works against God, attempting to change His law and actively persecuting His people.

However, Daniel's dream offers the assurance that this power's dominance won't last forever. A judgment day is coming when those who persecute will be defeated. On that day, "the greatness of the kingdoms under the whole heaven shall be given to the people, the saints of the Most High." Their kingdom, His kingdom, will be an everlasting kingdom.

Is the Little Horn "Antichrist"?

The little horn of Daniel 7 blasphemes God and persecutes His people. Could it also be the antichrist?

The Old Testament doesn't use the term *antichrist* at all, and the New Testament uses it only a few times. The term combines two Greek words: the preposition *anti* and the noun *christ*. *Anti* can carry the familiar meaning "against," but it can also mean "in place of"—which fits the biblical usage more precisely. Antichrist opposes Christ, but it does so specifically by trying to fill the position only Christ should fill in our spiritual lives. Antichrist, in other words, plays god.

Several New Testament passages help flesh out the picture of antichrist. In 2 Thessalonians 2, the apostle Paul prophesied

that this power would be instrumental in the great Christian apostasy (which both Daniel and Revelation also picture) that would occur before Christ's second coming. As predicted, during the Middle Ages, heresies, immorality, and corruption abounded in the church's power center, as well as among the various cults and offshoots that arose from it.

In one of the four Bible verses that use the term *antichrist*, the apostle John wrote that there are "many antichrists" (1 John 2:18). This term, then, doesn't point to any single person or organization. Every person or institution that tries to take the place of God, or the Messiah, or that coerces people to follow it shows that it bears the spirit of antichrist. Here the medieval Catholic Church, with its Inquisition, stands condemned—but so do those Protestants who, as soon as they had the political and military power to do so, forced their religion on the population under their control.

Revelation confirms this picture of the two basic characteristics of antichrist: the desire to displace God and the willingness to coerce religious practices (see Revelation 13). And it, too, portrays a multifaceted antichrist, picturing the "dragon," the "beast," and the "false prophet" as bearing that character. (See chapter 12. Notice that these figures are modeled on Daniel's beasts of chapter 7.) The "dragon," Satan, is the ultimate antichrist, whose spirit animates all the others.

So is the little horn antichrist? Yes—or more correctly, it's one of them, a major one. ▯

Daniel 8: A Ram, a Goat,

> **"**
>
> *For two thousand three hundred days;*
> *then the sanctuary shall be cleansed.*
> —DANIEL 8:14

and Another Little Horn
Good and Evil Go Head to Head

What You'll Learn

More details about the rise and fall of nations

- - - - - - -

Uncover more about the Little Horn power

- - - - - - -

The purpose of the Jewish sanctuary

CHAPTER 8 CONTAINS THE CENTRAL PROPHETIC VISION OF THE BOOK OF DANIEL. ALL THAT PRECEDES IT IS PRELIMINARY; ALL THAT FOLLOWS IS AN EXPLANATION OF IT. THE PROPHECY OF DANIEL 8 IS, IN FACT, THE LAST SYMBOLIC PROPHECY IN THE BOOK. THE VISIONS IN THE CHAPTERS THAT FOLLOW SIMPLY EXPLAIN AND EXPAND ON WHAT WAS REVEALED IN THIS VISION.

As in chapter 7, Daniel is the recipient of the vision—a dream that features more beasts. And like both the previous visions, this one comes in two parts: first the action in symbols and then an explanation by a heaven-sent interpreter.

Daniel wrote that, in this vision, he saw by a river near which he was standing a two-horned ram that pushed westward, northward, and southward. He said no beast could "withstand" this ram. He "did according to his will and became great" (v. 4).

Then a male goat with "a notable horn between his eyes" came from the west, moving so fast that he didn't touch the ground (v. 5). The ram challenged the goat, with disastrous results: The goat utterly defeated him. For a while, the goat dominated the area. Soon, however, his notable horn was broken and four horns grew in its place.

As Daniel continued to watch, he saw another horn appear on the scene, "a little horn which grew exceedingly great" (v. 9). This horn challenged heaven itself and "the Prince of the host," God's sanctuary (or temple) and its sacrifices. And, Daniel wrote, this little horn "cast truth down to the ground" (vs. 10–12).

The prophetic drama ended with a conversation. A "holy one" asked how long the little horn's battle against heaven would go on—when it would end. And a second "holy one" replied:

> "For *two thousand three hundred* days; then the sanctuary shall be cleansed" (v. 14).

Verses 13 and 14, but particularly verse 14, are the focus of this central chapter and thus of the whole book.

Gabriel's Commission

At this point the high drama had ended, but the vision had not. Daniel wrote that while he was trying to fathom what he had seen, he heard someone commission the angel Gabriel to "make this man understand the vision" (v. 16).

Gabriel began his explanation by telling Daniel the time this vision concerned: "the time of the end," "the latter time of the indignation" (vs. 17, 19). Then he began to identify the actors in the drama—and he couldn't have been more specific:

> "The ram which you saw, having the two horns—they are the kings of Media and Persia. And the male goat is the kingdom of Greece. The large horn that is between its eyes is the first king. As for the broken horn and the four that stood up in its place, four kingdoms shall arise out of that nation, but not with its power" (vs. 20–22).

A "beast" in Bible prophecy represents a political power.

Gabriel is also the angelic being who appeared to Mary and revealed she would give birth to the Messiah.

As in the vision of the previous chapter, the animals here represent empires. In describing the two animals of chapter 8, Daniel gave a pocket history of the empires they represent. He said the ram that represented Medo-Persia had two horns, one of which "was higher than the other, and the higher one came up last" (verse 3).

Remember: The horn that was "higher than the other" is a similar symbol of the bear in chapter 7 that "was raised up on one side" (v. 5).

The Medes attained regional power before the Persians did. But the Persians soon overtook them and assumed the superior position in the empire.

Daniel's description of the Greek Empire is just as concise—and just as accurate. The goat with the notable horn came from the west, traveling so fast his feet didn't touch the ground (chapter 8:5).

Gabriel said, "The large horn that is between its eyes"—the horn that was broken off when the goat was at the peak of its strength—"is the first king" (8:21; 8:8). This represents Alexander the Great, who, having founded the Greek Empire, died while still in his prime. The four horns that arose in his place are "four kingdoms [that] shall arise out of that nation, but not with its power" (verse 22).

These horns represent the Cassandrian, Lysimachian, Ptolemaic, and Seleucid kingdoms within the Greek Empire, which were established by Alexander's generals after his death.

> **Remember:** The scene here reminds us of the portrayal of speed in chapter 7—the leopard that had four wings.

Why the Differences?

As you've probably noticed, there are strong parallels between Daniel 8 and Daniel 2 and 7. (See also the chart on page 37.) But there are also enough differences to raise some questions ...

FIRST, WHY DOES THE VISION OF DANIEL 8 BEGIN WITH MEDO-PERSIA AND NOT BABYLON? The answer lies in the fact that by the time God gave Daniel the vision of chapter 8, Medo-Persia was already casting its shadow over Babylon, whose rule was soon to end.

SECOND, WHY ARE THE NATIONS REPRESENTED BY DOMESTIC ANIMALS (RAMS, GOATS) IN CHAPTER 8 WHEN CHAPTER 7 PICTURED THESE EMPIRES AS CARNIVOROUS BEASTS? Notice that the character of these creatures hasn't changed—they're still aggressive and domineering (see vs. 4, 7). But the focus of this chapter is on the sanctuary, God's temple. Rams and goats were sanctuary animals used as sacrifices in temple services. Their use here emphasizes the fact that God's place of worship plays a major role in this chapter.

THIRD, WHY DOES THIS VISION JUMP DIRECTLY FROM THE GREEK EMPIRE TO THE LITTLE HORN POWER, SKIPPING OVER ROME FROM DANIEL 2 AND DANIEL 7? To begin, we must observe that, just like the preceding two visions, this dream reaches all the way from Daniel's time to the end of the world

(see vs. 17, 19). Next, we must note that in each of the preceding visions, the fourth power continues on in one form or another to the end of time: In chapter 2, the iron of the legs is diluted with clay in the feet, but it's still there. And the little horn in chapter 7 wouldn't be much of a threat if the beast from whose head it arose were dead.

In other words, both the beast in Daniel 7 and its horn—pagan and Christian Rome—have the same character and carry on the same activities; that is, aggression against God and His people. They both do the work of antichrist. Chapter 7 portrays that antichrist role through the little horn. That's why God chose to use the same symbol in chapter 8—*but in this prophecy the horn represents both phases of the world's fourth great power up to the time of its destruction.* Like Daniel 7's fourth beast, Daniel 8's little horn is "fierce" and "mighty" and destroys "many" (8:23–25; 7:7, 19, 23). And like the little horn in Daniel 7, Daniel 8's little horn becomes great (8:9; 7:20). He magnifies himself in his heart (8:25; 7:8, 25) and persecutes the saints (8:24; 7:21, 25).

Investigating the Little Horn

Daniel 8 adds even more detail about the little horn's activities and its intentions, making its identity as antichrist even more apparent.

In the first place, Daniel ties the little horn to the original antichrist, Satan himself, who caused some of the angels to fall into sin (compare verses 10 and 11 with Isaiah 14:12–14; Revelation 1:20; 12:4, 7–9).

In its description of the little horn's opposition to the "Prince of the host" and the sanctuary and its services (the daily sacrifices, etc.), Daniel 8 sees the future work of both pagan

> **Remember:** The term antichrist can carry the familiar meaning "against," but it can also mean "in place of"—which fits the biblical usage here more precisely.

and Christian Rome. Pagan Rome literally destroyed God's earthly sanctuary, the temple in Jerusalem, when it put down the Jewish rebellion in A.D. 70. It was also responsible for Jesus' crucifixion and for later persecutions of His followers.

Ancient Greek Corinthian helmet.
Molded out of bronze.

Clockwise: Alexander
the Great ancient Greek
Tetradrachm, circa 315
B.C. Darius II King of
Persia. Facing page:
The two-horned ram
and the male goat.

Unlike pagan Rome, Christian Rome's opposition to God, His sanctuary, and His people was often more subtle—though, of course, Christian Rome did carry out a vigorous and very literal persecution of believers.

Some statements in chapter 8 make it clear that this power worked through deception: "He cast truth down to the ground," "through his cunning he shall cause deceit to prosper under his hand" (vs. 12, 25). Basically, Christian Rome's deceit involved counterfeiting ...

- **It substituted a counterfeit Sabbath** for the Sabbath of God's Ten Commandments (see pg. 20).
- **It substituted a counterfeit system of priests and saints** for Christ's mediation on our behalf (compare 1 Timothy 2:5).
- **It substituted a counterfeit sacrifice** for the sacrifice of Christ. (It claims that the daily mass is "one and the same Sacrifice as that of the cross" [See Catechism of the Council of Trent for Parish Priests, John A. McHugh and Charles J. Calla n, trans. New York: Joseph F. Wagner, Inc., 1934, 258, 259.], while the Bible emphasizes that Christ's death on the cross was a one-time event. See Hebrews 9:25–28.)
- **It substituted a counterfeit gospel** for the true gospel, making our salvation a matter of works— of pilgrimages and penances and indulgences—rather than of resting in faith in what Christ has done for us.

The Little Horn's End

The vision of Daniel 8 ends on a similar note to that of the visions in Daniel chapters 2 and 7. Like the statue of chapter 2, the little horn is "broken without human hand" (8:25). Verse 14, the central verse of both the chapter and the book, explains that the little horn's depredations end with the "cleansing" of the sanctuary—or as other versions translate it, the "restoring" of the sanctuary.

These words carry a complex of ideas. The sanctuary was the place of mediation, of salvation (see sidebar on next page). The "restoring" of the sanctuary implies that it is once again functioning as God originally intended it to run—that the deceptions of the little horn have been unmasked, the antichrist having been unveiled, and that people are turning to Christ as their mediator; they've found again the gospel of righteousness by faith.

The "cleansing" of the sanctuary implies the end-time fulfillment in real life of an ancient Hebrew ceremony. God gave the sanctuary and its sacrificial system to Israel as a living illustration of His plan for saving sinners from death. This system of worship culminated in a special service that took place on the Day of Atonement (see Leviticus 16). On that day, the sanctuary—and by implication, its worshipers—was to be cleansed from all the sins people had confessed there

The Ark of the Covenant.

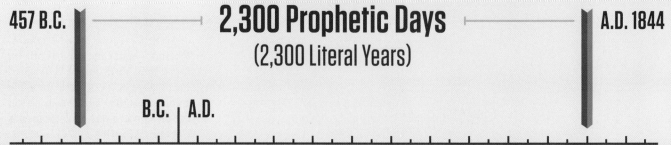

457 B.C. | **2,300 Prophetic Days** (2,300 Literal Years) | **A.D. 1844**

B.C. | A.D.

Daniel 8:14: *"For two thousand three hundred days; then the sanctuary shall be cleansed."*

This prophetic period began in 457 B.C. with Persian Emperor Artaxerxes' decree authorizing the rebuilding of Jerusalem. It stretched to 1844—a year that was to see the beginning of the cleansing, or "restoration," of the heavenly sanctuary and a change in Christ's ministry there.

through the previous year. On that day, no one was to work; all were to participate in the service. Anyone who ignored the service was deemed to have thereby declared that he or she had no need of God and was no longer considered one of His people, no longer a part of Israel. In other words, this day of cleansing was also a day of judgment.

As the New Testament book of Hebrews points out, these Old Testament services reveal Christ's ministry for us today. The Day of Atonement, which ended the religious year for the Israelites, speaks to us of the Day of Judgment that will end this world's history. Daniel chapter 7 says that it is this judgment that will bring the little horn—antichrist—to an end, free God's people from evil, and place them in His eternal kingdom.

The symbolic part of the vision of chapter 8 ends with a question and an answer. The question is: How long is it going to be until that restoration, that cleansing? The answer is quite specific: "Two thousand three hundred evening-mornings" (v. 14).

As this chapter closes, Gabriel confirms the accuracy of this prophecy. He says, "The vision of the evenings and mornings which was told is true" (v. 26). He's about to explain this to Daniel, when Daniel, perhaps overcome at the thought that justice won't be done until "many days in the future" (v. 26), faints. So the chapter ends with the words, "I was astonished by the vision, but no one understood it" (v. 27), which was Daniel's way of saying, "To be continued ..." Chapter 9 will unlock the mystery of the 2,300 days of Daniel 8:14. ▯

> The Day of Atonement and the sanctuary service are worth learning about because they are symbols of the work of Jesus Christ.

What Is the Sanctuary?

The whole book of Daniel centers on the statement in chapter 8:14: "For two thousand three hundred days; then the sanctuary shall be cleansed."

Just what is this "sanctuary"?

At the same time God gave Moses the Ten Commandments, He gave him plans for a portable structure that was to be the center for Israel's worship (see Exodus 25). God also told Moses what services were to be carried out in this building and in the temple that succeeded it when Israel eventually settled in Palestine. Through these services, He intended people to learn about His plan for saving them from sin and its ultimate consequence, eternal death.

As Daniel 9 shows, however, the prophecy of chapter 8:14 extends well into the 19th century. Neither Israel's wilderness sanctuary nor its permanent temples existed at that time. Obviously, then, God had something else in mind—and the New Testament book of Hebrews tells us what.

Hebrews says that none of Israel's services could actually clear the worshipers' consciences before God (Hebrews 9:9). They were merely copies (or illustrations) of Christ's work to save sinners—which was to be carried out in the true sanctuary, which is in heaven (see 9:11, 23). It is this heavenly sanctuary to which Daniel 8:14 speaks.

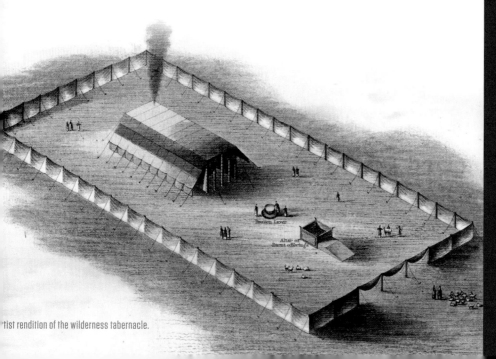

Brazen Laver

Altar of
burnt offering

An artist rendition of the wilderness tabernacle.

Daniel 9
Messiah the Prince
Daniel Witnesses Christ's First Advent

What You'll Learn

How Daniel pinpoints the first coming of Jesus

- - - - - - -

What was to become of the Jewish nation and temple after Christ

- - - - - - -

How Daniel 9 confirms Daniel 8

- - - - - - -

What happened in 1844

"Three Wise Men." Steve Bridger.

❝❞

And he informed me, and talked with me, and said, "O Daniel, I have now come forth to give you skill to understand."

—DANIEL 9:22

DANIEL 9 CONTAINS WHAT MANY BELIEVERS CONSIDER TO BE THE MOST SUBLIME PROPHECY OF THE OLD TESTAMENT—A PROPHECY OF THE MESSIAH, JESUS CHRIST. AMAZINGLY, NOT ONLY DID THIS PROPHECY LAY OUT THE PURPOSE OF HIS INCARNATION, BUT IT ALSO SPECIFIED WHEN HIS MINISTRY WOULD BEGIN AND END.

The prophecy of Daniel 9 differs significantly from those of chapters 2, 7, and 8. In this chapter, there are no symbols—no statues and stones, no beasts and horns, no "times" or "evening-mornings." The language, while still rather cryptic in places, is to be taken literally.

In Daniel 9, the angel Gabriel continues his explanation of the symbolic vision given in chapter 8—an explanation that had been interrupted when Daniel passed out.

Remember that Daniel 8:13 and 14 contain the conclusion and climax of that chapter's vision. It is also the central point of Daniel's book. Daniel wrote that when this vision ended, Gabriel was ordered to "make this man understand the vision" (8:16).

Gabriel proceeded with an explanation of the beasts and horns, but when he tried to explain the 2,300 "evenings and mornings" (v. 26), Daniel passed out. Gabriel had only partially fulfilled his commission to explain the vision to Daniel.

The last vision Daniel had seen said that 2,300 "evening-mornings [days]" would pass till the sanctuary would be restored (8:14). Daniel probably knew that in symbolic prophecy, days represent years. So he must have been wondering if that prophecy meant that God had changed His mind since Jeremiah's time—in other words, did it mean that Jerusalem and the temple would continue to lie desolate for 23 more centuries?

Daniel knew that earlier prophets had warned that the sinful unfaithfulness of God's people would bring about Jerusalem's destruction. He also knew that those same prophets had said that Jerusalem would be restored when God's people repented. So, anxious to see God's people and the temple restored, Daniel prayed a beautiful prayer of confession and repentance that fills most of chapter 9. (Please take the time to read it for yourself!)

God responded to Daniel's prayer quickly: "While I was speaking in prayer, the man Gabriel ... reached me" (v. 21). This, of course, was the same Gabriel who had been helping Daniel understand the vision of chapter 8. Daniel wrote that Gabriel told him he had again been commissioned to give him "skill to understand ... the vision" (v. 22, 23). There is no vision in chapter 9, so Gabriel is clearly referring to the vision of chapter 8, which he had not yet fully explained. These two chapters are linked—particularly in the time elements involved.

Gabriel's Explanation

Four compact but loaded verses—chapter 9:24-27—contain Gabriel's explanation. Verse 24 serves as an introduction to the ideas contained in the next three verses. It specifies the time involved and what God planned to achieve during that time.

Gabriel started his explanation by referring to a period of "seventy weeks," or as the Bible margins explain, "seventy sevens." During this period the city, its wall, and its temple would be rebuilt and the Messiah would come. However, the rebuilding of the temple alone took about four years (see Ezra 4:24–5:2; 6:15), which would be 208 weeks, so it's clear that something more than 70 literal weeks was involved.

Sure enough, the Hebrew in which Daniel wrote this phrase implies what the Revised Standard Version translates as "seventy weeks of years." Daniel had been concerned about Jeremiah's "seventy years," but Gabriel turned his attention to a period seven times longer— "seventy weeks of years," or 490 years.

In biblical prophetic language, a day equals one year.

Why Did Daniel Pass Out? *About 10 years passed between the vision of Daniel 8 and the one in chapter 9. By that time, it had been a little more than 45 years since Nebuchadnezzar had destroyed Jerusalem and its temple and had taken its people captive to Babylon. This caused Daniel to feel very distressed. He had understood from the book of Jeremiah that the "desolations of Jerusalem" would last 70 years (9:2). But that time was nearly completed, and no actions were being taken to rebuild the house of God or Jerusalem.*

The rest of verse 24 tells what was to happen during that 490 years:

FIRST, THAT TIME WAS TO BE A PRO-BATIONARY PERIOD FOR THE JEWS. Their sin in going their own way rather than doing what God asked them to do had resulted in the destruction of their city and temple by the Babylonians. Now, in Daniel 9:24, God said He would give them one more chance to fulfill the role He had originally planned for them.

SECOND, SOMETHING SPECIAL WAS TO BE DONE "TO FINISH THE TRANSGRESSION, TO MAKE AN END OF SINS, TO MAKE RECONCILIATION FOR INIQUITY, TO BRING IN EVERLASTING RIGHTEOUSNESS." This is actually a picture of the work of Jesus—particularly His death and His ministry as the High Priest in the heavenly sanctuary, both of which are essential parts of God's plan to eradicate sin.

> *Remember: The heavenly sanctuary and Jesus' ministry were important parts of the prophecy in chapter 8.*

THIRD, THE FULFILLMENT OF THIS PART OF GABRIEL'S EXPLANATION WAS TO "SEAL UP VISION AND PROPHECY," confirming our faith in the accuracy of what Daniel wrote—particularly the prophecy of chapter 8.

AND FOURTH, THIS PERIOD WAS TO SEE THE ANOINTING OF THE "MOST HOLY." This term refers to the heavenly sanctuary. At His ascension, Jesus began His ministry for His people in that heavenly sanctuary, as the book of Hebrews makes clear.

Hebrews 9 indicates that Jesus began His ministry by inaugurating, or "anointing," that sanctuary—much as Moses inaugurated the earthly sanctuary before Aaron started his work as high priest in it.

Christ and Antichrist

Daniel 9:25–27 gives more details on the timing of Jesus' earthly ministry and death. These verses also reveal what was to happen to the city and temple that Daniel was so concerned about. And they relate all this to the antichrist power, which chapters 7 and 8 spoke about.

Each of these three verses divides into two parts. The first half deals with the time element and the Messiah, and the

> **The horn powers of chapters 7 and 8 are the antichrist.**

second half deals with the city, the sanctuary, and the antichrist, or desolator. This kind of alternation between two themes was a regular characteristic of Hebrew literature.

Verse 25 specifies the starting point for the time period involved: "the going forth of the command to restore and build Jerusalem." There were three decrees by kings of the Persian Empire that provided for the return of the Jews to their land and for the restoration of Jerusalem. The decree that most closely fulfilled Gabriel's specification was the one Artaxerxes issued in 457 B.C.

Verse 25 then goes on to say that from this starting point "until Messiah the Prince, there shall be seven weeks and sixty-two weeks"—a total of 69 weeks.

The New Testament clearly and repeatedly says that Jesus is the Messiah. And the Gospel of Luke tells us specifically when He was anointed. It was at His baptism, when God Himself announced Jesus' role and when the Holy Spirit "anointed" Him by descending on Him in the form of a dove (see Luke 3:21, 22).

Luke not only tells us how Jesus was anointed, but he also tells us when Jesus was anointed. John the Baptist began his ministry "in the fifteenth year of the reign of Tiberius Caesar, Pontius Pilate being governor of Judea" (v. 1), and Jesus was baptized soon after. That puts His baptism in A.D. 27—exactly 483 years (69 "weeks of years") after 457 B.C.!

The next two verses in Gabriel's explanation say,

> "After the **sixty-two weeks** Messiah shall be cut off, but not for Himself; … Then He shall confirm a covenant with many for one week; but in the middle of the week He shall bring an end to sacrifice and offering" (Daniel 9: 26, 27).

This 62-week period—which follows the seven-week period—ended with Jesus' baptism. Verse 26 then says that sometime after His baptism, Jesus would be cut off—that is, killed.

The next verse is even more specific: "In the middle of the week He shall bring an end to sacrifice and offering." Jesus' earthly ministry ended with His crucifixion in A.D. 31—three-and-a-half years after it began at His baptism. Jesus died in the middle of the seventieth "week" of Daniel's prophecy. And just as Gabriel told Daniel, His death brought an end to "sacrifice and offering" (see Hebrews 10:4–9).

When Jesus died, the curtain in the temple dividing the holy and most holy compartments was ripped in two, from top to bottom, signifying the end of the sacrificial system. {See chart on facing page.}

No Longer His Nation

Gabriel's explanation doesn't specify an event that would mark the end of the 490 years, but verse 24 does indicate that those years were a probationary period for the Jewish nation as God's special people. Unfortunately, instead of fulfilling

> ## *"Seventy weeks of years are decreed concerning your people and your Holy city."* —Daniel 9:24

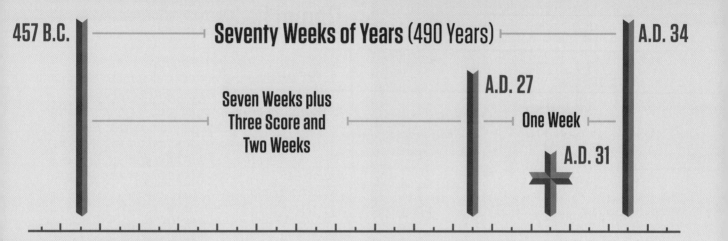

457 B.C. ——— **Seventy Weeks of Years (490 Years)** ——— **A.D. 34**

Seven Weeks plus Three Score and Two Weeks

A.D. 27

One Week

A.D. 31

Artaxerxes' decree authorizing the rebuilding of Jerusalem (457 B.C.) marks the beginning of this prophetic time period. In A.D. 27, at the beginning of the final seven years of the "seventy weeks of years," Jesus was baptized and His public ministry as the Messiah began. In the middle of the final week, in A.D. 31, He was crucified ("cut off," making "an end to sacrifice and offering"). And in A.D. 34, the governing council of the Jews confirmed their rejection of Christ by condemning Steven to death—thus ending their probationary time period. From that point on, the Christian church broadened its mission, reaching out to the Gentiles as well as Jews.

ospective tomb of Artaxerxes I in Naqsh-e Rustam, Iran.

God's desire that they serve as His emissaries to the world, and particularly, instead of accepting His Son, Jesus, the Messiah, when He came, they delivered Him to the Romans for execution.

For three-and-a-half years after Jesus' death, His disciples continued to preach mainly to the Jews. But then the official council of the Jewish nation, the Sanhedrin, began a persecution of the Christians who lived in Jerusalem; they initiated this persecution by stoning to death the deacon Stephen. Consequently, the Christians scattered—and began to take the good news to the Gentiles instead. The execution of Stephen, then, which occurred about A.D. 34, marks the end of the 490 years.

> Scholars believe that the stoning of Stephen by Jewish leaders confirms the accuracy of the 490-year prophecy.

Jesus had preached to the Jews for three-and-a-half years in person and for another three-and-a-half years through His disciples. He had confirmed God's special covenant with them for a "week"—or seven years (v. 27). Now the gospel was being preached to the Gentiles too, and people—Gentiles and Jews alike—would become God's "nation," not because of their ethnic background, but because of their relationship with Jesus.

And what became of the city of Jerusalem and the antichrist—the desolator? Verse 25 says that the city would be rebuilt, but "in troublesome times," which it was (see the books of Ezra and Nehemiah). Then "the people of the prince who is to come shall destroy the city and the sanctuary [or temple]. ... And on the wing of abominations shall be one who makes desolate" (vs. 26, 27). Jesus spoke of this "desolating sacrilege" of Daniel's prophecy, and warned, "When you see Jerusalem surrounded by armies, then know that its desolation has come near" (Luke 21:20; Matthew 24:15).

Like Daniel 7 and 8, chapter 9 ends on a more satisfying note. The conclusion of Daniel 9 says that God's purpose will eventually prevail; the "decreed end" will ultimately be "poured out on the desolator," as the Revised Standard Version translates verse 27. God will rescue those who have trusted in Him, and He will build a New Jerusalem that will never be destroyed. ◘

The message of the 2,300-day prophecy centers on Christ's ministry of forgiving sins in the heavenly sanctuary. Since 1844 this message was to be proclaimed to all the world.

Daniel 9 Confirms Daniel 8

Gabriel gave the explanation in chapter 9 to help Daniel understand the vision of chapter 8. It was the time element in the vision that Daniel didn't understand. What does chapter 9 tell us that throws light on chapter 8?

First, chapter 9 gives the starting point for the 2,300 "evening-mornings" of chapter 8:14. Daniel 9:24 says, "Seventy weeks are determined." These 70 weeks are cut off from a larger quantity of time—the 2,300 "evening-mornings." Since no starting point was given for that period, we can comfortably presume that both start at the same point—457 B.C.—otherwise, Gabriel's explanation would not help.

Second, Daniel 9 confirms that the 2,300 evening-mornings, or days, of chapter 8 are symbols that represent literal years. Both the language and the content of Daniel 9 indicate that its "seventy weeks" are years. If these 490 years are cut off from the 2,300 evening-mornings, then the latter must be years also. One could not cut 490 years out of 2,300 literal days!

Scholars agree that seventy weeks, 70 times 7, equals 490 years in prophecy.

So the 2,300 evening-mornings prophecy began in 457 B.C. and extended for 2,300 literal years. Consequently, it reached its conclusion in A.D. 1844. That's when Jesus' ministry as a high priest in the heavenly sanctuary began to be restored to prominence again. That's when He began His Day of Atonement for the cleansing of the heavenly sanctuary. That's when God's final judgment began.

Finally, Daniel 9:24 says that the 490-year prophecy is to "seal up vision and prophecy." It does just that for the 2,300-year prophecy of chapter 8. Jesus began His ministry as the Messiah, the anointed one, right when Daniel 9 said He would. And His death came right in the middle of the last seven of those 490 years. Thus the accuracy of the 70-week prophecy puts the seal of dependability on the larger 2,300-day prophecy.

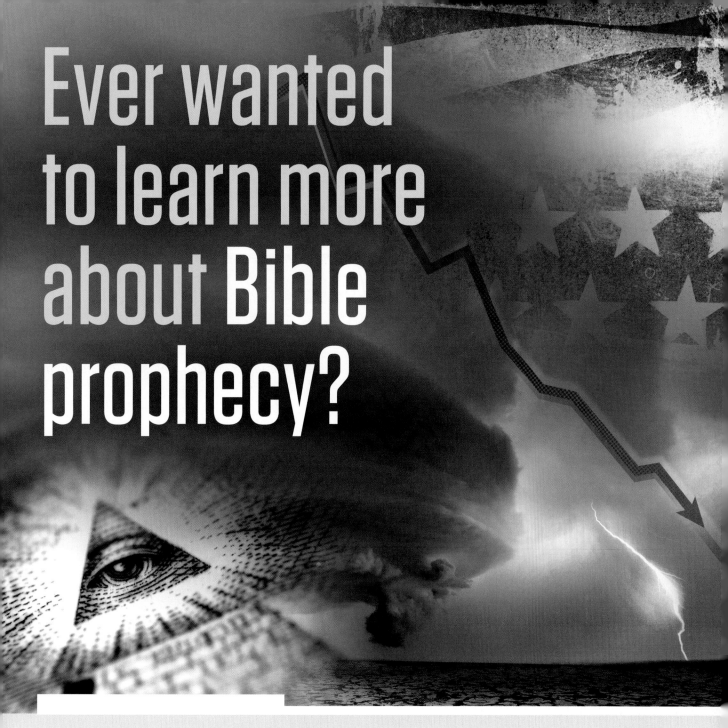

Ever wanted to learn more about Bible prophecy?

Then visit the number 1 Bible prophecy resource on the web!

BIBLE PROPHECY TRUTH is a powerful, simple-to-use website resource designed to help people from every background to clearly understand the major prophecies of Scripture—including more in-depth study of Daniel and Revelation—and how it affects you today! If you ever thought the mark of the beast, Armageddon, the tribulation, and other Bible topics were next to impossible to understand for yourself, Bible Prophecy Truth gives you all the keys you need to unlock these amazing prophecy secrets. Yes ... you can know the future! Visit **bibleprophecytruth.com** today.

BIBLEPROPHECYTRUTH.com

Daniel 10–12: Daniel's Last Prophecy

A Time of Trouble, A Final Deliverance

> " *Let no one deceive you by any means; for that Day will not come unless the falling away comes first, and the man of sin is revealed, the son of perdition.*
> —2 THESSALONIANS 2:3

What You'll Learn

More details on the antichrist

- - - - - - -

How the Messiah gains victory after being "cut off"

- - - - - - -

Details of the Messiah's eventual rescue of God's people in the last days

DANIEL 10 THROUGH 12 FORM A UNIT. GIVEN IN LITERAL BUT SOMEWHAT CRYPTIC TERMS, IT COVERS MUCH THE SAME GROUND AS THE REST OF DANIEL'S VISIONS—ENDING WITH A PROMISE THAT WILL GIVE YOU STRENGTH AND FAITH!

Chapter 10 in Daniel serves as an introduction to this final prophecy, while chapters 11 and 12 contain the prophecy itself. Chapter 11 begins with a sketch of Middle Eastern history from Cyrus's time to that of Alexander the Great. It becomes more detailed as it deals with the powers that followed Alexander, and it closes with events that take place during the very last days of earth's history.

Differing Interpretations

Just how this prophecy covers events between the Greek Empire and the end of time, however, is a matter of some dispute among Christian interpreters.

1. Some believe that following the detailed section on Alexander's successors (chapter 11:5–13), the prophecy becomes "sketch like," only outlining the character and work of the antichrist power through the Middle Ages and on to the end.

2. Others say the prophecy continues on in detail, picturing the career of Antiochus Epiphanes—a notorious persecutor of the Jews—and covering the Maccabean revolt that ended his rule over Judea. Many of these interpreters say that Epiphanes serves as a type, or example, of the antichrist who plays such a large role in the events that conclude with Armageddon.

We don't have room to offer an in-depth analysis of every view, so let's touch on the highlights of this chapter and then leave you to study further if you like.

In the midst
of Daniel's
sometimes
frightening
and mysterious
prophecies,
the promise of
the Messiah's
return brings
hope and peace
to those who
believe.

A Prince and the Kings

Chapter 10 begins with a two-verse description of "a certain man clothed in linen" (vs. 5, 6). Compare this description and the reaction of Daniel and his companions (v. 7) to the description of Jesus in Revelation 1:13–15 and in Paul's conversion experience (Acts 9:3–7). Obviously, in his vision of "Michael," the "prince" of the Jews, Daniel encountered Jesus Himself. Jesus appears again in the vision as "Michael," the prince of the Jews (Daniel 10:13, 21, 12:1; see also 9:25, 26). Chapter 10 goes on to reveal that history involves more than human striving. Behind the scenes, spiritual powers are at work to direct events on earth for good or evil (10:13, 20).

Daniel 11:2–4 says that after the "three more kings" who were to follow Cyrus on the throne of Persia, there would be a fourth king—richer and stronger than them all—who would fight with Greece. This is a reference to Xerxes. Verse 3 speaks of "a mighty king," a reference to Alexander the Great, and verse 4 speaks of the fourfold division of his kingdom that earlier visions of Daniel had also predicted.

> Michael also appears in the Bible as an archangel, but He is no more an angel than is Jesus simply a man.

> Daniel saw the vision of chapter 11 during Cyrus's reign in 539–530 B.C.

Verses 5 and 6 begin the detailed section of the prophecy. In Old Testament times, God's people were the Jews, who lived in Palestine. "The king of the South," then, was Egypt—the major power south of Palestine. And "the king of the North" was, variously, Babylon, Syria, and Rome—powers that approached the land of the Jews from the north and that were equally enemies of God and His people.

In New Testament times, God's new people, the Christian church, were no longer geographically centered—so we should expect the kings of the North and the South to be the *religious* equivalents of the old enemies. In other words, we shouldn't try to define the enemies of the church in terms of geography.

Machiavellian Schemes

Daniel 11:5 then refers to Ptolemy I of Egypt and Seleucus I of Syria. And verse 6 tells of the doomed attempt to establish peace between these two kingdoms by the marriage of Ptolemy II's daughter, Berenice, to Antiochus II of Syria—who was already married. When Ptolemy II died, Antiochus II took back his first wife, who then engineered the death of Berenice, her child, and all her attendants.

More detailed prophecy of this nature follows through much of Daniel 11. But note in this portion of the prophecy references to "a vile person" (v. 21), "the prince of the covenant" (v. 22), "damage" done to "the holy covenant" (vs. 28, 30), and the "abomination of desolation" (v. 31)—all terms signifying the antichrist power that opposes God's people in the last days.

As the vision progresses, the portrait of the antichrist power becomes increasingly clear. Verse 36 says, "Then the king ... shall exalt and magnify himself above every god, shall speak blasphemies against the God of gods." This line parallels what

When Ptolemy II died, Antiochus II took back his first wife, who then engineered the death of Berenice, her child, and all her attendants.

chapters 7 and 8 said about the little horn power. And as to the first line, compare it to what Paul wrote in 2 Thessalonians 2:3, 4, about the antichrist yet to come:

> "Let no one deceive you by any means; for that Day will not come unless the falling away comes first, and the man of sin is revealed, the son of perdition, who opposes and exalts himself above all that is called God or that is worshiped, so that he sits as God in the temple of God, showing himself that he is God."

As Daniel 11 concludes, it tells of the antichrist's attack on God's people, symbolized by his military foray against them: "He shall go out with great fury to destroy and annihilate many. And he shall plant the tents of his palace between the seas and the glorious holy mountain" (vs. 44, 45). The antichrist power would plant his forces between the Mediterranean and the "mountain" in Jerusalem on which the temple was built—in Israel, in other words. But remember, in the New Testament era, an attack on "Israel" represents an attack on the church, God's worldwide people.

But there is hope! As did all Daniel's previous visions, this one also ends with the destruction of this power that fights against God and His people: "He shall come to his end, and no one will help him" (11:45). How? "Michael shall stand up" (12:1) to take action. And though "there shall be a time of trouble, such as never was since there was a nation," "at that time your [Daniel's] people shall be delivered, everyone who is found written in the book."

Daniel 12 contains some "appendices" (which aren't dealt with here), but the main part of this prophecy closes with promises of a resurrection to come and with an assurance that the saints will enjoy God's kingdom forever (vs. 2, 3). ▫

What does this mean for you today?

Daniel's visions picture a continuous struggle on the earth. Nations rise against nations, and tyrants direct people's attention and worship away from God to themselves. But through it all, behind the scenes, God is also constantly at work. When Jesus pictured times of trouble like these, He said: "He who endures to the end will be saved" (Matthew 10:22). That sums up Daniel's message too. We prepare to endure the troubles of the end time by learning to trust God now.

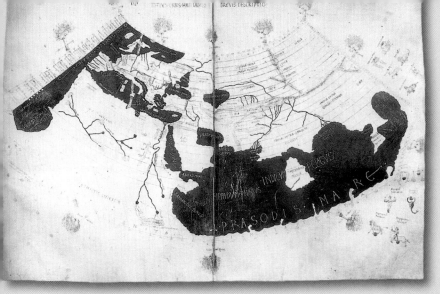

A 15th-century manuscript copy of the Ptolemy world map, reconstituted from Ptolemy's Geographia (circa 150), indicating the countries of Serica and Sinae (China) at the extreme east, beyond the island of Taprobane (Sri Lanka) and the Aurea Chersonesus (Malay Peninsula).

This clay cylinder is inscribed in Babylonian cuneiform and is an account by Cyrus, king of Persia (559–530 B.C.), of his conquest of Babylon in 539 B.C. and capture of Nabonidus, the last Babylonian king. British Museum.

Damaged Roman copy of a bust of Seleucus I, Louvre.

Parallels in Daniel's Visions

Chapter 2	Chapter 7	Chapter 8	Chapters 11, 12
BABYLON Gold head (verses 37, 38)	**BABYLON** Lion (verse 4)		
PERSIA Silver chest (verse 39)	**PERSIA** Bear with one shoulder higher (verse 5)	**PERSIA** Ram with one horn higher (verses 3, 20)	**PERSIA** King (11:2)
GREECE Brass thighs (verse 39)	**GREECE** Leopard with four heads (verses 5, 8, 21)	**GREECE** He-goat with large horn, horn broken, four horns (verses 5, 8, 21)	**GREECE** Mighty king, kingdom broken into four parts (11:3, 4)
ROME Empire—legs of iron (verse 40) Divided—feet of iron and clay (verses 41-43)	**ROME** Empire—beast with iron teeth (verses 7, 23); Divided (verse 24); Little horn opposes God and His people (verses 21, 24, 25)	**ROME** Empire (verse 9) Little horn opposes God and His people (verses 9-12, 23-25)	**ROME** Opposes God and His people (11:31)
KINGDOM OF GOD Earthly power broken without hands (verse 45) Stone becomes a mountain (verses 44, 45)	**KINGDOM OF GOD** Dominion to the saints (verses 44, 45)	**KINGDOM OF GOD** Earthly power broken without hands (verse 25)	**KINGDOM OF GOD** God's people delivered (Chapter 12:1-3)

The Book of
Revelation

John the Revelator on the island of Patmos.

Introduction to the Book of Revelation
The Revelation of Jesus Christ

" "

Now I tell you before it comes, that when it does come to pass, you may believe.
—JOHN 13:19

What You'll Learn

Who wrote this mysterious prophetic book

Why Revelation is part of the Bible

How the book of Revelation applies to you today

THE BOOK OF REVELATION FEATURES STRANGE AND VIOLENT IMAGERY: A DRAGON, A BEAST, A HARLOT, LOCUSTS THAT STING LIKE SCORPIONS, BLOOD, EARTHQUAKES, HAILSTORMS, AND LAKES OF FIRE. AT TIMES, IT CAN SEEM DISCOURAGING AND EVEN A LITTLE REPULSIVE. BUT ITS DEPICTION OF A NEW EARTH—IN WHICH SORROW AND PAIN AND DEATH DO NOT EXIST—OFFERS HOPE FOR EVERY READER SEEKING UNDERSTANDING.

Who Was John the Revelator?

During the latter part of his reign, the Roman emperor Domitian (A.D. 81–96) tried to establish his claim to deity by forcing his subjects to worship him. Refusal brought punishment, including exile and execution.

Domitian's persecutions brought Christianity face to face with the fiercest external threat it had known. Its resources were limited, and of the original leadership—the 12 apostles—only one, John, remained. Worse, he had been exiled to the rocky, barren Island of Patmos, awaiting the fate of other believers. More than ever, the church needed encouragement.

Revelation was written around A.D. 90.

God gave John visions that fill this book to meet that need. Revelation places the troubles Christians face in a bigger picture of the struggle between good and evil, and particularly, of the outcome of that struggle. In his introduction to the book, John called it "the Revelation of Jesus Christ, which God gave Him to show His servants—things which must shortly take place" (chapter 1:1). In other words, the encouragement Revelation supplies comes in its picture of the future.

Although John wrote down the visions in this book, its title is actually "The Revelation of Jesus Christ."

Still, much of that picture is pretty dark. Revelation's first half portrays the Christian church's spiritual decline, which the apostle Paul also wrote about in 2 Thessalonians 2:3. It's in the second half of Revelation that the real encouragement comes—a turning of the tables. God intervenes, bringing to justice the apostate Christian church and the political and economic powers with which it illicitly allied itself.

Revelation ends on a very bright note. It says that when Christ returns, He will bring a "reward" for those who have patiently endured the oppression, who have steadfastly kept "the commandments of God and the faith of Jesus" (see 22:12; 14:12). That reward? God's new creation, where He will live with the saved in a perfect world unmarred by evil.

Revelation's central message calls its readers to "hang in there." Those who remain faithful to God will face tough times. But in the end, they'll be glad they stuck it out.

Revelation's Roots

It doesn't take long for most readers to notice that Revelation resembles the Old Testament book of Daniel. Like Daniel, John's visions are full of strange creatures and other unusual imagery, which are explicitly said to be symbols representing a physical reality (e.g., 17:15, 18). And like Daniel's prophecy, Revelation is "apocalyptic" prophecy, meaning it's particularly concerned with the cosmic struggle between Satan and God. It means that this book portrays the world from the viewpoint of the final judgment, when all are either on God's side or against Him.

> The book of Revelation is deeply connected to the book of Daniel.

Revelation's imagery exhibits a strong relationship to the Old Testament. The dragon and beasts of chapter 12, for instance, are composites of the beasts of Daniel 7. Revelation also draws from Isaiah, Jeremiah, the Minor Prophets, and particularly Ezekiel—as well as from the rest of the Old Testament. Even images from the Creation story appear in it. And so do themes based on major events in the history of Israel, such as the Exodus and the ravages of Babylon, the actual and symbolic oppressor of God's people.

Revelation's use of these themes and imagery tells us that, like the rest of the New Testament, the author looks for the fulfillment of the Old Testament's end-time prophecies in the New Testament's equivalent of the nation of Israel—the Christian church. Revelation calls the church Christ's "kingdom" (1:6 NIV; cf. Exodus 19:6). As biblical scholar Hans LaRondelle notes, "This forbids any effort to apply the [Old Testament] sense of the Hebrew names and geographic places ... according to their old-covenant ethnic and local restrictions" ("Armageddon: Sixth and Seventh Plagues," *Symposium II, 383*).

In other words, Revelation's focus is fixed upon Christ and His New Testament people. Yes, John used the geography of Palestine and the names of ancient Israel's enemies—but in Revelation, these are symbols representing what the church and its modern-day persecutors will experience.

Don't Be Dogmatic

Just before His crucifixion, Jesus prophesied that one of the disciples would betray Him. Then He said, "Now I tell you before it comes, that when it does come to pass, you may believe" (John 13:19). That statement says something important about prophecy. God doesn't send prophets to satisfy our curiosity about the future. He sends them to strengthen our faith—"that when it does come to pass, you may believe."

This principle speaks to how we interpret Revelation. We can identify with some certainty how prophecy has been fulfilled in history, recognizing that it strengthens our faith in Scripture and in God's ability to accomplish His will. But when we come to the parts still to be fulfilled, humility becomes particularly important. We might be able to sense the general approach the fulfillment will likely take, but there's no room or need for dogmatism as to the specifics.

John wrote his prophecies for the believers of his day. But he meant them for us, too, on whom the end of the world is come. John pronounced a blessing on "he who reads and those who hear the words of this prophecy, and keep those things which are written in it; for the time is near" (1:3). We can share in that blessing. ℝ

Fortification walls surrounding the Monastery of St. John the Theologian in the town of Hora on Patmos Island, Greece.

Prologue	7 Churches	7 Seals	7 Trumpets	Great Controversy
(1:18) Introduction	(1:10 to 3:22) Christ counsels His church, at war, scattered in many cities.	(4:1 to 8:1) Christ shields His afflicted people.	(8:2 to 11:18) Severe judgments warn the world.	(11:19 to 14:20) Trials of the true Mother and her children.
• Testimony of Jesus. 1:2 • Blessed is he who reads. 1:3 • Behold, He is coming. 1:7 • I am the Alpha and the Omega. 1:8	• Christ walks among seven lamps. 2:1 • Tree of life. 2:7 • Open door. 3:8 • Christ sits on His Father's throne. 3:21 • New Jerusalem comes down from heaven. 3:12 • I am coming soon. 3:11	• Heaven opened. 4:1 • Rider on white horse followed by riders on variously colored horses. 6:2–8 • Souls of martyrs, under altar, ask for judgment. 6:9, 10 • White robes. 3:21 • Kings, generals, etc., ask to be killed. 6:15, 16	1. Earth, 8:7 2. Sea. 8:8, 9 3. Rivers and fountains. 8:10, 11 4. Sun, moon, and stars. 8:12 5. Darkness, bottomless pit, locusts. 9:1–11 6. River Euphrates. 9:13–21 7. Loud voices: The kingdom is Christ's! 11:15–18	• True mother, dressed in white. 12:1, 2 • Her children keep the commandments. 12:17 • Woman in the wilderness. 12:14 • Beast with 7 heads, 10 horns. 12:3; 13:1–4 • Fallen is Babylon! 13:8 • Testimony of Jesus. 12:17

Historical Half The Great Controversy in Progress

What You'll Learn

LET'S ADMIT IT: REVELATION IS A DIFFICULT BOOK TO UNDERSTAND! IT'S EVEN HARD TO KNOW ITS BASIC MEANING WITH JUST A SIMPLE READING, AS WE CAN WITH THE GOSPELS. SOMETIMES EVEN CAREFUL STUDY DOESN'T ALWAYS PRODUCE SATISFACTORY RESULTS. RECOGNIZING ITS USE OF OLD TESTAMENT IMAGERY DOES A LOT TO ILLUMINATE ITS MEANING. BUT DETERMINING THE ORGANIZATION OF THIS BOOK—ITS STRUCTURE—DOES EVEN MORE TO HELP US UNDERSTAND IT ...

The underlying structure of the book of Revelation

- - - - - - -

Deeper connections between Revelation and the Old Testament

- - - - - - -

The two halves of Revelation

Revelation's structure is based on that of Hebrew poetry. In this age, and particularly in the West, we do most of our writing in prose. We tend to think of poetry as "art" and, therefore, marginal to the more important matters of life. But that was not the case in Bible times. One-third of the Old Testament was written as poetry, as a look at one of the modern versions of the Bible will show. The prophets recorded much of their messages, which were so important to the author of Revelation, as poetry.

Like our poetry today, that of ancient Israel expressed emotions and used figurative language. Occasionally, their poetry, like ours, made use of similar sounding words. But most often, Hebrew writers constructed their poetry on other kinds of parallelism—especially parallelism of meaning or a thought. This is

"synonymous parallelism," in which the second or succeeding lines repeat the thought of the first line in different words; for example:

"Israel	does not	know,
"My people	do not	consider"
(Isaiah 1:3).*		

Or it might be "antithetical parallelism," in which the succeeding line stands in contrast to the first line; for example:

"A soft answer	turns away	wrath
But a harsh word	stirs up	anger"
(Proverbs 15:1.)		

A "chiasm" is a particular form of parallelism. In a typical chiastic structure, one thought (**A**) is presented; a second thought (**B**) is added;

* Illustrations of biblical parallelism and chiasmus come from Lee J. Gugliotta, *Handbook for Bible Study* (Hagerstown, Md.: Review and Herald, 1995), 36, 38

velation's Organization

7 Last Plagues	Fall of Babylon	Millennium	New Jerusalem	Epilogue
(15:1 to 16:21) Very severe judgments punish the world.	(17:1 to 19:10) Downfall of the false Mother.	(19:11 to 21:8) Christ enthrones His resurrected people.	(21:9 to 22:7) Christ rewards His church, at peace, gathered into one city.	(22:8-17) Conclusion
1. Earth. 16:2	• False mother, dressed in purple. 2:1	• Heaven opened. 19:11	• Christ is the eternal Lamp. 21:23	• I, Jesus, sent this testimony. 22:16
2. Sea. 16:3	• Her children are harlots. 2:7	• Rider on white horse followed by riders on white horses. 19:11-16	• Tree of life. 22:2	• Blessed is he who keeps. 22:7
3. Rivers and fountains. 16:4	• Woman in wilderness. 17:3	• Souls of martyrs, resurrected, are enthroned as judges. 20:4-6	• Gates never closed. 21:25	• Behold, I am coming soon. 22:12, 20
4. Sun, moon, and stars. 16:8, 9	• Beast with 7 heads, 10 horns. 17:3	• White robes. 19:14	• Throne of God and of the Lamb. 22:1, 3	• I am the Alpha and the Omega. 22:13
5. Darkness on the throne of the beast. 16:10, 11	• Fallen is Babylon! 18:2	• Kings, captains, etc., are killed. 19:17-21	• New Jerusalem comes down from heaven. 21:10	
6. River Euphrates. 16:12-16	• Testimony of Jesus. 19:10		• I am coming soon. 22:7	
7. A loud voice: It is done! 16:17-21				

Eschatological Half The Great Controversy Consummated

The word "chiasm" comes from chi, the name of the Greek letter X, which has the shape one might imagine a chiastic poem to have.

then follows a third thought (**B'**), which stands in some kind of parallelism—synonymous or antithetic—to (**B**); and finally, a fourth thought (**A'**) parallels in some way to (**A**), completing the structure. The following example shows a three-element chiasm:

A *"Ephraim*
B *shall not envy*
C *Judah, and*
C' *Judah*
B' *shall not harass*
A' *Ephraim"* (Isaiah 11:13).

Poetry pervades the Old Testament, and chiasms abound throughout. Consequently, it's not difficult to believe that the writer of a New Testament book so full of references to the Old Testament

Bible scholars have counted about 300 references to the Old Testament in the book of Revelation.

would also use one of its prominent literary forms to structure his own book. But the fact that this structure fits Revelation—that it works—makes this suggestion even more convincing.

The four major prophecies of Daniel parallel one another, each beginning in the prophet's time and portraying the political and religious developments that lead to the end of the world and the establishment of God's eternal kingdom.

Similarly, the first half of Revelation, its historical section, contains four major prophetic visions that begin in the prophet's time and reach to the end of the world—Christ's second coming, when God intervenes to end evil and establish His kingdom. The second half of Revelation also consists of four parts. These focus strictly on end-time ("eschatological") events, detailing the fate of those who have persisted in their rebellion against God and the "reward" of those who have remained faithful to God.

Like Daniel and 2 Thessalonians 2, Revelation presents the spiritual decline of the church. The visions of the

seven churches and seven seals tell the story of that decline. The vision of the seven trumpets are the warnings God sends to call people from that downward track to one that offers a better end. The vision of the dragon, sea beast, and land beast/false prophet reveals the roots of that decline and what those who persist in it will do to the faithful. Chapter 14—the focus of Revelation, the center of the chiasm—highlights the central issue in the cosmic battle of good and evil, the grounds of the decline. And the rest of Revelation, its eschatological half, reveals how God will deal with the unfaithful and then with the faithful. **R**

Don't be troubled by the *fact that the chapter divisions in Revelation don't fit the outline exactly. Those chapter divisions are not John's; they were added more than a thousand years after he completed his writing.*

The Seven Churches

Christianity's History

> Be faithful until death, and I will give you the crown of life. ... He who overcomes shall not be hurt by the second death.
> —REVELATION 2:10, 11

PHESIANS 4 SAYS THE CHRISTIAN CHURCH IS LIKE A BODY OF WHICH JESUS IS THE HEAD. ITS MEMBERS ARE HIS HANDS AND FEET, COMMISSIONED TO GO WHERE HE SENDS AND DO HIS WORK. ONE WOULD EXPECT, THEN, THAT JESUS WOULD BE QUITE CONCERNED ABOUT THE WELFARE OF HIS BODY, THE CHURCH. CHAPTERS 2 AND 3 OF REVELATION CONTAIN LETTERS JESUS DICTATED TO SEVEN CHURCHES IN THE ROMAN PROVINCE OF ASIA (WHAT IS NOW TURKEY)—THE CHURCHES IN EPHESUS, SMYRNA, PERGAMOS, THYATIRA, SARDIS, PHILADELPHIA, AND LAODICEA.

Follow Along: Revelation Chapters 1–5

If John, recording these letters from Jesus, were to have sent a letter carrier from Patmos, his island of exile, to those churches, the messenger would have started with Ephesus, a port on the mainland closest to Patmos. Then he would have taken a road that traveled a circular route through Smyrna, Pergamos, and the other cities in the order in which Revelation names them, ending with Laodicea.

What You'll Learn

The complete history of the Christian church

- - - - - - -

The era of the Christian church in which Christ will return

- - - - - - -

The church to which Christians belong today

Mosaic in St Mark's Basilica depicting the angels standing guard over the seven churches of Asia.

No doubt the contents of Revelation were read in those churches, so the messages the book contains obviously made sense to those members. And it seems unlikely that Jesus, who called Himself "the Truth," would have confused the members of those churches with messages that didn't actually fit their situations.

There were also, however, churches in other nearby cities in Asia that could easily have been included in this route but were not. Why were they left out? For one, Revelation is full of sevens: seven trumpets, seven seals, seven plagues, and so forth. The repeated combining of the number seven with symbols implies that this number is also to be understood as symbolic. In Scripture, seven represents completeness. These seven churches represent a "complete" picture of Jesus' church and His people on earth.

In other words, not only did Jesus'

messages to the seven churches speak to those churches, but they also fit the spiritual needs of every individual believer and congregation throughout the Christian era. All of these messages have value for all churches today. Some parts might apply more than other parts, but each is worth our study.

And there's more. Revelation builds on the visions of Daniel, which portrayed history from that prophet's time to the end. Revelation does the same; in its "complete" picture of the Christian church, it portrays the church from John's time to the end. In fact, in introducing the messages to the seven churches, Jesus specifically told John to "write ... the things which will take place after this" (1:19). Just as John's messenger would

have gone progressively from church to church delivering the messages, so the

> **Revelation is full of sevens: seven trumpets, seven seals, seven plagues, etc. In Scripture, the number seven is the prince of numbers and represents completeness.**

prophecy moves sequentially from era to era, starting with John's day and progressing to the end.

Before turning to the individual messages, note one more point: Each of these messages was built on the same general pattern. Jesus began each one by

THE SEVEN CHURCHES OF ASIA MINOR

GREECE

ASIA MINOR

AEGEAN SEA

PERGAMUM
THYATIRA
SMYRNA
SARDIS
EPHESUS
PHILADELPHIA
LAODICEA

John's letter to the seven churches would have likely followed this route and mimics the seven eras of the church through history.

identifying Himself in a way particularly appropriate to the needs of the church or era it represents. As a rule, the body of each message contains commendations of the church's spiritual strengths, insights on its weaknesses, counsel as to how it can correct the problems, and warnings about what will happen if the faults are not corrected. And each message concludes with promises to those who overcome the problems cited.

Ephesus — A.D. 31-100
Jesus praised the Ephesus church for its perseverance and good works and for having tested and repudiated false teachers that beset the church toward the end of the first century A.D. These false

While John's vision of the seven churches specifies eras of the Christian church through history, it is not a time prophecy. The dates suggested here are only approximate, helping to establish rough correlations of prophetic periods with historical eras.

teachers, particularly the "Nicolaitans" (verse 6), appear to have taught that deeds of the flesh do not affect the purity of the soul and consequently have no bearing on salvation.

But some 40 years had passed since Paul had first brought the gospel to Ephesus. A whole new generation now

comprised the church and its leadership. And while they were carefully maintaining correct doctrine, they had lost their "first love" (v. 4).

What the Ephesian church was experiencing must have been occurring in many other first-century churches as well. Losing the "first love" experience has always been a temptation for second and third-generation believers. No doubt that's why Jesus chose Ephesus to represent the situation of the whole Christian church through the apostolic era.

Smyrna — A.D. 100-313
The message to the church in Smyrna differs from most of the others in that it contains no reproof. Jesus had nothing but encouragement for this church, which faced persecution (v. 10).

Jesus' encouragement came first in His introduction of Himself as one who had experienced such troubles and had come out of them (v. 8). And it reappeared in the counsel and promise with which He closed the message: "Be faithful until death, and I will give you the crown of life. ... He who overcomes shall not be hurt by the second death [the one from which there is no resurrection]" (vs. 10, 11).

Early in the second century A.D., the emperor Trajan established what stood as the official Roman policy toward Christianity until Constantine issued an edict of toleration in A.D. 313. Roman officials were not to hunt down Christians, but if people were brought before them for

other offenses and were discovered to be Christians, they were to be executed unless they recanted. Throughout this period, Christians lived constantly with the possibility of discovery and death. And while Trajan had ruled that officials were not to hunt down Christians, some later emperors, particularly Diocletian and Galerius, carried on aggressive campaigns against the church.

Pergamos — A.D. 313-538
Jesus commended the church of the Pergamos era for holding "fast to My name" and for not denying "My faith" even in the midst of persecution (v. 13). During the period represented by Pergamos, various church councils established the orthodox Christian understanding of Jesus' divinity and humanity. Ancient church historian Theodoret said of the various bishops arriving for the first of these councils that some came without eyes, some without arms, which had been pulled from their sockets, and others with their bodies maimed in other horrible ways. These were people who had suffered for remaining faithful to their profession of Christ.

But Jesus rebuked the church at Pergamos for tolerating the insidious heresy of the Nicolaitans, which the Ephesians had rejected (v. 15). And another dangerous evil, "the doctrine of Balaam" (v. 14), was beginning to influence this church as well. To obtain royal favor and wealth, the ancient prophet Balaam had sold out the truth God wanted him to proclaim and led God's people into idolatry and immorality (see Numbers 22–25).

Constantine's edict of tolerance, which ended the persecution the Christian church had been enduring, ironically brought new dangers: both the influence of a "friendly" state and compromise with the paganism that had previously been the church's enemy. The era of the church of Pergamos saw the beginning of the great "falling away," or apostasy, that Paul had prophesied would happen before Jesus' second advent (2 Thessalonians 2:3).

Thyatira — A.D. 538-1565

During this period, the Christian church was responsible for many of the good things happening in society. It ran the hospitals, orphanages, schools, and missions. And among its members were faithful Christians—such as St. Francis of Assisi, the Waldenses, and John Wycliffe—who revealed God's love and upheld His Word.

But Jesus rebuked Christianity at large for allowing "that woman Jezebel ... to ... beguile My servants to commit sexual immorality and to eat things sacrificed to idols" (v. 20). Scripture calls the time of Jezebel's influence one of the lowest points in Israel's history (see 1 Kings 16:30, 33; 21:25, 26). As with Balaam, the matter was one of leaders tempting God's people into unfaithfulness and spiritual adultery.

In His message to the church of Thyatira, Jesus said, "I gave her [Jezebel] time to repent of her sexual immorality, and she did not repent" (Revelation 2:21). Of the last portion of this period, Cambridge historian Owen Chadwick wrote, "Everyone that mattered in the Western Church was crying out for reformation"—cries that went unheeded by the official church.

The "great tribulation" and death of which Jesus warned in this message (vs. 22, 23) might have seen their fulfillment in such tragedies as the bubonic plague, which killed 40 percent of the population of Europe, the Hundred Years' War, the revolts of the agrarian and urban poor, and the Thirty Years' War, which is estimated to have caused 10 million deaths out of a population of 18 million in Germany alone!

Sardis — A.D. 1565-1750

Jesus had little good to say about this church, which had "a name that you are alive, but you are dead" (chapter 3:1). Christianity experienced a great revival in the early years of the 16th century through a renewed understanding of justification by faith. But almost immediately the revival descended into a period of violent doctrinal controversy. To many it seemed more important to express justification by faith in precise terminology than to experience it in their lives. The various religious movements soon adopted rigid creeds that locked people into formal "head" religion that did little for their hearts.

Jesus did note, however, that there were "a few names even in Sardis who have not defiled their garments; and they shall walk with Me in white, for they are worthy" (v. 4). Perhaps He had in mind people like John Bunyan, who wrote that gospel-

proclaiming book *Pilgrim's Progress*; the Pietists Spener and von Zinzendorf; and the Moravians, who stimulated a renewed interest in missionary outreach.

Philadelphia — A.D. 1750-1844

As with Smyrna, Jesus had only positive things to say about this church. During the last half of the 18th century and the first half of the 19th, revivals swept across England, France, and America, sparking intense missionary outreach to other parts of the world. British Christians sent missionaries throughout the expanding British Empire.

The year 1793 saw the founding of the British Missionary Society by William Carey, and other missionary societies followed in Holland, Germany, and America. Less than a decade later, in 1804, the British and Foreign Bible Society was founded, and others arose as well.

This period also saw the birth of the Sunday school movement, the establishment of orphanages, growing pressure from Christians in Britain and America for the abolition of slavery, and the founding of church-related colleges. All these movements were characterized by the initiative and involvement of laity, interchurch cooperation, and self-sacrifice.

Laodicea — A.D. 1844-the End

In contrast to the message to Philadelphia, which contained only commendation, Jesus' message to the Laodicean church contains only warnings. He characterized Christianity in this period as being "lukewarm" and self-deceived—"because you say, 'I am rich' ... and do not know that you are wretched, miserable, poor, blind, and naked" (vs. 16, 17).

Jesus' counsel (v. 18) is particularly revealing, because the Laodiceans thought they had in abundance the very things He told them they needed to obtain. Laodicea was a prosperous commercial center. Nero offered financial aid when an earthquake destroyed the city, but the citizens turned his offer down, saying they had sufficient resources to handle the situation. One of the reasons for this prosperity was their commerce in the fine woolen garments for which their area was renowned. And a famous school of medicine just outside Laodicea kept the citizens supplied with eye salve.

The point of Jesus' message, of course, was that the Laodiceans' complacency and self-satisfaction were dangerous because they were unfounded. They made a great profession of religion, but their practice fell far short. But Jesus' warning was motivated by good will. He said, "As many as I love, I rebuke and chasten. Therefore be zealous and repent" (v. 19). And in the next verse, He indicated that He'd taken the initiative; in fact, He'd done as much as He could: "Behold, I stand at the door and knock. If anyone hears My voice and opens the door, I will come in to him and dine with him, and he with Me (v. 20)."

This message that combines warning and invitation is the last of the seven. That means it extends right up to Jesus' second coming. In other words, it's for our age; Jesus was speaking to you. Will you open that door for Him to enter your heart? ®

Mosaic found in Laodiceia. Laodiceia was situated at a distance of 6 mi from Hierapolis (Pamukkale) and of 4 mi from the village Eskihisar. It was founded in 261-285 B.C. by Antiochus II.

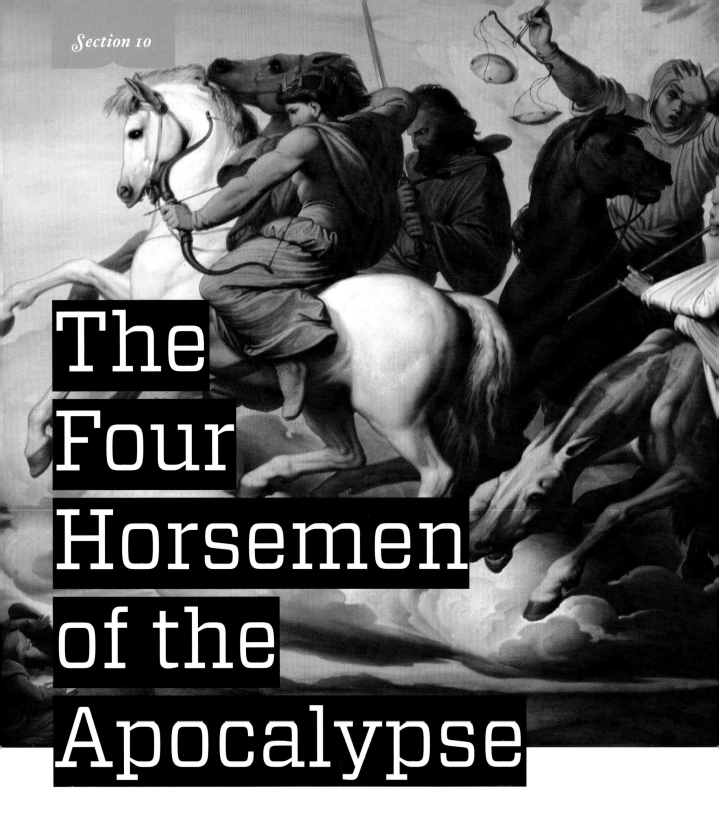

The Four Horsemen of the Apocalypse

> *Now I saw when the Lamb opened one of the seals; and I heard one of the four living creatures saying with a voice like thunder, "Come and see."*
> —Revelation 6:1

"Four Horsemen of the Apocalypse." Edward Jakob von Steinle.

WHAT DOES THE FUTURE HOLD FOR YOU? JOHN'S VISION OF THE SEVEN CHURCHES PROVIDED ONE VIEW OF COMING EVENTS. HIS VISION OF THE SCROLL SEALED WITH SEVEN SEALS LOOKS OVER THE SAME TERRITORY FROM ANOTHER PERSPECTIVE. AND IT IS HIGHLIGHTED BY A VIEW OF THE REWARD TO BE ENJOYED BY THOSE WHOSE FAITH IN GOD ENDURES THROUGH THE GREAT TRIBULATION HE FORESAW.

Follow Along: Revelation Chapters 4–7

What You'll Learn

| Why the scroll was sealed with seven seals | The only person worthy of breaking those seals and why | The meaning behind the silence in heaven |

Introducing the vision of the churches was a scene in which John saw Christ walking among seven candlesticks. The vision of the seven seals took John to the heavenly sanctuary, where stands God's throne. Chapters 4 and 5 of Revelation describe the scene, picturing in detail the courtiers—particularly four "living creatures" and 24 elders—and their worship.

Revelation 5 introduces the theme that will be developed through the next several chapters: "a scroll written inside and on the back, sealed with seven seals" (v. 1). The context of Revelation 4 and 5 is the enthronement of Christ after His resurrection. Jesus was now in heaven and approached the Heavenly Father. Revelation 6 and 7 focus on what happens as these seals are broken; however, it doesn't tell us what this scroll is and what comprises its contents. But two Old Testament passages that underlie this symbol give us some clues.

- Ezekiel 2:8 pictures a scroll that has been written on the inside and out, which the prophet is told to eat (cf. Revelation 10). Ezekiel tells what was written on the scroll he was given: "Lamentations and mourning and woe"—contents that accord well with what happens as the seals on John's scroll are broken.

- The other Old Testament passage related to John's scroll is the last chapter of Daniel. As the angel gave Daniel his final instructions and encouragement, he told him to "shut up" and "seal" his book "until the time of the end," when "knowledge shall be increased" (Daniel 12:4; see also verse 9).

Therefore, it's likely the sealed scroll John saw in God's hand contained the prophecies that reveal the events leading up to Christ's return, prophecies that include events that will cause mourning and woe in those who oppose God. In Daniel's time, these events were still far in the future, so the book was sealed "until the time of the end." But by John's day, these were "things which must shortly take place" (Revelation 1:1), and his instructions were to write about these things (v. 19).

The New King James Version uses the word "book" in Revelation 10 and Daniel 12, but in Bible times all "books" were scrolls.

Needed: A Seal Breaker

But the scroll was sealed with seven seals. That meant each of the seals had to be broken before John could open and read the scroll and reveal its contents—the events that are to usher in God's eternal kingdom. This explains his distress when "no one in heaven or on the earth or under the earth was able to open the scroll" (chapter 5:3; see also verse 2).

Having been made anxious by the lack of a qualified "seal breaker," we appreciate all the more the introduction of the "Lion of the tribe of Judah, the Root of David," the "Lamb . . . having seven horns and seven eyes" (vs. 5, 6). That this figure represents Christ is emphasized by references to His death and the redemption it has obtained and to His elevation to the throne, where He receives worship along with God.

With the scene set, the action begins: The Lamb starts breaking the seals. The seals are broken sequentially, and the results of each described before the next is taken up—an indication that they portray historical progression. The fact that the cry of the martyrs in the fifth seal comes as a consequence of the actions of the horsemen of the previous seals also indicates that the seals are broken sequentially rather than simultaneously.

> While the seals function sequentially, the action begun under one seal might continue well after the breaking of the next.

At the breaking of the **FIRST SEAL**, John saw a white horse whose rider "went out conquering and to conquer" (chapter 6:2).

Throughout Revelation, white is the color of Christ and His church (see 1:14; 2:17; etc.). And in Revelation's chiastic structure, the first seal's white horse with its conquering rider is paralleled by that of chapter 19, where the rider is obviously Christ. But there are also differences. The rider of chapter 19 wears a crown of royal rule and completely vanquishes His foes.

The crown of the rider of Revelation 6 is the wreath of victory (a stephanos), and the events under the seals that follow this first one make it clear that the victory obtained is only preliminary. This seal is best understood as representing Christ's victory at the cross and the early spread of His invisible kingdom through the church He established.

A stephanos is a wreath awarded as a prize to the victor in a public contest, or as a token of honor, especially in recognition of some public service.

Three Troubling Horsemen

In this vision of the seals, the remaining three horsemen of the Apocalypse picture troubled times. When the **SECOND SEAL** was opened, John saw a "fiery red" horse whose rider was allowed to "take peace from the earth," with the result that people killed one another (chapter 6:3, 4).

The opening of the **THIRD SEAL** disclosed a black horse whose rider carried scales for the measuring and selling of the grains used for making bread—a sign of severe famine. And the opening of the **FOURTH SEAL** revealed a "pale" horse upon which sat "Death, and Hades [or the grave] followed with him. And power was given to them over a fourth of the earth, to kill with sword, with hunger, with death, and by the beasts of the earth" (v. 8).

As you saw in the vision of the seven churches, the four horsemen of Revelation show God's work on earth beginning well but soon running into trouble. New Testament scholar Jon Paulien develops the picture:

> "First, there was the initial, rapid expansion of the church throughout much of the then-known world. The succeeding period brought division and compromise in the face of persecution. The loss of a clear understanding of the gospel followed as the church settled into an earthly kingdom in the years after Constantine. Finally, the Dark Ages of spiritual decline and death engulfed Christendom" (*Symposium I*, 234).

In the covenant God established with His people in the Old Testament, He warned that the disobedient would suffer war (sword), famine, and pestilence. Those who responded with rebellion to the warnings these "curses" brought would someday feel their full effects. Those who remained faithful to God or repented of their wandering might suffer persecution, but they would know His salvation.

The opening of the fifth seal marks the turning point in this time of trouble. And in it and the sixth seal, we catch glimpses of these two groups, the obstinate and those who have turned to God.

"How Long, O Lord?"

At the opening of the **FIFTH SEAL**, God's people, the "martyrs," cry for help: "How long, O Lord, ... until You judge and avenge our blood on those who dwell on the earth" (v. 10). John relayed the answer that was given them—it was just "a little while longer" until God's plan reached full fruition.

Connected with the opening of the **SIXTH SEAL** are the cosmic signs that both Old and New Testament prophecies

This scroll would certainly include Daniel's prophecies, but might more generically represent all the prophecies God has given regarding end-time events.

The limited scope of the horsemen's activities (to "a fourth of the earth") indicates that we're not seeing here the plagues and destruction of the end time.

Read Joel 2:30, 31 and Matthew 24:29-31 for more insight into these cosmic signs.

indicate would mark earth's final days and the second coming of Christ: a great earthquake, darkening of the sun and moon, and the falling of the stars.

As the last of these signs reveal the imminence of Christ's return, rather than welcoming what to Christians is "the blessed hope," the rebellious cry out in fear of what is to them "the great day of His wrath" and try to hide from the Lamb (vs. 15–17).

Next, in Revelation 7, John's attention was turned from the seals that were being broken open to a people who are being sealed. This tangent contains God's answer to the martyrs of the fifth seal. John saw...

> "... a great multitude which no one could number, of all nations, tribes, peoples, and tongues. ... These are the ones who have come out of great tribulation. ... The Lamb ... will shepherd them. ... And God will wipe away every tear from their eyes" (vs. 9, 14–17).

Signs of Christ's second coming according to the sixth seal include earthquakes, darkening of the sun & moon, and the falling of the stars.

In other words, though the people of earth will go through a time of terrible trouble, God has marked—sealed—those who are His. This interlude between the sixth and seventh seals offers hope by revealing the results of God's plan—the salvation of His people, the time when their suffering will be forever ended.

This section of Revelation ends with the brief statement that at the opening of the **SEVENTH SEAL** "there was silence in heaven for about half an hour" (chapter 8:1). The number seven represents completeness. The sixth seal brought the signs of the imminent return of Christ. And Jesus said that when He returns, all the angels will accompany Him.

Apparently, then, the opening of the seventh seal marks the completion of earth's history and of God's work for human beings—the second coming of Christ, which leaves heaven temporarily silent because all its inhabitants have come to rescue God's people on earth. What better ending could one find to a vision of seven seals!

Matthew 25:31 says, *"When the Son of Man comes in His glory, and all the holy angels with Him, then He will sit on the throne of His glory."*

Seven Angels and Seven Trumpets

NO SOONER HAD JOHN'S VISION OF THE SEVEN SEALS CONCLUDED THAN ANOTHER VISION BEGAN. LIKE THAT OF THE SEVEN SCROLLS, THIS VISION BEGAN IN THE HEAVENLY SANCTUARY. JOHN SAW AN ANGEL OFFERING INCENSE "WITH THE PRAYERS OF ALL THE SAINTS" (REVELATION 8:3) ON THE GOLDEN ALTAR IN GOD'S PRESENCE—A SYMBOL OF CHRIST'S INTERCESSORY MINISTRY FOR THOSE WHO HAVE CHOSEN TO PLACE THEIR LIVES IN HIS HANDS.

FOLLOW ALONG: Revelation Chapters 8–11

This vision also involves the number seven, which indicates that it, too, was intended to reveal earth's history through the end of time. The central symbol of this vision is the trumpet. The book of Joel contains the key passage for understanding why this symbol is used here. Joel 2 begins with these words:

> Blow the trumpet in Zion,
> And sound an alarm in My holy mountain!
> Let all the inhabitants of the land tremble;
> For the day of the LORD is coming,
> For it is at hand.

Joel goes on to warn of an army of locusts that threatens God's people. And then he tells how they should respond to the trumpeted alarm:

> "Now, therefore," says the LORD,
> "Turn to me with all your heart, ...
> Return to the LORD your God,
> For He is gracious and merciful"
> (verses 12, 13).

In Revelation, as in Joel, the sounding of the trumpet calls God's people to repentance and renewal of their relationship with Him in view of the judgments that are about to fall on the earth. And these are the judgments of the last days—the final judgment.

In ancient Israel, the seven monthly "new moon" feasts climaxed in the Feast of Trumpets (the first day of the seventh month of the religious year). And the sounding of the trumpets during this religious festival ushered

> *Then I saw another sign in heaven, great and marvelous: seven angels having the seven last plagues, for in them the wrath of God is complete.*
> —REVELATION 15:1

in the Day of Atonement, the ceremonial holy day by which God depicted His ultimate judgment day. The sounding of the trumpets served to remind the Israelites that they had but a few days left before they must stand before God's judgment seat. Those who refused to prepare for that experience were cast out from among His people forever.

Trumpets and Plagues

Revelation's chiastic structure is nowhere more obvious than in the parallel visions of the trumpets and the plagues (chapter 16). The first of each concerns the earth; the second, the sea; the third, the rivers and springs of water, and so forth, right on through the two series. But there is one clear and consistent distinction:

The destructive forces released under the plagues are universal, while those released under the trumpets are restricted. For example,

• When the second trumpet sounds, "a third of the sea became blood; and a third of the living creatures in the sea died, and a third of the ships were destroyed" (8:8, 9).

• But when the second plague is poured out on the sea, it becomes like blood, and every living creature in it dies (16:3).

As in the seals, the partial destructions of the trumpets signal that these are preliminary warning judgments—as contrasted with final, retributive judgments.

The text makes clear also that the trumpets, like the seals, are sequential rather than simultaneous. The sounding of each trumpet is followed immediately by the action it introduces, and only then is the next trumpet sounded. And each trumpet that follows the first is intro-

....

Aya Sofya, or Haghia Aghia Sophia, was the greatest Christian cathedral of the Middle Ages, later converted into an imperial mosque by the Ottoman Empire, and is now a museum.

duced by the word "then," an indication of chronological sequence.

The vision of the seven churches depicts the spiritual decline of God's people from the establishment of Christianity until just before Christ's return. When God's Old Testament people reneged on their spiritual commitments, God, as a last resort, sent them warning calls to repentance via the harassment of their enemies, the Assyrians and Babylonians.

That's exactly the picture this vision of the trumpets conveys regarding God's New Testament church and its oppressors. This vision showed what God would do to call His wan-dering people back to Him. In his book *Outline Studies in Revelation*, Professor Edwin Thiele

makes the fol-lowing summary of the seven trumpets:

[1] The first trumpet symbolizes the Divine judgments that came upon *Jerusalem and the Jewish nation* when it set itself against Christ and His followers; **[2]** the second symbolizes judgments upon the *western Roman world*; **[3]** the third fell upon the professed *church of Christ* when it allowed itself to become defiled and sent forth streams of death rather than life; **[4]** the fourth was the ensuing *darkness of the Middle Ages*; **[5]** the fifth constituted the *Mohammedan scourges* that swept over the Middle East and into Europe; **[6]** the sixth consisted of the scourges that continued under *Turkish control* of large sections of Asia, Africa, and Europe.

The Trumpet Sound

The symbolism in this vision extends beyond the trumpets themselves, of course. The "hail," "fire," and "blood" of the **FIRST TRUMPET** are biblical symbols of battle. And "trees" and "grass" represent God's people. In this trumpet, judgment begins with the house of God. The **SECOND TRUMPET'S** "mountain" is the biblical symbol for a nation, and the "sea" represents masses of people—fit symbols for the Germanic nations' attack on the Roman Empire.

In the **THIRD TRUMPET**, the "great star" named "Wormwood" that fell from heaven represents Satan. And the "springs of water" are the sources of spiritual life. Here we see the teachings of Christ corrupted, hindering His work on earth. This was fulfilled during the Middle Ages. And **TRUMPET FOUR**, which affects the lights in the heavens, sees this attack extended to the heavenly ministry of Christ, the Light of the world.

The **FIFTH TRUMPET** depicts the attack of the Islamic Arabs on the Christian world. Some interpreters, using the principle that in biblical prophecy a day represents a year of literal time, see in the line "their power was to hurt men five months" a reference to the Arabs' attempts throughout a 150-year period to take Constantinople, the capital of what remained of the Byzantine Empire and headquarters of the eastern branch of Christianity. Some also see this period as a reign of secular atheism.

The **SIXTH TRUMPET** continues with representations of the Islamic Turks. Its "fire, smoke, and brimstone" might well represent their use of gunpowder, which enabled them to do what the Arabs hadn't been able to do—capture Constantinople. There is also support for this trumpet marking the rise of end-time Babylon.

When the **SEVENTH TRUMPET** sounds, "loud voices" in heaven announce, "The kingdoms of this world have become the kingdoms of our Lord and of His Christ, and He shall reign forever and ever!" (11:15). Earth's history ends. God terminates the rule of the nations that oppressed His people, and He sets up His kingdom of justice and peace that shall rule forever.

Verse 19 speaks of the temple of God being opened so that the Ark of the Covenant can be seen. The only time a human saw the ark was on the Day of Atonement, which, as we have noted above, represented the final judgment. And verse 18 confirms this interpretation when it says that with this trumpet comes "the time of the dead that they should be judged, and that [God] should reward [His] servants ... and should destroy those who destroy the earth."

"The two witnesses/lampstands represent God's Word in the Old and New Testaments, which gives light to the world and testifies to *His love.*"

The date A.D. 538 is significant as it marks the date that the eastern remnant of the Roman Empire decreed the bishop of Rome head of all Christian churches. The decree became effective in A.D. 538 with the defeat of that last Arian power.

A Bittersweet Book

As in the vision of the seven seals, an interlude interrupts this vision between its sixth and seventh parts. In a takeoff on Ezekiel's vision, an angel handed John a little "book," or scroll, and told him to eat it. But while Ezekiel was simply told his scroll would taste sweet as honey, Revelation's angel told John the scroll would be as sweet as honey in his mouth, but that it would also make his stomach bitter. (See Revelation 10:8–11; compare Ezekiel 3:1–4.)

Then, after telling John to measure the temple of God, another reference to the Day of Atonement judgment, the angel related the story of two witnesses, which he described as being two olive trees and two lampstands that stand before the Lord (11:4). These witnesses were to prophesy for "one thousand two hundred and sixty days" (v. 3)—the same period for which the previous verse says the "Gentiles" will "tread the holy city underfoot." Then the "beast that ascends out of the bottomless pit" will kill these witnesses and "their dead bodies will lie in the street of the city that is spiritually called Sodom and Egypt" for three-and-a-half days, at which the people of earth will rejoice. But ultimately, God will resurrect them and bring them up to heaven, while a great earthquake will destroy a tenth of the city and kill seven thousand men, causing those left alive to give glory to God (vs. 7–13).

The two witnesses/lampstands represent God's Word in the Old and New Testaments, which gives light to the world and testifies to His love. The 1,260 days of Gentile domination of the Holy City represents the 1,260 years God's people would suffer oppression by people who have aligned themselves against God. Daniel 7 makes clear this period extends from A.D. 538 to 1798. Its closing years saw the epoch-changing French Revolution.

But that "earthquake" was followed by God's resurrection of His two witnesses. As we noted when looking at the sixth church, the 19th century was characterized by great religious awakenings and by the strongest missionary movement since the time of the apostles. And it saw the development of various Bible societies, which began the still-continuing effort to make the gospel available in every language spoken on this globe. God's two witnesses couldn't have become more alive!

And what of the bittersweet little book? Some scholars understand it to represent the "Second Advent Awakening" of the 19th century, a time in which faithful Christians believed they found in the

"Napoleon Crossing the Saint-Bernard Pass" on May 20, 1800. Jacques-Louis David.
Facing Page: The colossal Tuscan colonnades at St. Peter's Square, Vatican, Rome.

> During the French Revolution (1793–1798), the revolutionaries sought to de-Christianize the whole nation— discarding the Bible as antithetical to the Enlightenment.

Bible's prophecies of the end times, and particularly in Daniel's time prophecies, evidence that Jesus was coming in their lifetime. This message stirred a great revival on the North American continent. The failure of their hopes on October 22, 1844, appropriately represented by the scroll's ultimate bitterness, became known as the Great Disappointment.

What was to them a disappointment, however, becomes an additional reason for us to hope. It adds further confirmation of the accuracy of the prophecies of Revelation—prophecies that tell us we truly are living in the time of the end, the days just before Jesus returns to set up His glorious kingdom. ◪

. . . .

Napoleon Bonaparte was a French military and political leader who rose to prominence during the latter stages of the French Revolution and its associated wars in Europe. He sent General Alexander Berthier to Rome where on February 16, 1798, he took the pope captive and decreed that "the pope should no longer exercise any function."

The Heart of Revelation
Battle of the Ages

> " "
>
> *Now a great sign appeared in heaven: a woman clothed with the sun, with the moon under her feet, and on her head a garland of twelve stars. Then being with child, she cried out in labor and in pain to give birth.*
> —REVELATION 12:1, 2

What You'll Learn

Who is the woman, child, and dragon of Revelation 12

The sea and land beasts of Revelation 13

The three angels' messages of Revelation 14

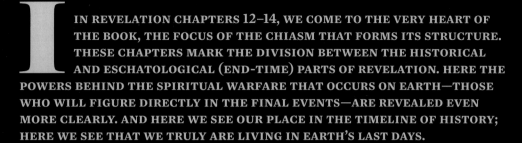

IN REVELATION CHAPTERS 12–14, WE COME TO THE VERY HEART OF THE BOOK, THE FOCUS OF THE CHIASM THAT FORMS ITS STRUCTURE. THESE CHAPTERS MARK THE DIVISION BETWEEN THE HISTORICAL AND ESCHATOLOGICAL (END-TIME) PARTS OF REVELATION. HERE THE POWERS BEHIND THE SPIRITUAL WARFARE THAT OCCURS ON EARTH—THOSE WHO WILL FIGURE DIRECTLY IN THE FINAL EVENTS—ARE REVEALED EVEN MORE CLEARLY. AND HERE WE SEE OUR PLACE IN THE TIMELINE OF HISTORY; HERE WE SEE THAT WE TRULY ARE LIVING IN EARTH'S LAST DAYS.

FOLLOW ALONG: Revelation Chapters 11–14

As did the visions of the churches, seals, and trumpets, this vision originates from God's temple in heaven. The setting is God's throne room, the Most Holy Place of His temple and, specifically, the place where the "the ark of His covenant" is kept.

The ark is notable because it holds the Ten Commandments, which forms the foundation of God's government. The "lightnings, noises, thunderings, an earthquake, and great hail" mentioned in this verse remind us of the events at the giving of the Ten Commandments to Moses (see Exodus 20:18). As we will see, the conflict between God and Satan centers on God's law and His authority.

Revelation 12 introduces these three characters:

1. "a woman clothed with the sun, with the moon under her feet, and on her head a garland of twelve stars"
2. "a great, fiery red dragon"
3. "a male Child"

> The woman of Revelation 12 is best understood as representing God's people on earth, His faithful church.

Verse 9 comes right out and identifies the dragon. It is "that serpent of old, called the Devil and Satan." This identification indicates that behind chapter 12's symbolism lies, at least in part, the Genesis account of humankind's fall into sin.

The identity of the Child is revealed by the events chapter 12 narrates as happening to Him. He was threatened by Satan at birth (v. 4), destined "to rule all nations with a rod of iron" (a messianic role), and "caught up to God and to His throne" (v. 5). Clearly, this child represents Christ—the promised Seed who was to end the serpent's life by crushing his head (Genesis 3:15).

The Cosmic Woman

Who, then, is the woman of chapter 12?

Because she gives birth to Christ, we might first suppose she represents Mary. But the description in the rest of the chapter suggests otherwise for at least three reasons:

1. The woman of Revelation 12 was to experience intense persecution; there's no indication in Scripture that Mary was particularly persecuted following either Christ's birth or His ascension.

2. Like both the book of Daniel and the previous chapter of Revelation, this chapter speaks of a 1,260-day period of persecution. As we have seen before, the 1,260 prophetic days represent 1,260 literal years—a period that obviously couldn't apply to the earthly life of any individual.

3. This prophecy has a cosmic sweep that suggests it functions on a larger scale than any one person could fit.

In fact, the woman of Revelation 12 is best understood as representing God's people on earth, His faithful church. This "woman" and her "offspring" (v. 17)—the 144,000 who are "virgins," "not defiled with women" (14:3, 4)—comprise the theme against which Revelation 17 and 18 play the counterpoint of the harlot woman Babylon and her prostitute daughters.

> Scripture frequently uses a woman as a symbol of God's people; see, for example, Hosea 2:19, 20; Isaiah 54:1–8; Ezekiel 16:8–14; 2 Corinthians 11:2; Ephesians 5:21–23.

Clearly, Babylon and her daughters are not individual people but symbols of all who have been unfaithful to God and who have opposed His followers. That implies that the woman in Revelation similarly represents a group rather than an individual and, because she stands in clear contrast to the harlot, that she represents God's faithful people.

The woman, then, stands, first of all, for God's Old Testament people (Revelation 12:1–5), the Jews, who gave birth to Christ, the Messiah. Most of Revelation 12, however, concerns His people from the time of Christ on (12:6–17). So for the most part, this symbol represents His church from New Testament times to the end.

The first six verses of chapter 12 introduce the characters: God's people (the woman), Satan (the dragon), and Christ (the Child). These verses also introduce the themes of the drama: Satan wants to kill Jesus. But Christ will be protected and, in fact, exalted to a position of authority. Meanwhile, the woman, though under God's care, will experience persecution.

The next six verses of chapter 12 tell us that the conflict between good and evil that wracks the earth has also affected heaven: "War broke out in heaven: Michael and his angels fought against the dragon ... and his angels" (v. 7).

Michael is Christ—though this no more makes Him merely an angel than does the fact that chapter 5 calling Him a Lamb makes Him merely an animal.

Isaiah 14 and Ezekiel 28 suggest that Satan—"Lucifer," the "covering cherub"—was first cast out of heaven before Christ's incarnation. But he suffered his pivotal defeat at the cross, and this passage seems to have that battle primarily in mind. (See also John 12:31; Colossians 2:15; 1 Peter 3:22; Jude 6.)

These verses conclude with a warning meant for everyone on earth, the "inhabitants" of both "the earth and the sea." "The devil has come down to you with great wrath," it says, "because he knows his time is short!" (NRSV).

Revelation 12:13 picks up the theme verse 6 introduced: Satan's persecution of God's people. Again, the warning of impending persecution is accompanied by a promise of God's help. The woman is given wings so that she can fly into the wilderness—a reminder of the escape God provided Israel from slavery in Egypt to freedom in the wilderness. And when the "serpent" tries to drown the woman, the earth swallows the flood and so saves her. All this takes place during the period here called a "time and times and half a time" (v. 14)—a direct reference to Daniel 7:25 and the prophecy of the little horn's persecution of God's people for a "time and times and half a time," and, of course, a repeat in different terms of the 1,260 days of verse 6. (More about this period later.)

As the curtain descends on this scene of the prophetic drama, we see Satan "enraged" because his attempts to eliminate God's people have been foiled. But he's not ready to give up. Instead, verse 17 says, he starts "to make war with the rest of her offspring"—a group the verse characterizes as people who "keep the commandments of God and have the testimony of Jesus Christ."

Chapter 13: The Universal War

Revelation 12 ends with a warning about a war between Satan and God's people. Chapters 13 and 14 detail that war and the results it brings to both sides. The time frame these chapters cover begins essentially with the start of the 1,260-year prophecy—A.D. 538—and extends through end-time events right up to Christ's second coming.

The war described in these chapters will allow no neutral parties. Eventually, all the people of the world will follow and worship the first beast described here (vs. 3, 12, 16)—all, that is, except the "virgins" who have not fallen for the seductions of the "woman" Babylon and her harlot daughters, the "saints" who have kept "the commandments of God and the faith of Jesus" (14:4, 12).

John's description of the first beast of chapter 13 helps us to identify it. The parallels to the creatures of Daniel 7 are striking and are intentional. This beast, like those, rises from the sea. It is, in fact, a summary of them: part lion, bear, and leopard, and bearing the horns of Daniel's fourth beast.

> Revelation 19:9, 10; 22:6–9, make clear that the **"testimony of Jesus Christ"** is not the saints' testimony about Jesus, but rather the testimony that He has given to the church through the spiritual gift of prophecy, which 1 Corinthians 12 and 14 and Ephesians 4 indicate was to function continuously in the church. In other words, the spiritual gift of prophecy will be seen in God's end-time church.

In John 4:22, Jesus says, *"Salvation is of the Jews."*

Verse 4 suggests that when Satan rebelled against God, a substantial portion of the angels joined him. (Stars, in Revelation, often represent angels—see chapter 1:20.)

Remember: *Daniel's four beasts represented the empires of Babylon, Medo-Persia, Greece, Rome, and the 10 horns, the Germanic tribes that would overthrow Rome. The crowns on the horns probably indicate that this prophecy concerns the time of their sovereignty. The seven heads and ten horns of chapter 12 show its close connection to Daniel's empires (Satan, the dragon, is the power behind all the thrones represented), and the crowns on the heads likely indicate that the action of that chapter takes place during the time of the empires rather than of the Germanic tribes.*

The woman and dragon of Revelation 12.

Chapter 13:3 pictures an attempt on the sea beast's life: "I saw one of his heads as if it had been mortally wounded." In 1797, the French revolutionary government wrote to Napoleon that the "Roman religion" would always be "an irreconcilable enemy of the Republic," and so it asked him to "destroy, if possible, the center of unity of the Roman Church." Napoleon sent General Alexander Berthier to Rome, where, on February 15, 1798, he took the pope captive and decreed that "the pope should no longer exercise any function."[1]

Popes had been taken captive before this incident but never in an attempt to destroy the Roman Church itself. A century later, Joseph Rickaby, a Jesuit priest, observed that when this pope passed away as a French prisoner, "half Europe thought ... that with the Pope the Papacy was dead."[2]

But Revelation said this "deadly wound" would be healed. In time, in other words, the world would again see the rise of a "Christian" religious institution that used political power to obtain the worship of "all who dwell on the earth," all "whose names have not been written in the Book of Life of the Lamb slain from the foundation of the world" (v. 8).

In chapter 17:5, John called this apostate Christian body "the mother of harlots." Apparently, in the end times, the problem won't be limited to one institution. However pure its origin, any cult, sect, or church that attempts to force its understanding of Christianity on other people comes under God's condemnation.

Beast from the Earth

As the vision continues, John sees a second beast arise and aid the first one in achieving its goals. This second beast comes up "out of the earth," which signifies several things:

- For one, it suggests that what follows moves beyond Daniel's vision, which was limited to creatures of the sea. Revelation's account offers more details than what Daniel gave.

But while the make-up of Revelation's "sea beast" relates it to the empires and nations of Daniel's prophecy, it most closely resembles Daniel's little horn power. It wields both religious and political power:

- It accepts worship (vs. 4, 8) and uses civil force to accomplish its purposes—"authority was given him over every tribe, tongue and nation" (v. 7).
- It blasphemes God and His tabernacle (sanctuary) and then makes war on the saints.
- And, as in the case of Daniel's little horn, God allows it this rule for a 1,260-year period.

Daniel 7 clearly links the beginning of this period of persecution with the fall of the Roman Empire. At that time, the medieval Christian church was the leading force in Western civilization, the dominating religious-political entity. We've already noted the church-sponsored violence of the medieval period. As for the rest of John's description, that church directed people's attention away from God with claims that the pope was, literally, God on earth. And in place of Christ's once-for-all sacrifice for us and His continuing ministry in the heavenly sanctuary, it substituted masses, indulgences, pilgrimage, and other meritorious works.

References
1. A. Aulard, *Christianity and the French Revolution*, Lady Frazer, trans. (London, 1927), 151.
2. Joseph Rickaby, "The Modern Papacy," in *Lectures on the History of Religions* (London: Catholic Truth Society, 1910), vol. 3, lecture 24, p. 1.

- Second, the fact that one beast arises out of the sea and one out of the earth emphasizes the worldwide scope of this prophecy. Chapter 12:12 contains a similar thought: "Woe to the inhabitants of the *earth* and the *sea!* For the devil has come down to you" (emphasis supplied). It is the same earth that saved the woman from the flooding waters of the dragon in Revelation 12.

- And third, some commentators have seen in this beast's earthly origin a clue to its identity. Revelation 17:15 indicates that in some symbolic prophecies, water represents multitudes of people. Beasts arising from the sea, then, represent nations or empires built in the populous areas of the world—which is certainly true of the empires of Daniel 7 and of the first half of Revelation 13. Conversely, a beast that comes up out of the earth would represent a nation or empire arising in a relatively unpopulated area, such as the Western Hemisphere was before the Europeans arrived there. This interpretation is particularly fitting because of the timing of this part of the vision. The land beast becomes active after the healing of the sea beast's deadly wound—in other words, sometime after 1798. So this line of reasoning suggests the land beast represents the United States.

John described this beast as having "two horns like a lamb" (v. 11). Everywhere else in Revelation where a lamb is mentioned, it represents Christ. The land beast, then, appears to be Christian. But the very next words reveal its true character:

John said that it "spoke like a dragon," that it causes those who dwell on earth "to worship the first beast, whose deadly wound was healed," and that it encourages them to make an image to the sea beast and then brings that image to life (vs. 11, 12, 15).

The sea beast uses political power to enforce its demands for worship. With the land beast's aid, this "image of the beast" mirrors its original. Their methods

Read Matthew 24:24 and 2 Thessalonians 2:9–12. Through the rest of Revelation, the beast with the lamb-like horns is called the "false prophet." See chapters 16:13; 19:20; 20:10. With the dragon and the sea beast, it comprises an evil counterfeit trinity that stands in opposition to the Divine Trinity.

are those of Satan: miracles, deception, and coercion—the very things both Jesus and Paul warned of in relation to the end of the world.

Revelation says this beast will use both economic coercion (v. 18) and, ultimately, the threat of death (v. 15). Those who succumb to the earthly beast's pressure and worship the sea beast "receive a mark on their right hand or on their foreheads" (v. 16). This "mark of the beast" figures prominently in chapter 14.

Chapter 14: Spotlight on Hope

What a relief the next verses of Revelation bring! After all the talk of war and deception and people knuckling under the pressure to worship someone other than God, John points to a group who has proven faithful—the 144,000, whom we saw also in chapter 7. As in that chapter, the portrayal of this group forms a little interlude in the prophecy, giving us hope by assuring us that despite all the pressures being applied, God's grace can enable people to remain faithful, "undefiled" by the temptations of false religion.

Some people will sing a new song before God's throne. Some will "follow the Lamb wherever He goes" throughout eternity.

Having been reassured that a sizable number of people will withstand the wiles and coercion of the dragon and the two beasts, John was shown what heaven would do during the time of the beasts. John wrote that he saw three angels flying "in the midst of heaven," each bringing a message of warning to earth's inhabitants.

The **FIRST ANGEL**, John said, has the "everlasting gospel to preach to those who dwell on the earth—to every nation, tribe, tongue, and people" (14:6). When Jesus listed for His disciples the signs that would indicate His coming was near, He said, "This gospel of the kingdom will be preached in all the world as a witness to all the nations, and then the end will come" (Matthew 24:14). God's final warning, then, is a gospel message. It will tell all people about His coming kingdom of peace; it will tell them how they can prepare to enter that kingdom.

The American Colonial Flag, designed during the American Revolutionary War, features 13 stars to represent the original 13 colonies.

In Revelation 11–14, *some commentators have seen clues to the earthly identity of the land beast that arose after 1798.*

The angels of Revelation 14 are symbols of God's end-time people, who, like Noah and the other prophets of old, deliver God's final warning.

John pictured an angel carrying this warning message to all the people of earth. But Jesus commissioned His followers to bear the gospel message to the world: "Go therefore and make disciples of all nations ... and lo, I am with you always, even to the end of the age" (Matthew 28:19, 20; see also Acts 1:8). The angels of Revelation 14 are symbols of God's end-time people, who, like Noah and the other prophets of old, deliver God's final warning.

The first part of this warning calls earth's inhabitants to worship the Creator God "for the hour of His judgment has come" (v. 7). The end-time judgment for which the fifth seal pictures the martyrs appealing has begun (Revelation 6:9–11).

When Scripture speaks of a people's relationship to God, "fornication" refers to unfaithfulness, to putting one's faith in something other than God and accepting false doctrines.

The **SECOND ANGEL'S MESSAGE** warns that the great city Babylon "is fallen" (v. 8). Babylon was ancient Judah's greatest oppressor, the city-state that not only conquered God's Old Testament people, but also broke up their nation, destroying their cities, including Jerusalem, and taking most of the population into exile.

But Babylon's threat to God's people came not only in its oppression. When Babylon fell to another empire's army, the new emperors allowed the exiled Jews to return to their homeland and restore their nation. The majority of the Jews, however, had become comfortable in Babylon. Rather than face the struggle of rebuilding a nation, they stayed in their adopted homeland. Thus, this second message warns of the intoxicating wine of Babylon's "fornication."

Daniel said that Babylon's greatest ruler, Nebuchadnezzar, had accepted God. But later rulers of that nation returned to their heathen gods. That's what made Babylon a harlot. And the Jews who remained in Babylon faced the strong temptation to compromise their religion and adapt to local beliefs. No doubt, many did.

Of course, the Babylon against which Revelation warns is not that ancient city. It's the Babylon of this time. The message says that the time of God's judgment has come; the oppressors of His people have fallen. It's time to leave, to go home. See Revelation 18:1–4.

This message warns against staying in Babylon, against compromising one's faith in God to enjoy the comforts and luxuries available to those who conform to the demands of contemporary society and of "Christian" religious institutions that have drifted away from God.

The Wine of God's Wrath

The **THIRD ANGEL'S MESSAGE** tells what will happen to those who stay in Babylon. It says that those who drink the wine of Babylon will also drink the wine of God, the wine of His wrath (14:10). In other words, they will suffer the eternal death that comes to those who continue in sin. They will be burned up in the fires that God will use to cleanse the earth when He is ready to restore the paradise He originally intended this planet to be, a paradise in which sin and pain and death will never again exist.

This part of the vision closes with another look at the "saints." Their "patience," or endurance, is pointed out, and they are identified as "those who keep the commandments of God and the faith of Jesus" (v. 12), emphasizing their faithfulness to true religion.

The reference to the commandments of God returns to a theme we've seen before in this part of Revelation. This vision opened with a reference to the Ark of the Covenant (11:19), the temple furniture that held the Ten Commandments. And chapter 12 ended by identifying the end-time remnant of the true church as commandment keepers.

These faithful commandment keepers stand in contrast to those who worship the beast and his image and receive his mark on their foreheads or on their hands (v. 9). This plays off the first commandment's prohibition of worshiping other gods and the second commandment's warning against bowing down to the image of any creature of heaven, earth, or the sea.

> Herodotus said that a runaway slave who got the mark of Hercules at a temple in Egypt became the slave of that god, and even his former owner wasn't allowed to lay hands on him (*Persian Wars*, 2.113).

And just what is this **mark of the beast** that Revelation warns us about? In ancient times, devotees of various gods bore permanent marks, brands, on parts of their bodies. The marks identified them as under the supernatural protection of those gods. Therefore, the beast powers use a mark to distinguish their adherents from the faithful Christians who have refused to turn from their allegiance to God. It is the intention of the beast powers to flush out these faithful ones and then to wipe them off the earth.

Interestingly, while Revelation uses literally hundreds of Old Testament ideas and themes, it never quotes directly from the Old Testament. The closest it comes to doing so is in chapter 14:7, when it calls us to "worship Him who made heaven and earth, the sea and springs of water." This is nearly a direct quotation from the fourth commandment, the Sabbath commandment.

As the commandment itself says, and as Revelation 14:7 reminds us, God gave the seventh-day Sabbath to serve as a perpetual reminder that He made us. In fact, He said He gave the Sabbath as a sign "that you may know that I am the LORD your God" (Ezekiel 20:20). It is because God made us that He has a right to our worship. The Sabbath functions as a sign, a mark, a seal, of our recognition of His authority.

On the other hand, complying with the sea beast's demands for worship means recognizing its authority as superior to God's. Significantly, the medieval Christian church claimed the change of the day of worship specified in God's Ten Commandment law (from Saturday to Sunday) is a mark of its authority.

The observance of these different days of worship certainly distinguishes in a simple way the different worshipers. Ultimately, however, the issue is not the day of worship; it is the matter of whose authority one recognizes.

When the warning messages of the three angels have been preached to "every nation, tribe, tongue, and people," a harvest begins. Like the parable of the harvest that Jesus told, by which He represented the final judgment at the end of the world (see Matthew 12:24), this harvest has two parts.

• The first gathers in God's own people (14:14–16).
• The second deals with those who have turned from God (vs. 17–20).

Here the metaphor of the previous verses changes. Earlier, the unfaithful were warned they would drink the wine of God's wrath. Here they become that wine—thrown into the "great winepress of the wrath of God," from which runs an immense quantity of blood.

The vision of Revelation 12 to 14 reveals the great battle going on between Christ and the dragon, Satan. It says the battle concerns the allegiance of the people of earth; it concerns whom they recognize as the rightful ruler of the universe, whose law they will obey. It tells us the outcome of the battle and, in its picture of the 144,000 and of the harvests, the results for each side. And most important, it tells us that every human being will end up on one side or the other—and that ultimately it's our choice. Choose wisely!

Catholic leaders meeting at Council of Trent during the Counter-Reformation.

Petrus de Ancharano: *"The pope can modify divine law" (see Lucius Ferraris, Prompta Bibliotheca, 8 vols. [Venice: Caspa Storti, 1772], art. "Papa, II"). At the crucial Council of Trent, which formulated the church's response to the Reformation, the archbishop of Reggio claimed, "The Sabbath, the most glorious day in the law, has been changed into the Lord's day … by the authority of the church" (Mansi, Sacrorum Conciliorum 33:529, 530).*

UNLOCK
DANIEL & REVELATION
... more great books and DVDs for further study!

Walking Through Revelation DVD Set

Popular prophecy teacher Doug Batchelor guides you, chapter-by-chapter, through the prophecies of Revelation in this video series, unraveling all its mysteries and secrets. This easy-to-follow DVD set will make your study of Bible prophecy even more productive and exciting!

DV-WTR $39.95

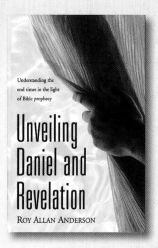

Unveiling Daniel and Revelation

Famed prophecy expert Roy Anderson clearly reveals the behind-the-scenes meaning of last-day events found in Daniel and Revelation, helping you understand exactly what's happening in our world right now and how you can be ready for Armageddon.

BK-UDR $19.99

Hidden Truth Magazine

Packed with colorful graphics and fascinating Bible facts, this eye-opening study magazine presents seven of the most misunderstood biblical subjects in a captivating way—covering prophecy, heaven, hell, salvation, and more.

BK-HT $2.25

God Cares: The Message of Daniel & Revelation Book Set

The ancient Bible books of Daniel and Revelation speak directly to you today! Discover how God still acts in human history and has provided all the information you need to know about the last days. A sweeping panorama and detailed Bible prophecy study set from C. Mervyn Maxwell.

BK-GCS $31.99

The Prophecy Code DVD Set

Pastor Doug Batchelor clearly explains the simple principles for understanding Bible prophecy in this complete, comprehensive 20-part DVD series. Learn how to intelligently unlock the many fascinating symbols of Daniel and Revelation along the way!

DV-PCS $99.95

Call us toll free:
800-538-7275

AFBOOKSTORE.COM
LIFE-CHANGING CHRISTIAN RESOURCES

AMAZING FACTS

Armageddon and the Final Plague

What You'll Learn

The scope and timing of the seven last plagues

- - - - - - -

The identity of the kings of the east

- - - - - - -

The nature of the battle of Armageddon

THE FOUR VISIONS THAT MAKE UP THE FIRST HALF OF REVELATION PARALLEL ONE ANOTHER, EACH REVEALING DIFFERENT ASPECTS OF WHAT WOULD HAPPEN FROM JOHN'S DAY TO CHRIST'S SECOND COMING. THE VISIONS IN THE SECOND HALF OF REVELATION FOCUS SOLELY ON END-TIME EVENTS ...

FOLLOW ALONG: Revelation Chapters 15, 16

The first four visions of Revelation, the historical ones, show us why there must one day be a final judgment. The eschatological, or end-time, visions outline the consequences of this final judgment for both the rebellious and the faithful. The last four visions of Revelation also form a small chiasm within the larger chiasm of Revelation. This small chiasm's theme is the outcome of the choices the rebellious and the faithful have made:

1. FOCUS ON PUNISHMENT
   A The plagues, 15:1–16:21.
   > **B** Circumstances related to the plagues: Fall of Babylon, the false mother, 17:1–19:10.
   > Plague angel shows John the great harlot, 17:1–19:8. John attempts to worship the angel, 19:9, 10.

2. FOCUS ON REWARD
   B' Circumstances related to the holy city: The millennium, 19:11–21:8.
   > **A'** The holy city: Descent of New Jerusalem, the Lamb's bride, 21:9–22:21. Plague angel shows John the Lamb's bride, 21:9–22:7. John attempts to worship the angel, 22:8, 9 (*God Cares* 2, 425).

A Song of Victory

The first verse of chapter 15 introduces us to the subject of this vision: "the seven last plagues" in which "the wrath of God is complete." In the next two verses, John wrote of seeing "those who have the victory over the beast ... standing on the sea of glass. ... And they sing the song of Moses ... and the song of the Lamb." These elements—the plagues and the song of victory sung beside the sea—tell us this vision is based on a familiar Old Testament story: the redemption of Israel from slavery in Egypt.

> As Yahweh [God] vindicated His covenant and liberated Israel from the house of bondage by means of a series of plagues, so Christ will bring about the final deliverance of His faithful people by sending again a series of plagues (Hans K. LaRondelle, "Contextual Approach to the Seven Last Plagues," *Symposium II*, 143).

Other translations picture these people standing "beside the sea" as they sing these songs. See, for example, the New Revised Standard Version.

"The Great Day of His Wrath." John Martin, 1853.

> Then the fourth angel poured out his
> bowl on the sun, and power was given
> to him to scorch men with fire.
>
> —REVELATION 16:8

As was the case in the previous visions of Revelation, the action in this vision proceeds from the heavenly temple.

Chapter 15 concludes with the observation that "the temple was filled with smoke from the glory of God ... and no one was able to enter the temple till the seven plagues" were completed. Revelation 22:11 says a time is coming when people will no longer be able to change. Those who are unjust will be unjust still, and those who are holy will be holy still. This last verse of chapter 15 indicates that the plagues will fall during that time. When no one can enter the temple, Christ's gracious work of interceding for sinners will have ended.

Chapter 16 then goes on to describe the effects as the individual plagues are poured out. Chapter 14 introduced the expression "the wine of the wrath of God." It's that wine the angels carrying the bowls deliver. That there are seven plagues also speaks of their fullness, their completeness.

It was noted earlier that in their content and in their place in Revelation's structure, the seven trumpets parallel the plagues. The trumpets were limited in their effect. They functioned as wake-up calls to earth's inhabitants, calling them to repentance so they needn't suffer the full effects of the judgment to come. By the time of the "seven *last* plagues" (chapter 15:1, emphasis supplied), however, everyone has decided either for or against God. There's no further intercession in the temple. The time of mercy, of God's grace, has passed. In these plagues God begins to carry out the verdict of His judgment.

Like the Plagues of Egypt

The first five plagues strike the persons and environment of those who have rejected God and oppressed His faithful followers. These plagues resemble closely those that fell on Egypt. And the

results are much the same. Just as Pharaoh ultimately refused to acknowledge God and repent of his evil ways, so those who experience these plagues, rather than seeking God's mercy and grace, stubbornly refuse to repent. They're firmly committed to their rebellion against Him. Pharaoh's persistent rebellion resulted in his death, and that of his army, in the Red Sea. The rebellion of the end-time opposition of God, later chapters of Revelation say, will result in their death in a lake of fire.

With the sixth and seventh plagues, the imagery changes. Revelation continues to portray what God will do to rescue His faithful followers from those who would destroy them.

In Bible times, wine was usually served diluted. Chapter 14:10 warns that on the Day of Judgment, the wine of God's wrath won't be watered down; it will be served "full strength."

But the scene shifts from Egypt and Pharaoh and the Red Sea to "the great river Euphrates" (v. 12) and "the great city" "Babylon" (v.19).

Nebuchadnezzar's defeat of Judah—his destruction of Jerusalem and its temple and depopulation of the land through death and exile—make Babylon the ultimate embodiment of evil in the writings of the Old Testament prophets. So Babylon's fall and the subsequent release and return of the Jewish exiles play a role equally important in salvation history as Israel's redemption from Egypt.

Daniel, Isaiah, Jeremiah, and the Greek historians Xenophon and Herodotus tell us how it happened. Cyrus united the Medes and the Persians, nations to the east of the Babylonian Empire. Eventually their combined forces laid siege to Babylon, capital of the empire. But Babylon was a strongly fortified city with ample stores of food, and the Euphrates River, which ran through the middle of the city, supplied it with plenty of water. Gates over the river kept enemy armies from slipping into the

"Inferno." Steve Creitz.

city via the riverbed.

But the Medo-Persian army attacked Babylon when the Euphrates was low. In addition, according to the Greek historians, the Medo-Persian forces actually diverted the river to drop it even lower. So Cyrus's soldiers were able to slip under the river gates and, in a surprise attack, defeat the overconfident defenders of Babylon!

The sixth and seventh plagues of John's vision are portrayed in the terms

Kings from the East

At this point, the rest of Revelation develops the picture briefly sketched in the sixth and seventh plagues. We'll close this section with a brief look at a few of the details given in those two plagues.

Cyrus and his generals were kings from the east who were the agents of Babylon's defeat—and thus also agents of the return of God's people to the Promised Land. Isaiah wrote of Cyrus in messianic terms (e.g., Isaiah 45:1). Significantly, the east gate of the temple Ezekiel described was permanently shut "because the LORD God of Israel has entered by it" (Ezekiel 44:2; also 43:4). Christ and the heavenly armies are the "kings from the east" of Revelation 16:12.

"Three unclean spirits" appear in the sixth plague (vs. 13, 14). These three spirits are demonic counterparts to the three angels of chapter 14. The angels proclaim the gospel to all nations, inviting people everywhere to join God's side in the great cosmic conflict that is about to begin. The demons work on behalf of the false trinity, gathering the kings of "the whole world to the battle of that great day of God Almighty."

Finally, the sixth plague says these forces gather for the final war at "Armageddon." For some people, the term Armageddon means a devastating global war. For others, it means a specific end-time war in the Middle East involving the Russians, Africans, Chinese, or nations of the West.

The term itself doesn't give us much help in determining the nature or location of this war. There is no place named Armageddon. The word might mean something like "mountain of Megiddo," but Megiddo is on a plain. Probably, like most of the other names in Revelation, it's meant to be symbolic. Only the context can help us understand it correctly.

1. In the sixth plague, the battle is called "the battle of that great day of God Almighty" (v. 14). This is a biblical term for the universal judgment day of God.

2. "The kings ... of the whole earth" are called to this battle. Chapter 19:19 says they're all united with the beast against Christ and His army.

3. As noted earlier, the sixth and seventh plagues describe parts of the same event: the fall of Babylon. Revelation 17–19 elaborates further on this event. Those chapters, then, enlarge our understanding of the Bible's "battle of Armageddon." In the next section, you'll be looking at that part of Revelation.

It seems clear the Bible doesn't picture Armageddon as a battle between earth's nations. It will certainly involve actual bloodshed on earth. Ultimately, however, it's a battle between good and evil, a battle between the forces of Satan and those who have adopted his methods on the one hand and the Lamb and those who have sided with Him on the other. ⟨R⟩

The Wrath of God

The Bible says God is love. Sometimes we find it hard to reconcile that statement with passages like those in Revelation that vividly picture His "wrath." How can He be a God of love if He's also a God of wrath and does such terrible things to people?

God doesn't dislike those who experience His wrath. Both the Old and New Testaments are consistent in portraying God as taking no "pleasure in the death of the wicked" (Ezekiel 33:11; see also 2 Peter 3:9). But sin is evil because it hurts people, the innocent as well as the guilty. It breaks relationships, and it breaks hearts. God's wrath is His determination to rid the universe of the pain and death sin has brought. And sin exists only in "free moral agents"—intelligent beings who have the power of choice. That means that to rid the universe of sin, God must rid it of those who harbor sin—those who have refused His grace and clung to sin rather than to Him.

---

of this story. Verse 12 says the sixth plague will dry up the Euphrates to prepare the way of the kings from the east—an image obviously based on the drying of the Euphrates that facilitated the attack of the Medo-Persian army. The seventh plague follows with pictures of Babylon's destruction: the biggest earthquake this world has ever seen, the division of the city, and the statement that Babylon was remembered before God, receiving "the cup of the wine of the fierceness of His wrath" (v. 19).

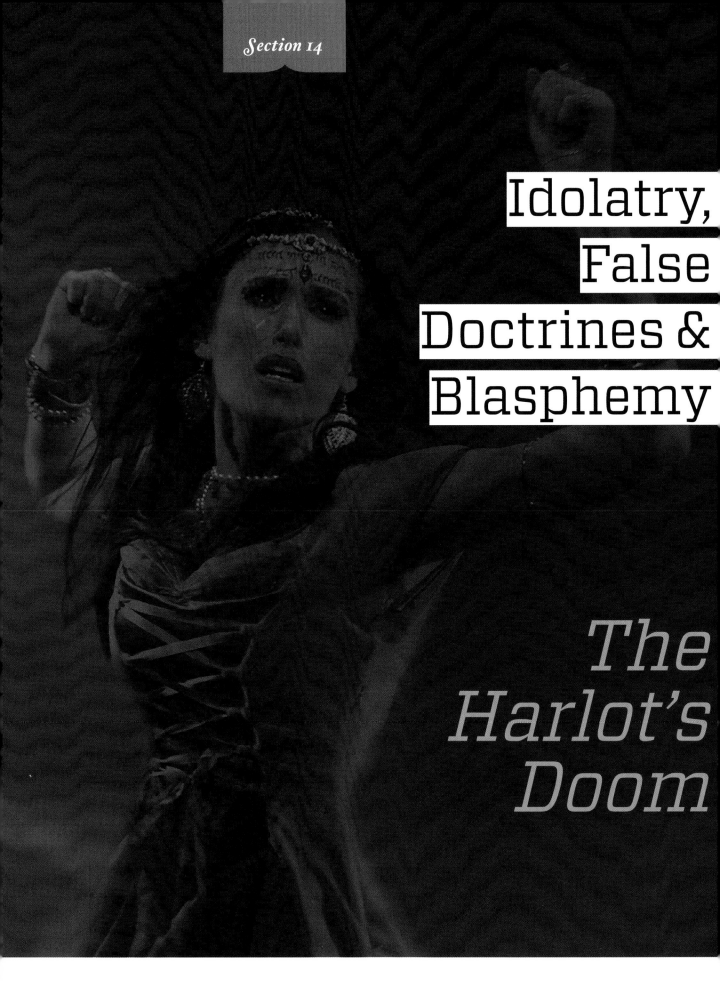

Idolatry, False Doctrines & Blasphemy

The Harlot's Doom

> ❝❞

MYSTERY, BABYLON THE GREAT, THE MOTHER OF HARLOTS AND OF THE ABOMINATIONS OF THE EARTH.

—REVELATION 17:5

What You'll Learn

More information about the identity of God's enemies

- - - - - - - -

What God's enemies will try to force His people to do before Armageddon

- - - - - - - -

The seven songs of judgment

REVELATION 15 AND 16 INTRODUCED GOD'S RESCUE OF HIS FAITHFUL FOLLOWERS USING THEMES AND IMAGES TAKEN FROM THE STORIES OF THE REDEMPTION OF ISRAEL FROM EGYPT AND BABYLON. CHAPTERS 17 AND ON, WHICH YOU'LL EXAMINE HERE AND IN THE TWO FOLLOWING CHAPTERS, EXPANDS THIS OUTLINE, DESCRIBING IN MORE DETAIL THE DESTRUCTION OF THE OPPRESSORS AND THE NEW PROMISED LAND GOD MAKES FOR HIS FAITHFUL.

In another of Revelation's chiasms, John saw the destruction of the evil powers in the reverse order of their appearance in his visions: Babylon dies first (chapters 17, 18), then the beast and the false prophet (chapter 19), and finally, Satan, the dragon (chapter 20).

The parallels between these sections on the fates of the wicked and the righteous become particularly evident when you compare Revelation 17:1, 2 with chapter 21:9, 10 and chapter 19:9, 10 with chapter 22:6–9.

FOLLOW ALONG:
Revelation Chapters 17, 18

Revelation 16 pictures Babylon as a city. Chapter 17 calls it a harlot (v. 18). Here Revelation is using Old Testament imagery (e.g., Isaiah 1:21; Hosea 2:2, 4; Jeremiah 3:1–3, 8, 9; Ezekiel 16:15–34). It was the nations of Israel and Judah that these Old Testament prophets were calling harlots—God's own people who had turned themselves into unfaithful idolaters. The harlot Babylon of Revelation's end-times, then, must represent not some foreign political oppressor, but the church—Christian people gone bad. And these false Christians persecuted God's faithful people!

The picture Revelation paints in chapters 17–19 adds a further detail, a new element, to our understanding of the God-opposing forces of the end times. Revelation 17:1 portrays the harlot sitting "on many waters," which verse 15 says represent "peoples, multitudes, nations, and tongues." Verse 3 says the

> "I saw the woman, drunk with the blood of the saints and with the blood of the martyrs of Jesus. And when I saw her, I marveled with great amazement."
>
> —REVELATION 17:6

harlot sits on a blasphemous scarlet beast that has seven heads and ten horns. Verses 9 and 12 say the heads are also mountains and the horns are kings. Daniel's prophecies make clear that heads, mountains, horns, and kings all represent one thing: nations. In other words, the peoples and multitudes on which the harlot sits—that support her—are not amorphous masses but rather organized political bodies.

Here, then, is the new element that these chapters add to our understanding of the end times: The opposers of God and His faithful followers are made up of the combined worldwide forces of religious and political institutions!

Unchristian Coercion

As chapters 13 and 14 reveal, these powers will try to force all the people of the world to worship as they command. But while they claim to be Christian, they really aren't.

Jesus rejected the use of force because, He said, "My kingdom is not of this world" (John 18:36; also Matthew 26:52). As Elijah learned in the cave in which he sought refuge from Jezebel, God speaks to people in the still, small voice of the Spirit rather than through threats of force. Some have thought to improve the moral state of the world by forcing people to conform to God's will. But Jesus said that it's what's inside a person that defiles; cleaning up the outside does little good (Mark 7:14). Jesus pointed Nicodemus to the new birth the Holy Spirit brings as the root of the only kind of religious change that counts with God (see John 3).

The "fornication" Revelation decries means both the acceptance by the nations of the world of the false doctrines that constitute Babylon's apostasy and the union of their powers with hers to enforce her decrees and demands. The fact that Babylon rides the beast indicates that the political powers support the apostate religious institutions and that the religious institutions control the political powers to their own ends. Verse 18 says, "And the woman whom you saw is that great city which *reigns over* the kings of the earth" (emphasis supplied).

John wrote that this woman was "drunk with the blood of the saints and with the blood of the martyrs of Jesus. And when I saw her, I marveled with great amazement" (v. 6). That a pagan power would persecute the saints wouldn't have amazed John. His surprise came because it was a supposedly Christian power that was drunk with their blood.

But these chapters here are not primarily about Babylon's power. They're about its judgment and fall. The sixth plague indicates that the drying up of the river on which Babylon sits precipitates its fall. Chapter 17 pictures the same

event in different terms and makes it more explicit: "The ten horns which you saw on the beast ["the kings of the earth," v. 18], these will hate the harlot, make her desolate and naked, eat her flesh and burn her with fire" (v. 16).

In other words, Revelation says the nations of the world, all of which had united in support of the apostate Chris-

---

Historians Thomas and Gertrude Sartory wrote, "No religion in the world ... has on its conscience so many millions of people who ... believed differently. Christianity is the most murderous religion there has ever been."

---

tian religious institutions and tried to enforce their forms of worship, will turn against those institutions and destroy them. This is the first actual engagement of the battle of Armageddon.

Seven Songs

The rest of this portion of Revelation is comprised of seven songs—again arranged in a chiasm. They can be summarized in this way:

A Mighty voice of an angel: "Fallen is Babylon!"
  B Heavenly voice: "Come out of her, my people!"
    C Lament of the kings: "Alas! alas!"
    C' 'Lament of the merchants: "Alas! alas!"
    C' Lament of the seafarers: "Alas! alas!"
A' Voice of a mighty angel: "So shall Babylon ... be thrown down."
  B' Heavenly voices: Praise God for Babylon's fall (Maxwell, *God Cares*, 462, 463, slightly modified).

Like so much of the rest of Revelation, these seven songs are rooted in Old Testament prophecies (for example, Jeremiah 50, 51; Ezekiel 26–28). The **FIRST TWO SONGS** announce again Babylon's fall, call God's people out of her (they must both choose to leave and act on that choice if they are to remain God's

people), and call for her to be given the judgment she deserves.

In the **NEXT THREE SONGS**, the earth's kings, merchants, and seafarers mourn at the destruction of Babylon. Here it becomes evident that they didn't necessarily support Babylon because of religious conviction. Revelation says that "the merchants of the earth will weep and mourn over her, because no one buys their merchandise anymore" (chapter 18:11; also v. 19). They mourn the wealth they're losing because of Babylon's fall. They supported her because it was expedient; it was good for business; they profited by it.

Notice in several of these songs the theme of justice: "Render to her just as she rendered to you" (v. 6). Together, the religious and political institutions had enforced a boycott that forbade anyone to "buy or sell except one who has the mark or the name of the beast, or the number of his name" (13:17). Now the merchants, who had been part of that conspiracy, suffer because "no one buys their merchandise anymore" (18:11).

On a similar note, the last line of chapter 18:20, translated literally, reads, "God has judged her judgment against you." Babylon judged against the saints (against "you"). Now God has overturned that judgment. The Old Testament specified that the makers of false accusations must suffer the punishments they were attempting to pin on the innocent. God enforces that kind of justice. In the **SIXTH SONG**, the "mighty angel" spells it out: Babylon was responsible for the death of the martyrs; therefore, she must die (vs. 21–24).

Song of a Multitude

The final song, **THE SEVENTH SONG**, is sung by a "great multitude in heaven" (19:1). A "voice" in heaven—the 24 elders, the four living creatures, and those surrounding the throne—all call the servants of God on earth to praise the Lord for what He's done for them. He's judged the "great harlot who corrupted the earth; ... and He has avenged on her the blood of His servants shed by her." His judgments are righteous and true (v. 2). But wonderful as it is that God has put an end to the oppression of the saints, He's done more for them. He's invited them to the marriage supper of the Lamb (v. 9).

Who is this bride? In Revelation 21:2, John wrote that he saw "the holy city, New Jerusalem, coming down out of heaven from God, prepared as a bride adorned for her husband." This city, "arrayed in fine linen, clean and bright" —the "righteous acts of the saints" —(19:8), stands in contrast to Babylon, the harlot city. This "New Jerusalem" represents the people who will soon become its

"If a false witness rises against any man to testify against him of wrongdoing, then both men in the controversy shall stand before the Lord, before the priests and the judges who serve in those days. And the judges shall make careful inquiry, and indeed, if the witness is a false witness, who has testified falsely against his brother, then you shall do to him as he thought to have done to his brother; so you shall put away the evil from among you" (Deuteronomy 19:16–19).

inhabitants—Christ's faithful church, all the people who have chosen to trust and serve God in love, truth, and holiness.

Verse 7 says the Lamb's wife "has made herself ready." The church participates actively in her preparation. The grace of Christ does not permit us to take refuge in passiveness. Revelation continually solicits a response; it calls for endurance and obedience on the part of those who would, in the end, be counted God's faithful followers, those who wish to share in the reward of the righteous. (See, e.g., chapter 7:14; 12:11, 17; 14:12; 21:7.) R

The King of Kings Returns
The End of Evil and Death

> *And I heard a great voice out of heaven saying, Behold, the tabernacle of God is with men, and he will dwell with them, and they shall be his people, and God himself shall be with them, and be their God.*
> —REVELATION 21:3

I N THE PRECEDING SECTION, YOU SAW THAT ARMAGEDDON'S FIRST BATTLE IS DESCRIBED IN REVELATION 17:16. THE PASSAGE THIS CHAPTER COVERS, 19:11–21:8, PICTURES THE NEXT BATTLE OF THAT END-TIME WAR. IT PICTURES THAT CONFLICT AS A GRISLY SUPPER OF THE BIRDS, CONTRASTING IT TO THE WEDDING SUPPER OF THE LAMB THAT THE RIGHTEOUS WILL ATTEND.

FOLLOW ALONG: Revelation Chapters 19–21

"Coming King". Lars Justinen.

What You'll Learn

The two feasts of Revelation

- - - - - - -

The fate of Satan

- - - - - - -

What happens during the 1,000-year reign

This portion of Revelation continues the chronological end-time sequence begun with chapter 15 and corresponds to the seven seals.

1. Both start with riders on white horses
2. Both connect the martyrs with judgment.

First, the kings and mighty men and all people, free and slave, call for death to hide them from the Lamb. Second, the death wish of this group is fulfilled.

In the first scene of this section, John wrote that he saw a warrior from heaven who judges and makes war in righteousness. The warrior is clothed in a robe dipped in blood and wears "many" crowns on His head, in contrast to the crowns on the heads and horns of the beasts in earlier chapters. He's the supreme royalty of the universe, the "KING OF KINGS AND LORD OF LORDS" (v. 16).

John wrote that He's called "The Word" of God (v. 13), which is John's name for Jesus (John 1:1; 1 John 1:1). At the creation, the Word brought the universe into existence by speaking; now His speech becomes a sharp sword that destroys (v. 15).

The event these verses portray is Christ's second coming. Note verse 14: "The armies in heaven ... followed Him." Jesus said that when He returns, all the angels will come with Him (Matthew 25:31). Revelation says that He comes to tread "the winepress of the fierceness and wrath of Almighty God" (Revelation 19:15). Chapter 14:17 relates this treading of the winepress directly to the second coming.

The Conclusion of the Battle of Armageddon

Revelation 19:17–21 describes the main battle of Armageddon. Verse 19 depicts the two sides: "And I saw the beast, the kings of the earth, and their armies, gathered together to make war against Him who sat on the horse and against His army." As noted above, these are the very ones who had called for the rocks and mountains to hide them from Christ's face (compare v. 18 with chapter 6:15). Verse 18 makes sure we understand that this conflict is universal; it includes "all people."

Armageddon, then, is not merely a Middle Eastern battle, nor a war between all of earth's nations. In Armageddon, the powers of earth try to overthrow God's own forces, including those people who have refused to worship the beast or receive its mark (v. 20).

> Note that the warrior's blood must be His own, since the battle hasn't yet begun.

> **Some suggest** the conflict in chapter 20:8, 9 is to be considered part of Armageddon as well.

Like the striking of the nations with the sword, the second image in verse 15—ruling with a rod of iron—depicts destruction rather than simply firm governing; see Psalm 2:9. And the third image, that of the winepress, also is an image of death; compare Revelation 14:17.

The outcome is certain: "The beast was captured, and with him the false prophet. ... These two were cast alive into the lake of fire burning with brimstone" (v. 20). That's Revelation's way of saying the political and religious powers these figures represent will be destroyed, never to trouble the universe again.

"And the rest were killed with the sword which proceeded from the mouth of Him who sat on the horse. And all the birds were filled with their flesh" (v. 21). This image of the great supper of the birds was taken from Ezekiel 38 and 39. In that time, becoming food for animals of prey was the lowest depth of shame.

> *Ezekiel followed* his portrayal of the supper of the birds with a description of the new city and temple. Revelation follows this pattern; see chapters 19, 21, 22.

In these verses, then, Revelation explains what happens to the wicked at Christ's return. They're killed by the sharp sword, broken with the rod of iron, and trodden in the winepress of God's wrath. They become food for birds. (See also 2 Thessalonians 1:7–10; 2:8.)

So Revelation 19 pictures two suppers. All people are invited to the first, the marriage feast of the Lamb. Those who refuse to attend that supper become part of the menu of the second. God offers only these two options. We must choose one or the other. (See Matthew 22:1–14.)

Satan's Fate

After His coming, then, Christ has taken the righteous to heaven, there to live and reign "with" Him for a thousand years (20:4).

The wicked are all dead. The beast and false prophet are gone forever, and Babylon has been destroyed. That leaves only "that serpent of old, who is the Devil and Satan," (v. 2) unaccounted for.

John wrote that an angel from heaven "laid hold" of him, "bound him for a thousand years," and "cast him into the bottomless pit ... so that he should deceive the nations no more

An Israeli antiquities archeologist steps down to a 1,400-year-old winepress found near the kibbutz of Hafetz Haim, in central Israel. The unusually shaped press was exceptionally large and advanced for its time.

till the thousand years were finished" (vs. 1–3).

Essentially, Satan is bound by circumstances. He deceives the nations no more because there's no one left to deceive. The wicked are all dead, and Jesus has "taken" the righteous away to heaven. (See also Isaiah 24:21–23.)

The Millennium

The next three verses (Revelation 20:4–6) describe what the righteous are doing during this thousand-year period—the famous biblical "millennium." They live and reign with Christ, and judgment is given to them. Under the fifth seal, the martyrs cried out, "How long, O Lord, holy and true, until You judge and avenge our blood" (6:10). God has judged and avenged their blood. Now He's giving them the opportunity to judge too.

John wrote that judgment was committed to "those who had been beheaded for their witness to Jesus and to the word of God" (v. 4). The original recipients of Revelation were people facing death for their belief in Christ. John seems to have singled out the martyrs here especially to encourage those first-century Christians. But all who have professed the name of Christ, whether martyrs or not, have suffered the devil's ire. It is likely that all the righteous will do this judging.

It's not that they'll decide who's to be saved and who's not. That's all been determined before the second coming.

But there are three phases to the final judgment. The first is a pre-advent judgment (before Christ's return), which separates those who have falsely professed to be Christian from those whose profession is genuine. (This is the judgment spoken of in Daniel 7:9, 10, 13, 14; 8:14; 9:25; Revelation 3:5.)

Next comes the millennial judgment—in heaven—the time when the saints will judge the world and even the angels.

Apparently, before the wicked are destroyed forever, God will allow the righteous to review the case of every being in the universe, to determine that they have all been dealt with fairly. In a sense, the righteous are judging God. This judgment will establish for eternity their faith in His justice, His righteousness, and His love.

Final Judgment

Chapter 20:7–10 sketches out quickly the final, executive phase of the judgment. Here God acts to carry out the sentences He has pronounced and the saints have confirmed. Jesus said all people—both those who have done good and those who have done evil—will eventually be resurrected.

__The word "throne"__ is used 47 times in Revelation. When used of God's or Christ's throne, it always is situated in heaven. God comes to reign upon the earth only after the millennium (chapters 21, 22). Other passages in Revelation also picture the overcomers of the beast reigning in heaven. (See chapters 3:21; 4:1, 2, 6; 15:2.)

How do we understand chapter 20?

At Jesus' return, the angels gather the righteous from the four winds and then Jesus takes His people to be with Him where He is. That the righteous are taken from the earth at the second coming to celebrate the marriage of the Lamb in heaven becomes important to understanding the millennium described in chapter 20. (See Matthew 24:30, 31; John 14:1–3; cp. 1 Thessalonians 4:16.)

"Golden Balance." Lars Justinen.

The "Gog and Magog" of Revelation 20:8 come from Ezekiel's (chapters 38 and 39) description of the feast of the birds. They were the enemies of God's people who were to be destroyed in this judgment. Chapter 19:18 shows that in Revelation, they represent all the unrepentant people of the world.

"Do you not know that the saints will judge the world? And if the world will be judged by you, are you unworthy to judge the smallest matters?" —1 Corinthians 6:2

The "resurrection of life" occurs at His second coming. The "resurrection of condemnation" takes place at this time, the end of the millennium. It is this resurrection that releases Satan from his prison and enables him to go out to deceive all the nations of the world (vs. 7, 8). He can deceive again because people are again living on the earth.

The next two verses tell the end of the story. Satan gathers all the wicked of all ages of earth's existence together for a final attempt to overthrow God's kingdom. They surround "the camp of the saints and the beloved city," which chapter 21:2 describes as descending from heaven at the end of the millennium. But instead, fire comes down from God out of heaven and devours them.

In this brief scenario, we see the justice of the sentence the wicked receive and of the judgment they suffer. When they are resurrected, they don't repent of their sins and ask for mercy.

They persist in their rebellion and actually try to physically overthrow the God they've rejected.

Chapter 20:11–15 fills in some details to the ending these verses sketch out. (It ends with the same people being cast into the lake of fire, an indication that this section is an expansion on the previous scene.) John sees "the dead, small and great, standing before God," who is seated on a "great white throne" (vs. 11, 12). "Books were opened"—among them, the Book of Life—and "the dead were judged according to their works." "And anyone not found written in the Book of Life was cast into the lake of fire" (v. 15).

What's the purpose? Ever since Satan brought sin into the universe, God has allowed it to continue so people could see its true and ultimate nature.

If God had immediately destroyed sin and sinners, His created beings would have worshiped Him from fear of His power rather than from respect for His justice and love. Now, at the end of the millennium, everyone, even those destined to destruction, will admit that God was right all along. This final part of the millennial review strengthens the faith of the righteous. It's part of God's plan to see that

"Do not marvel at this; for the hour is coming in which all who are in the graves will hear His voice and come forth—those who have done good, to the resurrection of life, and those who have done evil, to the resurrection of condemnation." —John 5:28, 29

The Millennium

Beginning of the Millennium

- Second coming of Christ
- Resurrection of the righteous
- Destruction of the wicked
- Righteous taken to heaven
- Earth wracked by a great earthquake
- Satan bound to the desolate earth

During the Millennium

- Righteous in heaven; they judge the world and angels
- Wicked dead on the earth
- Satan "bound" to the earth

End of the Millennium

- New Jerusalem descends from heaven to earth
- Resurrection of the wicked
- Satan loosed
- Satan and the wicked attack the New Jerusalem
- Great white throne judgment
- Fire consumes Satan and the wicked; cleanses the earth

Earth Recreated; Eternity Begins

"affliction will not rise up a second time" (Nahum 1:9).

Death and the grave ("Hades") have no part in paradise restored, so Revelation pictures them being destroyed in the same lake of fire that eliminates sin and sinners from the universe (chapter 20:14, 15).

John ends this section with a brief portrayal of the new heaven and earth in which God will dwell with His people and in which there will be "no more death, nor sorrow, nor crying," nor pain (chapter 21:3, 4). He writes that God will "give of the fountains of the water of life freely to him who thirsts," and reminds his readers that those who overcome "shall inherit all things." But those who persist in their sin, he warns, "shall have their part in the lake ... which is the second death" (vs. 6–8).

That choice is ours too. ▣

Revelation 20 *tells us the fate of the devil.*

Paul wrote, *"We shall all stand before the judgment seat of Christ" (Romans 14:10, 11). And when writing to the Philippians, he said that the time is coming when every intelligent being of the universe will bow and "confess that Jesus Christ is Lord" (Revelation 2:10, 11). This "great white throne" judgment appears to be the only time when Paul's prophecies could be fulfilled.*

2 Peter 3 *also speaks of the cleansing fire and then the new heaven and earth.*

Paradise Restored

> " And God will wipe away every tear from their eyes; there shall be no more death, nor sorrow, nor crying. There shall be no more pain, for the former things have passed away.
> —REVELATION 21:4

No More Death, No More Sorrow

What You'll Learn

THE BOOK OF REVELATION HAS MORE THAN ITS SHARE OF DOOM AND GLOOM, WITH ITS DRAGONS AND BEASTS AND FALSE PROPHETS, ITS EARTHQUAKES AND HAILSTORMS AND LAKES OF FIRE. BUT THE REWARD FOR FAITHFULNESS JOHN DESCRIBED IN REVELATION'S LAST TWO CHAPTERS COMPENSATES FOR ALL THAT'S GONE BEFORE. THE NEW WORLD THAT GOD WILL CREATE FOR THE RIGHTEOUS TO ENJOY ENCOURAGES US TO HANG ON WITH PATIENT ENDURANCE TO THE COMMANDMENTS OF GOD AND THE FAITH OF JESUS THROUGH ALL THE TROUBLE THE DRAGON AND HIS ALLIES MIGHT BRING.

The purpose and design of New Jerusalem

The new Eden

The nearness of Jesus' return

FOLLOW ALONG: Revelation Chapters 21, 22

In Revelation's overall structure, chapters 21 and 22 parallel the vision of the seven churches. That vision pictured the church erosion down through history. These last chapters portray the church triumphant. The messages to the seven churches each concluded with a specific promise to those who would "overcome." These chapters reveal the fulfillment of those promises.

Previously, in another chapter, another parallelism involving this part of Revelation was introduced: The vision of the heavenly city New Jerusalem stands in a parallel of contrast to the earlier vision of the great earthly city Babylon. That city was the product of human hands—remember Nebuchadnezzar's boast, "Is not this great Babylon, that I have built for a royal dwelling by my mighty power and for the honor of my majesty?" (Daniel 4:30). It represented rebellion against God and the consequent oppression, suffering, and death. The New Jerusalem comes down from heaven entirely the work of God; humankind has nothing to do with building it. Along with it come life, joy, and light.

Both sections picture these "cities" also as women. Babylon is a harlot. It is Christianity become unfaithful, prostituting itself to the political and economic powers of the world. On the other hand, John saw the New Jerusalem as a pure bride—imagery representing the exclusiveness of the saints' relationship with Christ (see Revelation 19:7, 8; 21:27).

Jerusalem Restored

Revelation portrays the New Jerusalem as the fulfillment of God's promise through the Old Testament prophets to restore His people Israel, their city, and their land. Like Ezekiel, John was carried to "a great and high mountain" from which he saw the city. The features of that city—its high walls, square shape, gates named after each of the 12 tribes, and presence of the throne and glory of God—all are rooted in Ezekiel's visions.

But Revelation extends those Old Testament promises to include all people of the earth—all who will respond to the gospel invitation. Notice, for instance, that while the gates are named after the 12 tribes of Israel, the foundations of the

The gems and precious metals used as building materials no doubt are meant to convey both the value and beauty of what God has planned for His faithful people.

city are named after the patriarchs of the Christian era, the 12 apostles (21:14). Here John reminds us of Paul's statement that the Christian community is "built on the foundation of the apostles and prophets" (Ephesians 2:20).

Having described the exterior of the city, John moved inside. Immediately he exclaimed, "I saw no temple in it"

To see this parallel, compare Revelation 21:10 to Ezekiel 40:2. See also Ezekiel 40:2-5; 43:2-7; 44:6-14; 48:20, 31-34.

(chapter 21:22). One can imagine John's surprise. The temple was both the showpiece and the most important structure of ancient Jerusalem. In addition, most of the action in Revelation was specifically said to have originated from the heavenly temple. No doubt John expected to see the ultimate temple in this, the ultimate city of God.

The Old Testament tabernacle and the temples that succeeded it represented God's dwelling among His people. But while they represented His presence, they also represented separation.

Because of sin, people could not live in God's immediate presence; they could not look upon His face and live. So the temple contained a series of compartments separated by veils. Lay people could go no farther than the courtyard. There two veils stood between them and God's presence. The common priests could enter the holy places of the temples but were still separated by a veil from God's presence. Only the high priest had access to the Most Holy Place—the divine throne room where the Shekinah rested upon the mercy seat—and only one day a year after having carried out special rites and having surrounded himself with a thick cloud of incense.

The temple meant God's presence. But it was a dangerous presence, one from which the temple separated the people of God. John "saw no temple" in the New Jerusalem for two reasons ...

1. "The Lord God Almighty and the Lamb are its temple" (v. 22). The saints need no screening. They will have direct access to God.

2. The New Jerusalem is a cube: "its length, breadth, and height are equal" (Revelation 21:16). Its shape mirrors those of the Most Holy Places of the Old Testament tabernacle and temples.

In other words, the New Jerusalem itself is eternity's Most Holy Place, God's dwelling place, His throne room. But it's a Most Holy Place that all His people can enter. In fact, they will live there, directly in God's presence, forever and ever.

Here is the ultimate fulfillment of God's promise at the time of the Exodus: "I will walk among you and be your God, and you shall be My people" (Leviticus 26:12). Here is the fulfillment of the promise of "Immanuel"—"God with us." Now "the tabernacle of God is with men, and He will dwell with them ... and God Himself will be with them and be their God" (Revelation 21:3).

The New Eden

The New Jerusalem needs no other light source than the glory of God. "The nations of those who are saved shall walk in its light" (vs. 23, 24).

Another theme from the Exodus story: the pillar of cloud and fire that lighted Israel's way through the wilderness (Exodus 13:21).

Light was God's first creation. He brought it into existence before He made the sun, moon, and stars. God's new creation also features a light that eliminates the need for sun and moon. More than that, there is "no night there" (v.25). All that is dark and obscure is eliminated. The revelation of Christ is fully accomplished. All is definitively clear.

Revelation's description of the New Jerusalem closes with more imagery drawn from earth's beginnings. John saw "a pure river of water of life, clear as crystal, proceeding from the throne of God and of the Lamb"—reminiscent of the river that "went out of Eden" to water the earth. On both banks of this river grows Eden's tree of life, which supplies fruit throughout the whole year and the leaves of which are for the "healing of the nations" (Revelation 22:1, 2; compare Genesis 2:9, 10 and Ezekiel 47.)

The water of life and tree of life indicate humankind's continued dependence on God.

The tree of life—its fruit and leaves—is a reminder that only God is eternal, has life in Himself. Man's eternity is an eternity continuously received from God. ... God's gift will always be there to impart life (symbol of the tree) to heal man from his essential finitude (symbol of the leaves). ... Even in eternity all is grace.[1]

In another reference to the stories of Creation and the Fall, verse 3 says "there shall be no more curse." Here the reference is by contrast. The first man and woman succumbed to the serpent's temptation, and curses fell upon them, the serpent, and all creation. Now the serpent has been destroyed. Judgment has been rendered. The entire universe has confessed God's justice and His love. The faith of the citizens of the New Jerusalem has been established on such a firm foundation as never again to waver. So "affliction shall not rise up a second

Interestingly, the Greek word usually used for "tree" is *dendron*. But when writing of the tree of life, John used the word *xulon*—the word also used of the cross. John might have meant to suggest that the cross is a tree of life for earth's inhabitants.

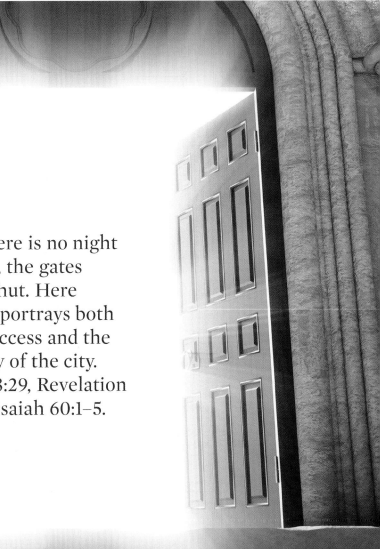

Because there is no night in paradise, the gates are never shut. Here Revelation portrays both continual access and the universality of the city. See Luke 13:29, Revelation 21:24, and Isaiah 60:1–5.

time" (Nahum 1:9). Consequently, "there shall be no more curse" (v. 3). And "they shall reign forever and ever" (v. 5).

"I Am Coming Quickly"

At the end of Daniel's series of visions, he was told to shut and seal his book until the time of the end (Daniel 12:4). His prophecies had little application to his own generation; they concerned mainly people who would live much later. In direct contrast, John was told, "Do not seal the words of the prophecy of this book, for the time is at hand" (Revelation 22:10). John's visions